BRIDGE THROUGH THE MIST

DENISE A. AGNEW

Copyright © 1999, 2008, 2016, 2024 by Denise A. Agnew

Cover Art Copyright 2024 by Scott Carpenter

ALL RIGHTS RESERVED.

This book is licensed for personal enjoyment only. This ebook may not be re-sold or given away for free to other people without the permission of the author.

This is a work of fiction. Names, characters, places, brands, media, and incidents are either the product of the author's imagination or are used fictitiously.

PRAISE FOR BRIDGE THROUGH THE MIST...

"Bridge Through the Mist is one story that can be read again and again…"
Fallen Angel Reviews

"Four hearts...an exceptional tale of medieval times...I highly recommend this to anyone looking for a lot of action, sizzling passion and a battle of wills that will keep the reader completely engrossed to the very last page."
Romance Studio

"The characters are very realistic. I had no trouble believing Alenna was a modern woman who suddenly found herself bound by the constraints of the early fourteenth century...secondary characters are so utterly alive they make this book a must read. I highly recommend Bridge Through The Mist."
Just Erotic Romance Reviews

DEDICATION

To my husband Terry, who has always believed in me and supported me every step of the way. You're my hero.

ACKNOWLEDGMENTS

Special acknowledgments must go to my Scottish friend and author Cait Miller, who snagged me one day at a conference and told me she loved the fact I had the Scottish accent right in this book. Thanks for all your help, Cait.

A huge thank you to Jennifer Tovar for reading through this story in 2024 and locating things that needed fixing. Your expertise and kindness is so appreciated. You're the best!

AUTHOR'S NOTE

The idea for this novel percolated in my brain in the mid 1990's but it wasn't until I moved to England in 1996 and visited the Tower of London that inspiration hit me hard. I knew I wanted this story to be a time travel, to feature an exciting Scottish highlander, and to involve archaeology in some manner. Visiting Scotland numerous times cemented my desire to complete the book. Bridge Through The Mist was first released in 1999 with a publisher no longer in existence and has gone through at least two other publishers after that who are also no longer in existence. This year I give you a reboot. I've tweaked only a few details. Enjoy this trip back in time to 1318 Scotland.

P.S. Beware. This book is erotic romance and is for those who appreciate a particularly hot book.

Denise A. Agnew
2024

SHE TRAVELS BACK IN TIME & INTO THE ARMS OF A WARRIOR...

When Alenna Carstairs is hurled through time into 1318, Scotland's medieval world brings her face to face with hot, sexy Tynan of MacBrahin. Infuriated with his barbaric manners, and yet sensing vulnerability within him, she vows to discover the heartbreak that has scarred his soul.

World-weary knight Tynan of MacBrahin lost two loves to the brutality of other men. He can't forgive himself for failing to protect the women who depended on him. When Alenna saves his life, her independent and courageous spirit stirs desires and admiration so strong within him he can't resist her.

A depraved baron soon wants Alenna for his own, and Tynan must find a way to conquer this powerful man to save her. Alenna struggles with soul-staggering desire for Tynan, but most of all, she must convince Tynan his love is not lethal, and she is the one who can bring shine to his armor again.

CHAPTER 1

*S*cotland, Present Day

To Alenna Carstairs, the rasp of trowel over hard earth sounded like the proverbial nails over a blackboard. The scent of damp earth assailed her nostrils and nausea rolled through her. She stopped removing the soil, thin layer by thin layer. The other archaeologists around her didn't halt the repetitive motion.

Scrape. Scrape. Scrape.

As she straightened from her crouched position in the test pit, unease gathered tight in her throat. She took a deep breath and wondered if another panic attack would beset her any moment. Queasiness swept through her in a wave. She pressed one hand to her stomach and willed it to stop roiling. Despite the chill in the air, perspiration broke out on her forehead.

Thick, tall curtain walls seemed to hang over her like sentinels. Mellow light played over the stones and gave the imposing structure the look of sandstone.

Since she'd first stepped into the castle two days ago, a vague discomfort plagued her. She couldn't say why, but it disturbed her to walk among old stones and ancient memories that whispered their secrets. Panicky feelings assaulted her when she worked in this part of the castle, near the Black Tower. She half expected the test pit to widen into a black hole and suck her into infinite space. Nausea rolled, threatening dire consequences.

I wish to hell the earth would swallow me up now.

Just what she needed. Barely a day left of excavation at MacAulay Castle and they'd finish the work.

Any minute she might have to run back to the van, leaving her friend Demi Arnold, Dr. Benedict and the rest of the small, mostly American amateur archaeology group to finish the day's work.

"You okay?" Demi asked, dropping her trowel on the ground.

Alenna smiled with effort. No sense in alarming Demi, who already hovered like an anxious mother hen. "I'm fine."

Dr. Benedict straightened from his crouch by the pit and pulled off his gloves. "Well, I'm taking a break. My back is killing me. Why don't we all head for the van and have something to drink. We're almost done for today anyway. We can come back in twenty minutes and cover the site."

The eight other people in their group quickly agreed.

The thought of drinking or eating didn't appeal to Alenna. "I'll stay and work."

Demi shook her short grey curls. "You don't look so good. Why don't you take a break? I was about to."

"I'll be fine."

Demi might as well be Alenna's mother. Demi was twenty-five years Alenna's senior and thin as a cat o'nine tails. "It's freezing out here. Maybe you should come back to the van. There's a creepy crawly flu going around."

"Are you kidding? I love working on the dig," Alenna said. "Besides, the tourists are having a lot of fun watching us."

The National Trust wished to attract more tourists into the castle and they believed the small group of amateur and professional archaeologists digging during hours the castle was open would be an attraction for the tourists. They had been right, but Alenna didn't exactly agree with the idea. More often than not, tourists became a distraction with their questions and incessant chatter. Luckily, no tourists roamed this part of the castle now.

Dr. Benedict twirled one end of his droopy white mustache and gestured to his crew. "Come on. Let's take that break."

"I'll be right there," Demi said as he trooped away.

Alenna noted the worried frown on Demi's face and knew her friend was concerned that Alenna didn't feel quite right. Well, she didn't, but breaking up with her fiancé and leaving her job could have a hell of a lot to do with it. Impulsiveness could really bite a person on the ass.

Initially, she'd wondered what possessed her to venture from the sun of her home in Sierra Vista, Arizona to the chill damp of the United Kingdom. Why not sunny Florida or balmy Hawaii? She'd left the U.S. at the end of August to participate in a once-in-a-lifetime archaeological expedition at MacAulay Castle in the border country between Scotland and England. Now, several days later, she wondered if she'd done the right thing. Sure, she'd see places she'd wanted to visit all her life, but this trip and the fees for participating in the dig didn't come cheap. But she needed a way to clear the cobwebs and find a fresh perspective in a mind full of shadows and doubts.

Hah. Remembering how flushed and excited her fiancé had looked when she caught him fucking another woman always caused her blood pressure to boil. Hostility toward her fiancé raged raw in her blood, and she didn't plan to spend the vacation of a lifetime brooding. The temper tantrum she'd had in front of the entire legal staff, though, had been a royal catastrophe. The one time in her professional life that she'd blown up secured her a fuchsia slip.

Not pink. Fuchsia. As if the startling color somehow signaled a greater transgression.

Alenna Carstairs doesn't break down.

Weakness is a fault.

Her mother had told her so, her father had told her so, and her fiancé had told her so.

Yeah, right.

Marshaling a reservoir of strength, Alenna stood. She ran a hand through her damp hair. A splatter of rain brought her back from maudlin thoughts.

She shoved her hands in the pockets of her lightweight coat. A drop of rain dribbled down the back of her collar and trickled under her sweater and flannel-lined jeans. September in Scotland proved to be damned cold.

Suddenly an image of her fiancé taking the other woman sprang into her head like a hydra from the depths of a water hell. Fiery, painful and nightmarish.

"Bastard," she mumbled under her breath.

Demi gave her a startled look. "Someone woke on the wrong side of the bed this morning."

"Humph."

"Hang in there. We're almost done for the day. Why don't we take my camera and do a tour of our own?"

Alenna grinned at her friend of ten years. Demi might be impulsive, but she was fun. And Alenna had discovered since the breakup with her fiancé that fun was something she didn't always recognize unless she was shoe-horned into it directly.

"You've got a deal," Alenna said as Demi helped her climb out of the pit. Alenna yanked off her gloves and dropped them next to the pit. "Where do you want to start?"

"How about close to the dungeon? I hear people have seen spooks around there."

Alenna felt a strange dread cover her like a shroud.

She'd been in the dungeon before.

Wait. No she hadn't.

"I've been in there before," Alenna said without stopping to think.

"What?"

"I think I've been in there before."

Demi wrinkled her nose. "No you haven't. We haven't had a chance to tour before today. Dr. Benedict has kept our noses to the grindstone."

"I've been in there. It's a really creepy feeling."

Demi smiled. "Wait a minute. Miss Skeptical is getting goose bumps from this castle?"

Alenna made a face. "Just because I don't believe in ghosts—"

"Okay, okay." Demi's smile turned cocky. "I'll make you a deal. I'll bet you that while you're excavating here, you'll see a ghost. If I'm wrong, I owe you five bucks…or pounds, as it were. If you're wrong, you owe me five big ones."

"It's a deal."

They shook hands and smiled. Alenna knew they wouldn't see evidence of ghosts or goblins. Quickly, she strapped her crossbody bag around her waist.

Demi moved toward the front of the castle, away from their excavation site. She angled her sophisticated digital camera to take a quick picture of a raven perched on one corner of a stone outcropping.

Alenna was vaguely aware of tourists straggling by. Their voices came as mere threads of sound and she felt a strange, almost unworldly detachment from everything around her. Almost as if she'd transformed into a specter herself.

"Alenna?"

She came back to awareness with a jarring snap.

"Are you sure you're all right?" Demi asked, walking toward her. Concern etched Demi's thin face.

Alenna forced herself to walk forward, placing one foot in front of the other as if dragging them through molasses. "I'm great."

A raven cawed, startling her, and as she looked for the bird, the watery sunlight disappeared under dense clouds. The resulting loss of light threw heavy shadows along the cobblestones beneath her feet, and the air cooled.

"The ravens are keepers of the castle," Demi said as they looked at the wooden raven house perched inside the entrance to the courtyard. "They watched over the MacAulays when they lived here hundreds of years ago."

"Kind of like the ravens at The Tower of London," Alenna said.

"Shades of Edgar Allen Poe," Demi said as she snapped a picture of the raven house. She gave a delicate shiver.

Alenna felt a growing unease, as if history reeled back like a giant scene ready to play out in front of her.

Demi looked around the castle. "Imagine how horrible it must have been to live here in the Middle Ages."

"It was awful," Alenna whispered as a knot of unease tightened around her throat.

A shiver of bone-deep cold racked her as her stomach did a drunken lurch. She wiped her sweaty palms on her jeans as her pounding heart thudded in her ears with a maddening pulse.

She started down the cobblestone lane to her left. "I think I'll stop in the tea shop and grab coffee or something. They make a better cappuccino than Dr. Benedict. Why don't you go on and explore?"

"Alenna—"

"I'll meet up with you later, Demi."

Sure, she felt rude walking off. "Unfailingly polite" was her middle name. Physically wobbly and mentally perplexed, she didn't want to embarrass herself by having a panic attack.

Alenna Carstairs never gives in to emotional displays. Everybody says so.

People who couldn't keep a lid on their emotions were just that...emotional. Sucking in deep breaths, she managed to reduce the butterflies doing barrel rolls in her abdomen.

Once inside the tearoom, she'd find warmth and settle the odd turmoil in her mind and heart. Somehow, though, these thoughts rang as hollow as if she'd said them out loud and the echo had bounced among the castle walls.

Her heart. What a laugh. After her broken engagement, she didn't plan on letting any man into her life for a long, long time. Shaking off thoughts of her failed engagement, she walked. Her steps made no sound. She glanced at the high walls, marveling at the stone's resiliency, at the way it stood strong and immovable through centuries of turmoil. But there was more.

Like a bad scent, dark and thick as smoke, a lingering malaise stained the atmosphere and almost knocked her over with its stench. She shuddered, puzzled by bizarre feelings.

She strolled until she noticed an archway in the wall. Curious, she decided to see where the doorway led. A cool blast of wind came from the opening and she pulled the collar on her jacket higher around her neck. As she looked through the arch, she spied an inner courtyard. A yeoman gave a tour to with a small group of seven. She joined the group.

"During the early 1300s this area was used for several different functions. A parade ground, for the occasional tournament, perhaps even for executions. Please follow me…"

She followed, listening to the yeoman's continuous story. "Of course, one of the more gruesome uses for a castle is to imprison your enemies. With great regularity, it is said, the enemies of the MacAulay's were jailed, including many thought to be witches or other poor souls in the wrong place at the wrong time."

As the yeoman ducked under an archway and the group

followed, Alenna's apprehension surged. Sick of her wayward emotions, she tamped it down and continued with the tour. The teashop idea went on the back burner.

As everyone passed through a wooden doorway, the blackness beyond seemed to swallow them.

She was the last one in the line, and a cold draft rolled up from the darkness and flowed around her. She stopped. A series of small stone steps led downward in a sharp spiral. Weak light from a narrow arrow slit window scarcely illuminated the way.

Although unnerved, she proceeded. The steps were few and when she emerged into the cluster of people huddled around the yeoman, she realized where they were. The cavernous area, dimly lit by torches placed in wide spaced intervals, had four cells with bars. Each small cell offered nothing but a dirt floor. Tiny barred windows at the top of the high ceiling allowed minimal light into the dank, dark dreariness.

The dungeon.

As she stood at the back of the group, she turned slowly, looking at the solid blocks of stone in this subterranean hellhole. While a tourist could see more if the room offered better illumination, the torches created more effective atmosphere. Stale, thick air settled into her lungs as she drew in a breath. As people milled about and kicked up tiny particles, she smelled the dust of the ages.

Although the yeoman chattered, she realized she hadn't heard a word. She was too absorbed in her mental meandering, her surroundings and the fact her nerves hopped liked Mexican jumping beans.

Prickly.

Hyperaware.

Her heart pounded with a slow, stirring dread in her chest. A sharp, dull throb started in her skull. She closed her eyes. Leaning against the wall for support, she hoped the strange disquiet would pass. Alenna tried to draw a steady breath, but it seemed little oxygen reached the barren prison.

The yeoman moved toward the center of the large room and continued with his tour speech. "The castle came under siege in 1318 by a Baron Ruthven who hated Baron MacAulay, the lord of this castle. It was during this time that a knight by the name of Tynan of MacBrahin betrayed Baron MacAulay. MacBrahin and the baron came to blows over a woman. Tynan was killed."

At his words, Alenna's throat tightened and hot tears surged into her eyes without warning. *God, oh God. This is ridiculous. Why do I feel like they are talking about someone I might...love?*

"Many people mourned the brave knight's passing," the yeoman said. "Especially the ladies."

"Why?" a woman in the back asked.

The yeoman cleared his throat and smiled conspiratorially. "Apparently he was quite a...well, to be delicate about it...quite a randy fellow."

A titter of laughter went around the dungeon, echoing eerily off the walls.

"What happened to the woman?" a man asked.

"No one knows," the yeoman said, his tone designed to convey drama.

Fear teased, like the tiny touches of a spider's legs, flitted over Alenna's skin.

Get out. She had to leave here before the nausea and tension overwhelmed, before the unbearable sadness she now experienced tore her to shreds.

She ascended the stairs swiftly, her heart slamming as if she'd been running a marathon. Once outside she slowed her walk. Beyond grateful, she smiled. She'd escaped the heinous place.

Tremors in her limbs subsided with the exercise, and she wondered if the strange claustrophobia was yet another ailment sent to plague her.

She hurried down the lane. She'd return to the test pit and accomplish a little more digging before everyone returned from their break.

When Alenna reached the excavation, she didn't bother to remove her waist pack. She stepped into the pit and reached for her trowel.

Scrape. Scrape. Scrape.

Clink.

Her trowel hit metal.

She grabbed a brush. When she glanced around to see if anyone would witness her discovery, there wasn't a soul in sight. Gingerly she brushed at the area until she saw the dull gleam of gold.

"I'll be damned," she whispered. "I'll be damned."

She used the brush to remove the remainder of the dirt from the metal. A gasp left her throat. *A ring.* A wide gold band, scratched and dented, lovingly cradled a large, pitted oval garnet stone. Without thinking about procedure, excited by her extraordinary find, she lifted it out of its dirty grave and slipped the jewelry on the ring finger of her right hand.

"Damn," she said when she realized what she'd done. Instead of leaving the ring as is and recording the find like a professional, she'd acted like an impulsive amateur. In other words, she acted exactly like what she was.

What the hell…she'd put it back and no one would be the wiser. She'd have to be more careful next time. The ring was too big and slipped sidewise on her finger. She turned it around so the garnet faced up again.

Before she could remove the ring, she heard the sound of animal hooves clamoring on the cobblestones behind her.

No sooner had she heard the sound than she noticed a strange mist had settled around the immediate area. A solitary patch of cold, cloaking fog. She couldn't see beyond the haze. Perplexed by the bizarre phenomena, she didn't move.

Seconds later a shout and the harsh whinny of a horse sounded right on top of her. She whirled in time to see a huge black horse rear on its hind legs. Simultaneous impressions and emotions bombarded her in milliseconds. The horse, which hadn't been there three seconds before, would crush her under its hooves. She would die here in this castle, far from home.

A man, cloaked in black, rode the powerful horse like a demon upon its back. She didn't have time to scream or to dodge out of the way. The horse's hooves came down and the world went black.

CHAPTER 2

A hand, rough with calluses, brushed Alenna's forehead. She knew she must be in heaven because she felt no pain.

But she changed her mind. Heaven wouldn't be this cold or as uncomfortably hard. Dazed, she lay without moving, amazed she'd somehow survived being trampled.

"Is she kilt, sir?" the voice of a young boy, accent as thick as oatmeal, asked.

"Nay. Damned silly wench appeared in front of Dragon. Where did ye come from, taet taupie?"

His question rippled over her skin like a physical touch. Deep and husky, the man's voice was easier to understand than the boy, but not by much. Certain peculiarities to his accent baffled her. She didn't understand some of his words at all. *Taet taupie?*

He pushed a hand under her shoulders and strong arms bore her aloft. A scratchy texture like heavy wool rubbed against her cheek, but beneath it lay warm, steel-strong muscle.

Wonderful. Run down by a horse, now lugged around by a yeoman? One of the people who enacted scenes from the past?

She tried to pry open her eyes, but deep lethargy weighed down her eyelids.

"Are you sure she is nae goin' to die, sir?" the boy asked.

"Clandon, have ye nothin' to do but plague me with clishmaclaver? Dragon dinnae run her down. I think she has fainted. I willnae ken until I have had a look at her."

Dragon? The man had been riding a dragon? God, she was dreaming. Only dreaming. In that case, she'd just wake up. Forcing her eyes open, she saw nothing but fuzzy shapes. Grey sky and a man cradling her to his chest. Light dazzled and hurt her eyes, so she closed them quickly. The man's movements as he walked were strong and sure. The guy had to be pretty damned strong to walk with her as if she weighed no more than a feather.

"Sorry, sir. 'Tis just that she is as strange as anythin' I have seen before me eyes. Be she a witch then, or a kelpie? Caithleen said there was a sightin' of the clootie on the berm this fortnight."

"We are too far from a loch for Caithleen to be seein' a kelpie, lad. And ye think if she was a clootie she would be lyin' in my arms this minute and not damnin' us both to hell?"

Clootie?

A kelpie, a witch and a devil wrapped in one? A pretty tall order.

"Her clothes are strange, sir."

"Mayhap she is from the south."

"Sassenach?" the boy asked, awe and a smidgen of disgust in his voice.

"Aye."

"Will his lordship have her kilt then?"

"Nay, Clandon. He doesnae slay mere women and children."

What the hell are they talking about?

Moments later the man said, "Open the door."

The groan of hinges long in need of oiling grated on her ears. Seconds later, she caught the woodsy scent of smoke.

"Stoke the fire," the man said.

Metal clanked and feet shuffled. The man laid her upon something lumpy and smelly.

"I will see to Dragon. Watch over the woman until I return," the man said.

"Are ye goin' to fetch his lordship?" the boy asked.

"Nay, Clandon. If she be an unimportant wench, do ye think his lordship would concern himself with her?"

"The steward, then?"

"Nay. For her safety, we best tell no one she is here. Let no one in these chambers until I return." She felt his heavy, warm hand upon her forehead. "She has a wee fever. Bring the fur from the chair."

A heavy material settled over her body and someone tucked it about her shoulders. Alenna barely suppressed a gag at the stench.

"Is she hurt?" the boy asked.

"I dinnae believe it is grave. Fetch some ale for her if she wakes and see that she no leaves here."

The clatter of the door announced his departure. She heard the boy moving around the room. The fire crackled as sparks spit off the wood. Sooty scents rose to her nostrils, stinging. She shivered—her feet and hands felt like blocks of ice.

More shuffling, the clank of metal.

Curious sounds…a shout…bustling activity from outside.

She had to see what the hell was happening.

And this time, with startling clarity, Alenna could see her surroundings. The ceiling above her was soot-stained stone. She lay on some sort of wooden pallet about the size of a double bed, piled high with furs for a mattress. Alenna wrinkled her nose and tried to ignore the odor. She propped herself up on her elbows.

While she wouldn't call the room large, she could see a bigger room off to the side. Besides this pallet, a well-worn chest of black wood sat in one corner, and a large, square, knotty wood table sat in the middle of the room with three chairs around it.

A young boy sat near the fire in a rickety-looking chair. Thin and not particularly clean, his face was a study in poverty and neglect. His short, dark hair looked greasy and lay limp and straight against his small head. He couldn't be much more than nine, if that. A ragged, torn, dirty white shirt covered his gaunt torso, and rough-looking brown pants protected his stick-like legs. His brown ankle boots had seen better days. Little guttersnipe described him to a capital T.

He turned and looked at her. His dark eyes widened, large in his small face. "Zounds!"

"Hi," she said, testing her voice. She licked her dry lips.

His brow furrowed and as he stared, he slowly stood and reached for a pitcher. He poured liquid into a small wooden goblet and headed for her, still wide-eyed.

Alenna sat up and took the goblet from him. She sniffed the contents of the cup. "Ale?"

"Aye."

"Okay. Interesting."

Like a frightened crab, the boy skittered back from her, bumping into a chair and almost tripping.

She managed a half-hearted smile. "It's all right. I won't hurt you."

She took a sip of the ale and choked on the sour taste. A small coughing fit seized her and a full minute passed before she could talk again. Maybe it would be better if she didn't drink the stuff.

Open-mouthed, the boy continued to stare at her.

Poor kid. Wasn't he taking his act a bit far?

The door opened with a loud creak. She started, spilling ale down the front of her jacket. "Damn it."

The door slammed shut. She opened her mouth to speak, but the sound strangled in her throat as she caught her first sight of the man standing inside the door.

"Aye, so I see ye are awake now," he said, in the husky, deep voice that belonged to the man who had carried her.

Nothing, in her wildest, most fantastical dreams could have conjured a male like this man. Okay. Maybe in her most outrageous, sex-filled evenings with her vibrator. Still, she'd never encountered a man like this one in real life. With her dating and almost-married record, she didn't think guys like this existed.

Most women would run in fear from him. A few inches over six feet, his sheer size swallowed the small room. Did a man this outrageously feral have a concept of tenderness? Of restraint? He looked ready to spring, to dominate. His brutishly handsome face arrested her. Time slowed, and all the fantasies she'd harbored about gorgeous men over the years dissolved, overwhelmed by the sheer male animal presence in front of her.

Unfastening the broach at his shoulder, he allowed his heavy brown cloak to fall open. Under the cloak, he wore a dark shirt of rough material open at the throat. The gap revealed a bit of muscled chest sprinkled with dark hair. Broad of shoulder, his powerful frame demanded attention. His black trousers revealed just enough with their cut to suggest strong thighs and calves. She licked her lips involuntarily. His gaze landed on her mouth and stayed for one stomach-dropping second, then glided over her body with a mix between curiosity and pure male appreciation. His hungry appraisal sent a coil of heat deep into her loins and a blush to her cheeks. She couldn't speak and she almost couldn't breathe.

Taking off the cloak, he settled it over a chair. Crossing the room, he stood next to her makeshift pallet. "Are ye deaf, then, lass? Or mayhap a mute?"

"No," she said softly, her throat feeling as parched as if she'd crossed the Sahara. His strange questions threw her, and she couldn't think of a retort.

His brow crinkled and she noted a deep scar ran down the right side of his forehead, as if he'd suffered a severe blow at one time and never had it stitched properly. He shoved a hand through his inky black hair and it fell about the top of his shoulders in thick waves.

Turning to the skinny boy, he said, "Clandon, ye had best get back to yer duties. And visit yer sister at the donjon to see how she fares."

Continuing to look at her as if she might decide to bite him, the boy nodded. He scrambled up from his chair and started for the door.

"She must be a witch, sir," the boy said, his voice squeaking in his excitement.

The man smiled slightly, a twinkle leaping into his eyes. Before the boy could open the door, the man clasped his arm. "Tell not a soul about the woman."

Tell not a soul about the woman.

A curl of apprehension wandered along her body.

"Aye, sir," the boy said in a whisper, and rushed out the door as if the devil were on his heels and fast closing.

Maybe the boy knew something she didn't. She looked at the door with longing. It really wasn't far, and Alenna wasn't that ill. She could dash by this big man and make a run for it.

No. The man had planted his solid bulk in her way. If he caught her, she knew she wouldn't be a match for him. He possessed a sheer, brutal power she felt could overpower if provoked.

"Why did you send him away?" she asked.

The man turned back to her. "His sister worries about him."

As he stared at her, Alenna shivered and realized that although her stomach no longer lurched like a drunken sailor, a heat wave invaded her. She pushed the pungent fur off her shoulders. Again his eyes traced over her, penetrating and searching. He didn't guard his emotions well, she realized. She saw unadulterated sexual interest overlaid by curiosity.

Sexual interest? Another warm wave settled over her and then she shivered. God, since when did extraordinary men like this enter her life?

Never.

"I wouldnae try to stand," he said, pinning her with a hard look. "Yer no well enough."

"I'm fine," she said, aware her statement sounded lame.

"Fine?" he asked, looking confused by her choice of words. "Ye no sound Scottish or English."

Hadn't the man spoken with an American before?

"I'm American."

"American?"

She sighed. "Look, I don't know what game you're playing here, but I'd really—"

"I dinnae play with ye," he said softly, with a hint of menace lacing every word.

"Then will you please tell me if you have a nurse or doctor here at the castle? Or maybe a first aid station?"

"Nurse? Ye have a child that needs a wet nurse?" he asked.

"No, no. I mean someone who helps the ill."

"Father MacDougald helps those that are poorly. And Elizabet helps those she can."

He squatted beside the pallet and stared at her as if she'd sprung from the floor like a demon from hell and he was a scientist sent to explore the oddity. Confusion lent sharpness to her feelings, and she was in no mood to play whatever game this man had in mind.

"Thanks for your help, but I think I'd better go," she said.

She shifted on the pallet and he reached out for her, his grip on her forearm tight enough to restrain but not enough to injure. She looked down at the multitude of white, thin scars crossing the back of his broad hand.

"Stay," he said.

"Let me go."

He removed his hand, but he didn't back away.

Despite her wariness at his close proximity, she had an unhindered view of how kind nature had been to him. Sculpted with an artist's hand, his nose was strong but not overly large. The cut of his mouth looked designed for kissing—not too full...not too thin. More disquieting than the unabashed way he stared at her was the smoldering, dark-as-night quality of his eyes. Framed by thick, black lashes, his gaze penetrated with an intensity that unnerved her down to the bones and made her feel as if he could read her every thought. Despite her desperation, a warm well of arousal stirred in her lower belly. Her vaginal muscles contracted and a tight, sweet longing pulsed inside her.

Oh, God. I really have gone nuts.

"What is this aid station?" he asked, once again bending the words awkwardly.

"You know. First aid." When he continued to stare at Alenna as if she'd lost her mind, irritation bolted through her in an impatient wave. She twisted at the waist so she could prop herself against the wall. "If you're worried I'll tell someone that your horse hit me—"

"Dragon dinnae hit ye." His tone came out certain, clipped and brooked no argument. "Ye fell in the path of my war horse."

War horse. This man played his part a little too close to that delicious, broad, muscled chest. "Look, I'm not out to sue anyone."

The man sighed. "Eh? What's this sue? His lordship willnae listen to anything against me, lass. He trusts my word above all else."

Who was this lordship? She recalled the guidebook said the

castle belonged to the National Trust. For over twenty years, no lordship had been in residence.

Every second that passed cemented her belief that this guy might be a few bricks short of a load.

Too bad. A man this hunky and he was loony as hell.

A ripple of caution twisted in Alenna's gut. If she escaped in one piece, she'd contact security and let them know one of the reenactment people had gone south on them. But obviously this man was in no mood for her to pop up, say "ta ta" and hightail it out the door. She'd have to make a run for it.

"Why didn't you want the boy to tell anyone about me?" she asked.

One corner of his mouth tilted in a smile far from amused. He shook his head. "Word of a strange young woman within the castle walls would spread fast."

"What? Why surely, with all the other tourists—"

"I dinnae ken what you mean by tour…tourists." He reached out slowly and touched the metal tab of the zipper on her jacket. "A strange thing, this cloak. And ye are wearin' a man's trews."

Alenna shifted away from him and swung her feet off the pallet. "I'd like to stand, please."

He twitched an eyebrow and nodded. "Risk it if ye will."

She stood slowly, gratified when everything stayed exactly as it should. "I think I'm fine now."

Time, as the cliché said, to get the hell out of Dodge.

Taking a chance, she headed for the door, her feet sprouting wings. She hit the door at the same time she heard him spit something that sounded like a curse.

Before she could fling the door open, the man's hands slammed down on either side of her head, bracketing her in and pinning her entire body from chest to toes to the door. Every tight, hard muscle of his body pressed against her. A lightning bolt of fear paralyzed her only for a moment. Then her body betrayed her. He smelled musky, like subtle man sweat. But it wasn't unpleasant and her heartbeat skittered in her chest. His chest braced against her, and under those trews his cock pressed aggressively into her mid-back. She shivered in pure sexual awareness. Her nipples tightened into points. Total, utter surprise and shame gathered inside her.

How in the hell can I feel like this? Horny and scared all at one time?

"What do ye think ye are doin'?" Deep with indignation, his voice whispered low in her ear, his warm breath tickling the back of her neck and her cheek. "Ye no can go out there."

She quivered once, his harshness and the wild feelings careening through her adding to her panic.

"Let me go!" She twisted toward him, trying to recall her self-defense training. She stomped on his foot.

He let out a bellow and another curse but he barely budged. Adrenaline pounded through her system and she aimed up with her knee. He was too fast. Blocking her aim at his groin, he leaned against her so her palms plastered against his broad chest. She sucked in a breath as his hips jammed against her and pinned her legs against the door.

This time his cock felt bigger. Bulging against his trews and pressing into her stomach in a way that screamed one thing.

Feral, unadulterated, pulse-pounding sex.

Fear slammed through Alenna. The heavy pressure of him against her forced the air out of her lungs. She looked up and realized the top of her head just peaked over his shoulder. Enveloped by his strength, she forced herself to relax, trying to give him the illusion she'd surrendered.

His dark gaze blazed with angry fire, his arms caging her to the door with a strength she'd never experienced. More fear poured through her system. Oh, God. What the hell did he have in mind? Maybe if she tried to reason with him, he'd release her. If he thought he could rape her, the bastard had a fight on his hands he wouldn't forget.

"Let me go and I won't scream," she said, attempting to lace her words with steel.

"Do ye really think anyone will come to yer aid if ye scream?"

"Of course."

"No one," he said quietly. "But ye dinnae need to fear me. I willnae force myself on ye."

"What do you call this?" she asked, wiggling against him.

She sucked in a strangled breath as he pressed his hips closer. His dark eyes perused her face with undeniable interest, his chest rising and falling, his lips parting. "I cannae help my cock responding to such a fiery woman. Make no mistake, my body wants ye. But I would never hurt a woman."

She snorted. "Right." She twisted again. "Let me go!"

"Ye dinnae ken the danger in goin' out there."

"What could possibly be more dangerous about being outside than in here with you?"

"Ye have nothin' to fear from me."

She sighed. "You're holding me against my will, and I don't know what your intentions are."

"'Tis my warrant, as a knight, to protect a woman's honor."

Alenna smirked, amazed at the historical crap he spouted and how he continued playing the part. "From what I've heard knights didn't try to protect damsels in distress. That is an overblown fairy tale."

His brow wrinkled, but he didn't say a word.

Exasperated, she continued. "Look, you don't have to keep playacting for me. "

Confusion once again marred his features. Slowly, he backed away a step so he no longer leaned against her and she took a deep breath. He remained watchful.

Despite being half afraid of him, she couldn't help the odd attraction to his raw maleness and the absolute certainty of his power. This close, even Alenna's consternation couldn't remove the dazzling impact of his masculinity. Resolutely, she shoved away the mystique of his magnetism.

Slowly, he reached up to cup her face in one rough palm and she flinched. "Ye are unwell."

"No. Let me out of here. Now."

"Have ye lost all sense? Ye have a fever, no meat on yer bones, and 'tis cold outside."

Alenna knew for a fact as a woman of medium height and medium weight that overall, her shape was ordinary. Maybe he liked plump women.

Was she out of her mind? What did she care what kind of woman he wanted? Alenna's mind raced to figure out how to deal with him. Thinking back to the numerous psychology courses she'd taken, she knew her first mistake had been to antagonize him. She needed to lure him into believing in her complacency then make a move to leave.

"All right," she said.

He moved back a little more, but continued to cup her face with his hand. His thumb traced over her cheek. "I willnae hurt ye. Dinnae be afraid of me."

She nodded as he continued to look down on her, his gaze tracing her face with a slumberous, rapt attention.

"What are you doing?" she asked, fear tightening her throat.

His palm dropped away from her face. "Why are ye here?"

"What?"

"Why are ye at this castle?"

"I'm with the archaeological dig." Her pulse beat a rapid tattoo as he watched her with wary attention.

"What is this arch...archaeological dig ye speak of?"

"Release me and I'll tell you."

She licked her lips again and he watched, the heat of his attention suffusing her body.

"Tell me," he said. "Are ye a spy for Ruthven?"

"I don't know anyone called Ruthven."

"I dinnae believe ye."

"I promise you, I'm not a spy." She could feel sweat running down her neck. "I'm a sort of tourist."

Anxiety pumped in Alenna's veins and quickened her heart. Her hands trembled and she clasped them in front of her tightly.

"What is this tourist?"

Humor him. She drew in a deep breath. "A person who travels to places for the purpose of sightseeing."

His hard expression didn't change. He put his hands on his hips. "Sight-seein'?"

"You know. Visiting castles like this place."

"Why?"

"I told you. Because…because we like to see ruins, visit grand houses to see the way people lived centuries ago."

Expelling a slow breath, he inched a little closer. "This castle is indeed very old, but not centuries. Why are ye tremblin'?"

"I'm not." Her heart crammed her throat and threatened to choke her. So much for staying calm.

"We've had spies the last few months tryin' to harm his lordship."

"Baron MacAulay?"

One of his dark brows quirked up. "Aye."

A little of Alenna's fear subsided and a possible explanation for his bizarre behavior came to her. "Are you an undercover police officer?"

Once again his face registered confusion. "I am Tynan of MacBrahin, one of his lordship's knights. My loyalty is to his lordship's household and all who take shelter within it."

Instantly Alenna remembered the yeoman's tale of the knight who had fought Baron MacAulay and died. This man didn't pretend he lived in the fourteenth century, he believed it. Now she knew, as some Brits would say, that he was a total nutter.

She glanced about the stark room, took in the dank scent of the chamber and the odors that didn't seem to fit with a fabricated scenario. Uneasiness filled her. Besides the crazy man in front of her, something else didn't feel normal.

She had to escape. Passing the time of day as if she hadn't a care in the world wouldn't win her release from this madman's chamber. She made her decision. Turning with the last of her strength, she grabbed for the door and flung it open.

CHAPTER 3

As she dashed out the door, Alenna almost landed in the path of a large white horse. The man atop the large stallion pulled back on the reins of the horse and swung from the saddle. He landed with a thud and clatter. Clad in chain mail, he sported a blond mustache and piercing blue eyes. Shorter than her captor by quite a measure, she wondered if he would be any match for the other man.

Before she could ask for help, Tynan wound his strong arms around her waist and pulled her back against him.

"She is half wild, Dougald, she is that," Tynan said.

The blond man smiled, his grin wide and friendly. Maybe he could help her. She pulled against the crazy man's grip. "Please this man is crazy—"

Alenna cut herself off when she took in the activity around her. She smelled smoke and saw a light tendril drift into the air. Around her the sounds built...a horse's whinny, the clang of metal upon metal, a shout from some part of the castle, a man's laugh. Sun slanted on the castle walls, not a cloud in the sky.

Not a cloud in the sky. How could that be? She remembered seeing a completely overcast sky just before Tynan's horse nearly ran her down. The odd mist that had enveloped the dig had disappeared.

"What...?" she said, bewildered as she noted the test pit she should have seen a few feet away had vanished. All the cobblestones seemed back in place. In fact, it looked as if they'd never been disturbed.

The man called Dougald stepped up, his gaze searching but still friendly. "Aye, but she is a tall one. Where did ye find her, Tynan?"

"Please," she said, pulling against Tynan's grip. "You've got to help me. This man is keeping me against my will—"

"Pay no mind to her, Dougald. She is half out of her mind with fever." Tynan tucked her closer. Like solid bands of steel, his arms held her captive. "I am keepin' her with me until she has her wits about her. 'Tis nae safe for her to wander the castle."

"'Tis nae safe for any woman to roam the castle with ye about." Dougald grinned, showing even white teeth and a captivating smile. He tugged off his coif, revealing his collar-length crop of straight, butter-gold hair. "Yer women are usually more willin'. Are ye sure ye dinnae want to pass her along to me like ye did the last one?"

Tynan's laugh rumbled up from his chest, vibrating into her body. "I dinnae pass her. She fell in love with yer ugly face and left me."

Dougald nodded. "Aye, she did that. She knew a better lookin' man when she saw one."

Leading his stallion over to the side to allow a man driving a small wagon to pass on the narrow cobblestone way, Dougald watched as Tynan released her waist and transferred his grip to her wrist.

Increasingly confused and angry at her predicament, Alenna said, "I realize in some places it's still acceptable to treat women like second-class citizens. But in the United States, we—"

"Quiet," Tynan whispered, his tone deadly and low. He pulled her against his side.

"She is a fair one, with a mouth on her. What do ye plan to do with her?"

"He's not going to do anything with me," she said, gritting her teeth.

The sound of several horses and the trundle of wheels grabbed their attention.

"'Tis his lordship," Dougald said, peering into the distance.

"Aye. He went out of the castle walls without our protection."

"What can he be thinkin'? Ruthven has men ready to attack if they find any sign of weakness. Will ye speak with him about it?"

"Aye, I will."

Alenna couldn't believe what she was hearing. His lordship. The sights and smells of a dream world.

Maybe…maybe…she wasn't in her world anymore.

No. Absurd.

Perhaps she'd slipped into a delusion. She didn't know which scared her more, time travel or losing her mind. She must be delirious. Otherwise she couldn't have this elaborate and crazy dream, with characters from a fairy tale. Please, God, let her wake up or revive from this fever of hallucinations.

Yet as she denied everything she saw around her, all the things in this world that hadn't been in hers, a dawning suspicion awoke within her psyche.

As her heart pounded with fear, Alenna moistened her parched lips. "What year is it?"

Both men looked at her as if she'd gone mad.

"Watch that one. She might give ye the evil eye," Dougald said.

"What year is it?" she asked again.

"'Tis the year of our Lord, thirteen hundred and eighteen," Dougald said.

She watched the small procession of people coming down the lane, and a sinking feeling settled in her stomach.

"Oh my God," she whispered as scanned the area.

The inner wall appeared much higher than she remembered. Beyond it stood a tower that hadn't been there before the horse had run her down.

Her legs wobbled. She would not faint. She had never fainted in her entire twenty-nine years.

If she did pass out, she'd be at the mercy of these men. Then again, if she let the black cloud hovering on the edge of her vision take over, maybe she'd wake and find herself back in the normal world.

The black cloud lowered and Tynan lifted her in his arms. As the world spun around, Alenna let the haze envelop her senses.

* * *

SOMETHING hard and warm encircled Alenna and she snuggled closer, burrowing for warmth.

Cold. Why the hell was it always so damned cold?

Her nose twitched as something tickled it, and she moved back a smidgen. Under her cheek she registered the soft exhalation of breath, the heat of skin and the scent of man.

Hot, hard man. Muscular and big.

In contrast, a slightly rough softness brushed against her body, like cozy flannel pajamas. Sure was a lot better than stinky fur.

Where was she? Her limbs felt weak, almost useless. An arm, rock-solid with muscle, tightened around her back. She felt a hand hot as a furnace light upon her brow and she flinched.

"Shhhhh. Be still."

Had she made a sound? Who had the gall to tell her to shut

up, anyway? Alenna struggled against the fuzziness in her brain and the mist threatening to overtake her one more time. A sound of fear escaped her throat, and tender hands stroked through her hair.

"Shhhhh. 'Tis all right. I am here."

The tender words, spoken in a gentle, unmistakably deep voice, brought memories back. Could she really have traveled back in time?

No, no, no, no!

The darkness came back.

* * *

BENEATH ALENNA'S cheek was warm flesh. Reaching out, she tried to feel her way through the fog and clamped down on something solid and rough with hair. She felt downward until she touched—

A very naked, erect cock. Hard as stone.

Oh, that was nice.

A man's deep moan growled near. His big palm clamped over her hand and held it against his firm manhood. Her fingers tightened around his length and he hissed in a breath and groaned. His entire body shivered.

The man sighed and before she could open her eyes, he slowly flipped her over on her back. His long, naked thigh insinuated itself between her legs and pressed tight against her folds. She gasped but he cut off her surprise with his mouth. She whimpered as his lips caressed hers and his tongue dipped warm and sensuously over her own. As he tasted her mouth, his hand came up without hesitation and caught her breast. He cupped it tenderly, his fingers toying with her cloth-clad nipple in a light caress. As her nipples peaked and ached with sweet arousal, she gasped into his mouth and writhed. The rough hair of his hard thigh pressed against her naked clit with a slow, maddening rhythm. Drugging kiss after drugging kiss consumed her with a wealth of erotic sensations. His tongue swept over hers repeatedly, and through the sensual fog she returned his caresses. Her tongue tangled with his, and she searched his muscled shoulders. Her touch swept down his broad ribcage and discovered his naked ass. He moaned as she touched him.

His cock pressed intimately to her thigh. One more movement. Just an inch or so and he'd have that glorious, naked penis pressed between her legs. For a few wild, unbelievable seconds, she wanted to shift and make room for his cock to plunge straight up inside her. Naked. Hard.

She parted her thighs in instinctive desperation. As his tongue continued to take her mouth, his lips ravenous, his hips lowered between her legs. Then, with a gentle push, he started to ease inside. The broad tip parted her and stopped. She throbbed high and hard, her womb seeming to clench, to ache.

Oh.

Oh yes.

Alenna's stomach clenched, her breath came fast, her heart pounding. She closed her eyes and became nothing more than feelings, nothing more than burning physical need. His mouth captured one nipple through the cloth, sucking deeply as he kept that glorious cock poised to thrust deeper, teasing her with promise.

With a startling, mortifying jolt she recalled where she was.

This wasn't some wild sex dream.

Her eyes opened and she pushed at his shoulders. "Oh my God!"

Tynan looked down on her, his eyes smoldering with hungry desire, his chest rapidly moving in and out. His words came husky and brutal with desire as he said, "Mother of God ye feel so good. So hot and wet."

Shocked down to the roots of her being, she wanted to come so badly, so much she almost...almost begged him to take her.

His fingers stayed secure around her nipple. He tugged it experimentally. A sweet, luscious jolt spiraled through her. Stunned, she watched as his gaze transferred to her other breast. His mouth lowered until it hovered over the tight bud. Without hesitation, he latched onto her and gave the nipple a hard suck right through the cloth. She whimpered, writhed against his cock. He tweaked and plucked the other nipple at the same time.

"Oh God." She gasped, as desire raged fiercely inside her body, demanding a delicious, burning release.

"Wait," she managed to gasp. "No."

He immediately halted, his eyes glazed with pure passion. He released her nipple, his fingers slipping away on a last caress that caused her to moan softly.

"Stop," she said. "I can't. This isn't...I don't know you..."

He eased back, his cock leaving the heated cradle, his gaze cautious. "Aye, ye know me."

As his cock left its place between her legs, her body screamed a protest. Her clit throbbed, wanted completion. Damn but she'd lost her mind. How could she act this way with a perfect stranger? When his hand slipped between her legs and his large fingers brushed across her clit, she gasped.

"Do ye crave release?" he asked, his voice a rough counterpoint to his gentleness. He caressed her folds, his long fingers tracing with fine precision. As he circled the tiny nub, she shuddered in pure pleasure.

She couldn't stand the teasing any longer. When his hand started to leave her, she grabbed his wrist and held him there. One part of her was mortified and yelling at her to stop, the other begged Alenna to have this one delicious thing before reality slammed into her life again.

Before she could change her mind, his eyes blazed with realization and his fingers moved against her flesh. She gasped as fire licked her veins and her clit ached with need. *Please.* She just needed this one thing. His mouth came down on hers, his tongue once more conquering with lush, deep strokes that sent sizzling desire shooting through her. His fingers returned to intimate exploration. She arched more fully into his caresses and he sank two fingers deep inside her. Alenna cried out in bliss against his mouth.

He stroked slowly in and out, stretching her inside, spreading her as he worked his fingers deeply within her channel. God, what would it have felt like if she'd let him thrust his cock like this? It was so good right now. So very, very good. She moaned into his mouth and yet he still kissed her. She squirmed under his touch. His fingers hooked a little inside her and found a spot she didn't know she had. When he caressed that place with a firm brushing, the tension escalated dramatically and she writhed and whimpered in total excitement. She wouldn't last long at this rate, her arousal already so high.

When Tynan released her mouth, she couldn't cease her groans of excitement. She could smell sex in the air, the musky scent adding to her frenzy. His breath panted, his own sounds of desire forcing the firestorm higher and higher. Tension drew taut inside her, coiling in a spiral.

She groaned, almost reduced to begging. She was almost there...

Alenna climaxed violently, her voice rising in a scream. He shoved his fingers deep as her pussy clenched hard, then convulsed as sharp, jolting pleasure overcame her. Shaking, she panted through the last exquisite aftershocks as his fingers resumed their leisurely caress deep inside her. It was too much. She grabbed his wrist to stop the teasing. His fingers withdrew from her sheath and a wave of self-consciousness slammed her.

Oh God. What had she done? How could she have let this stranger touch her this way?

His eyes gleamed with male, predatory satisfaction. He licked the two fingers that had been buried inside her, tasting her juices. "Hmmm, a woman's taste. So bonnie. I've never seen a woman find her pleasure so sweetly before."

More heat flushed her cheeks. She'd never seen a man lick his fingers clean of her essence, either. Renewed arousal threatened and Alenna took a deep breath as her heart continued to pound in her ears.

The soft seduction in his words surprised her. She shifted into sitting position to put distance between them, trying desperately to resurrect a sense of equilibrium.

As he sat up, she scooted back, no mean feat considering the narrow bed had no room to maneuver. She pulled the wool plaid blanket tight around her. The bed barely fit in the room. There was no fireplace and it was icy cold.

As he opened his eyes, she stared into his piercing gaze. Embarrassment washed through her like a sea wave and flushed her cheeks.

"I ken there is a fair draft in here. Would ye mind not taken' the feileadh breacan all for yer own?" he said gruffly as if he hadn't just brought her to the most incredible orgasm she'd experienced in a long time.

"The what?"

He touched the wool plaid she clasped taut around her. "This."

In a panic she assessed her garb. She no longer wore her own clothes. A thin garment made of a soft linen draped in heavy folds about her body and covered her from head to toe. A plaid served as a cover for both of them. Yet she felt naked—

She wasn't wearing a bra or panties.

His big, naked body crowded her.

Oh, oh my.

Naked somehow didn't describe the glory of his body. There should be another word to define a man this honed, this freakin' gorgeous. And his cock, still totally erect, pointed upward from a bush of dark hair. Framed by his muscular thighs, his cock caught her attention and held it. She couldn't look away.

"As pleased I am ye like my cock, lass, have ye lost your tongue?"

For a moment she thought Tynan meant he wanted her to lick his cock. More heat spilled into her face. She'd gotten herself into this mess and encouraged him. Responded to the wildfire passion he aroused. She'd never reacted this violently on any level to any man but Tynan.

"How did I...did you undress me?" she asked in a rush, indignation and shame flaming in her face.

To her surprise his dour countenance lightened and he laughed. The rich sound caressed her ears. "What if I were to say I did? Would ye run and caterwaul the way ye did earlier?"

"Earlier? What time is it?"

"Early in the morn." In the semi-darkness she saw his wide grin slip, until the grave look returned. "When ye fainted, I went for Elizabet and Johanna."

"Who?"

"Elizabet is a healer and Johanna is her daughter. They brought ye a shift and got ye settled in bed. When ye mumbled and tossed in your fever, I could see the plaid wouldnae keep ye warm. I tried the fur but ye tossed it away."

She wrinkled her nose. "It stinks."

A tiny grin twitched at the corner of his mouth. "Aye. That it does."

Tynan's explanation of how she'd gotten into this nightdress didn't explain everything that had happened to her in the last few hours, nor why he'd climbed into bed with her.

Well, okay. Maybe he'd climbed into bed with her so he could seduce her. And man, if she'd been any more addled, who knows what would have happened?

Well, okay. It had happened. He'd slipped his cock into her, even just a little bit. He'd brought her to climax. Yet her channel still ached as if it longed for the hard, ramming thrust of his large cock, and nothing else would completely appease her.

Her mind whirled with questions. Demi must be frantic about her by now. Why hadn't she discovered that she'd been taken hostage by this man and called the authorities?

Memory crashed in on her. Demi couldn't find her because she was no longer in her time...

"Dinnae look so worried," he said. "I was tryin' to keep ye warm. Ye were murmurin' about being cold."

"You were...you tried to take advantage of me while I was sleeping."

One dark eyebrow twitched upward. "Nay. I gave ye pleasure." He reached out and clasped her hand, then slipped it firmly around the base of his cock. He was still hard, still so hot flesh-to-flesh. A quivering started to multiply low in her stomach. "When a woman grips me like ye did, what do ye think crosses a man's mind?"

She jerked her hand under his and at first he didn't let her go. "Stop it. I was dreaming...I thought I was, anyway. I had no idea..."

He released her. He raked his hands through his ebony hair and it fell back to his bare shoulders in thick waves.

She'd guessed at his strength earlier, but now he was naked, she could see the rippling muscles in his arms and in the broadness of his hair-roughened chest and hard stomach. Across his abdomen was a red scar, as if from a recently healed wound. As Tynan turned a curious gaze on her, a stunning emotion captured her breath.

It nagged at her, begged her to form...like an elusive scent lingering in a room, the sensation almost came clear. Abruptly it vanished, leaving her with a sentient deja vu stronger than anything she'd ever experienced. Somewhere before this moment…before he'd almost run her down with his horse, she had met him. Where?

"Why do ye look at me that way?"

"Have I met you before?"

"I never set eyes on anythin' like ye in all my life, before yesterday."

She didn't know whether to be insulted or a complimented.

Disconcerted by his raw masculinity so close, she said, "I haven't seen anything like you before either."

"Humph."

When Tynan said nothing more and stared like Alenna was a prize salmon catch, she grew uneasy. She needed to make a plan. But how could she get back to her time? Her mind reeled with the implications. How had she come back in time in the first place? And why?

He left the bed and it displayed his nakedness even more gloriously. His cock stood proud and she caught a glimpse of his tight, bare ass.

Alenna, you are certifiable. Stop looking at him like this.

"You've got to let me go," she said.

"Nay," he said firmly. "If ye went now, no matter where it was, it would be far too dangerous. Word has been that the Ruthvens are comin' this way intent on killin' his lordship. Everyone has come within the castle walls. We think the Ruthvens and their supporters will be here any day. They will lay siege to the castle."

"War?"

"Aye."

The thought of being trapped in this place while a war raged settled a hard cold dread over her body.

"Come to the table and eat," he said. He walked to a chair across the small room and grabbed his trews. He drew them on swiftly, sat on the chair and put on his footwear with quick efficiency. "Tell me how ye happened to be in MacAulay Castle alone. Have ye no guidman?"

"Guidman?"

"Yer husband? A betrothed?"

"No...I don't have a man."

Alenna tensed. Despite the fact Tynan hadn't harmed her, she didn't completely trust him. She could tell him she'd come from another time, but she hesitated. Would he think she was crazy and have her thrown into the dungeon? The thought of being stuffed into that hellhole made her blood freeze. And nowadays it would be far worse than the sanitized version she'd seen before.

"Elizabet said ye came here for a special reason," he said.

When his words mirrored her thoughts, a tingle prickled her body like static electricity. "Special reason?"

"Elizabet is a wise woman. She knows many things that would brand her of the de'il. When first I came here, four years ago, she told me a woman would appear to me from a mist. She said ye were special and I must protect ye with my life. I dinnae believe her then, nor do I now." He walked to her and held out his hand. "Can ye stand?"

She allowed his warm hand to close over hers, and as she left the bed she drew the plaid around her. The floor beneath her bare feet felt icy. With her legs so weak, she felt grateful he held her hand. After she settled into a chair next to the table, he knelt by the fire and stoked it high and roaring. She watched him poke at the flames, mesmerized by the way the muscles moved in his back and shoulders and arms.

A wooden bowl sat on the table, partially covered with a piece of linen. Peaking into the bowl, Alenna saw a stew of potatoes and onions. The idea of eating the concoction didn't appeal and her stomach did a flip. She closed her eyes and pressed her hand to her midsection.

He squatted down next to her chair. "Are ye goin' to be ill?"

She took a deep breath. "No. I...would you have bread or some cheese? I don't think I can eat this."

He nodded. "Aye." After he'd retrieved a trencher and cheese and she discovered the taste was not bad, he settled into a chair across the table from her. "Who are ye?"

Disoriented and singularly scared at turns, Alenna didn't know how she wanted to answer him. When she remained silent, he stood and reached for his shirt, which lay looped over a chair. He pulled it over his head, covering his magnificent chest. After he sat down in a chair opposite her again, he leaned across the table, his gaze intent, as if by mere force of will he could see into her heart.

"Elizabet said ye were sent to save my life and I must protect ye."

She shook her head. "No. There's been a horrible mistake. I don't belong here."

"Ye are not from the village. Ye speak most strange."

How could she possibly answer his questions? If she came right out and told him she had traveled back in time, what would he do with her? If he'd planned to rape or murder her he would have done it long ago. And he'd taken the trouble to keep her warm. But just because he didn't intend her physical harm didn't mean everything was peaches and cream. She still couldn't trust him.

"I'm not from the village. As I said, I'm from a place far away."

"I heard ye speak of it. America?"

"Yes."

Silence stretched for a moment before Tynan said, "Ye aren't eatin'. Ye must build yer strength."

Alenna nodded and did as he suggested. Soon she felt better, and the fire in the hearth warmed the room.

Eager to stretch her cramped muscles, she stood and moved toward the small pallet next to the wall. As she sank to the pallet she said, "You said you are a knight. Yet you live in such… meager chambers."

His brow, with its deep scar, wrinkled as he frowned. "These chambers are fair large and guid. Most other knights have less. My rooms are grand."

She looked at the rushes on the floor, the linen coverings over the windows that barely kept drafts out, and the fireplace. "You don't have lands of your own?"

"Nay. I am not a noble."

"How did you come to be a knight for the baron?"

Tynan rose from the table and came toward her. As he advanced, her muscles tightened, as if readying her to flee. When he sat beside her, his closeness, coupled with the intensity of his regard, made her hyper-aware. She shifted a couple of inches away.

"Ye ask many a question without givin' any answers," he said. "I saw the strange cards ye have in the odd little bag you had with you. I cannae read them. There was something else in there. A hard, square thing. I've never seen the like."

The mention of her bag and the contents sent a jolt of fear and hope through her. *Her cell phone.* She could try and call someone. Maybe she would discover she'd lost her mind and this world she'd built was a part of that insanity. At least she could touch reality and not this medieval fantasy.

"Where is my bag?" she asked.

He moved to the other room quickly and returned with the waist pack. Alenna checked the contents and found the lip balm, wallet with her credit cards and money, and her comb were intact. Her smart phone was there, too. She grabbed it and quickly tried to turn it on. Nothing. He watched her as she messed with it. Every attempt to turn on the phone resulted in nothing. The battery appeared dead and it shouldn't be, because she'd made certain to power it up before her day started at the excavation.

"Damn it," she said. "Damn."

She didn't have a charger with her, either.

As she riffled through the bag again and realized something was missing. She looked down at her right hand.

"The ring!" she gasped.

"Eh?"

"The garnet ring! Where did you put it?"

He gave her a frosty, grim look. "I dinnae steal from ye, if that is what ye think."

"You must have taken it. It's gone. Give it back."

His frown turned to full-fledged anger, darkening his eyes. "I am not a thief. I dinnae take yer bluidy ring."

Wildly she thought about what could have happened. "Maybe I...maybe I dropped it somewhere. It was loose on my finger—"

"Aye. That is the way of it. Maybe when ye ran out of here earlier."

She thought back to her mad dash from the room. The last time she remembered seeing the ring was right before the horse almost ran her down and she'd toppled back into time. If it had fallen off her finger then, maybe it still lay on the ground outside.

Before she could say another word about the jewelry, he plunged ahead. "What is yer name?"

"Alenna Carstairs."

"Lady Alenna?"

"No. Ms. I mean, no. I don't have a title." She grimaced slightly at her stumbling words. Why did Tynan's presence make speaking coherently such a chore? Was it the deep concentration of his gaze? Or that fabulous body so close? Remembering what his mouth and fingers had felt like on her breasts and the way that fabulous thigh had felt against her clit, made her want to squirm.

Get a grip, Alenna.

"Alenna," he said, soft and light. As if it were a mere breath on his lips. "'Tis a bonnie name."

A tremor of pure female satisfaction drove her to smile widely. "Thank you."

Feeling warm, she let the plaid fall from her shoulders. As he perused the front of her gown closely, she felt her nipples peak against the material. Self-consciousness flooded her face with heat, and she crossed her arms over her chest. The way this man looked at her was scary.

No. Scary was too light a word.

She took a deep breath. Maybe if he checked the items in the bag again, he'd believe her if she told him she'd come from the future. The paper money with Queen Elizabeth's countenance should prove she wasn't from his time.

She shifted and cleared her throat. Though she already knew his name, she asked once more, "What is your name again?"

"Tynan of MacBrahin." The sound rolled off his tongue with a slightly guttural accent that intrigued her every minute more she listened.

Once again her gaze locked with his in a battle of wills. "I assume I must call you Sir?"

"Nay, ye can call me Tynan if it suits ye."

She twined her fingers tightly in the plaid. "Where are you from?"

"Glenfinnan. In the Highlands."

"You speak English well," she said, then realized how bizarre her statement sounded.

"'Twas not always so," he said, apparently taking no offense at what she'd said. "I speak Gaelic, but I learned English over these four years I have been at the castle. I dinnea learn it as well as I would like, but 'tis enough to take me through day by day."

"When did you come to the castle?"

"As I said before. Four years ago. For such an ill woman, ye ask a lot of questions."

"I feel good now. Thank you for the meal."

When Tynan reached out to her, she moved back. He made a noise that sounded half laugh and half scorn. He touched her forehead. "Why dinnae ye sleep more? Ye still are hot."

Weariness was returning. What she *should* do was figure a way out of her predicament. But where did one start when it came to time travel? Thinking about the idea made her head throb. She'd never believed in the possibility of something so incredible.

There must be some reason she'd been sent here, but she had to return to her time. Anything else was unthinkable.

"Alenna?"

The quietness of his voice startled her. "Yes?"

"Are ye fashed about bein' in the room with me?"

She shook her head, even though she lied.

He lifted one dark eyebrow and it wrinkled the deep scar on his forehead. She mused that the mark could have made him less attractive, but instead it gave him a tangible air of danger that was wildly intriguing.

"Only fallen women worry naught about their virtue."

Slivers of resentment moved through her. "It's none of your business—"

Tynan reached out, grasping her arm in a grip that was stern, but not tight enough to cause pain. "Ye should worry. There are many who would prey upon a woman within this castle."

"Including you?" she asked, indignant. "You almost took me."

"Aye. I was dazed from sleep. With a beautiful woman in my bed, the temptation was fierce. But not all men would have a care for your virtue."

She wanted to smile. Her virtue. Well, little did he know...

"I can take care of myself," she said.

His smile lifted one side of his mouth in a sarcastic twist. "I wouldnae be so sure about that."

A slow burn of irritation and fear pushed her up from the bed and out of his grasp. "I'm a grown woman. I'm twenty-nine years old and I've spent a large portion of my life getting along without a man to guard me every step of the way."

He made an aggravated sound in his throat and stood. Toe to toe, he stared down at her. Her heart did a strange jump and suddenly she wasn't sure she was getting enough air.

"I am three-and-thirty and in my life I have seen many horrors. Not the least, the fate that could befall a woman without a man to protect her. I have seen women raped and murdered by men with no souls. Ye have no knowledge of what a woman like ye would do to a man with no sense of honor and decency to hold him back."

"I can fend off the advances—"

He grabbed her shoulders and pulled her flush against him, startling a little gasp out of her. "Can ye?"

"Damn it," she said in frustration and fear, yanking back from him and finding his grip too tight for her to dislodge.

He loosened his hold enough to quickly slip his arms about her waist and press her close to him. "Do ye think every man would be honorable enough to stop when ye asked him?"

"Please let me go," Alenna said quietly, hoping her tone would convince him she didn't want to fight. Besides, she didn't know what he had in mind. Obviously acceptable behavior between men and women in 1318 would be different than twenty-first century morals.

"Do ye think, if I were some knave on the street, ye could ask me in that soft, sweet voice to let ye go and it would be that simple?" One of his hands came up and tangled in her shoulder-length hair. He leaned down to sniff her hair and his warm breath tickled her ear. She shivered against him, alarmed when the sensation excited her more than frightened her.

"Ye smell fair sweet. Ye have no feelin' for how ye look?"

"What do you mean?" Alenna strained back against his arms

but his muscles wouldn't give an inch. Instead, he pressed one hand to her bottom and cupped her. She let out an outraged gasp. "Get your hand off my—"

"I saw the way Dougald looked at ye. Though he is an honorable man, he would be sore tempted to touch ye as I am now."

Genuine fear grew within as he snarled his fingers into her hair. She knew if she moved too suddenly that it would hurt like blazes.

"Why are you doing this?" she asked. "An honorable man would have released me by now."

"To show ye how dangerous it is for a woman who takes no care."

"So you mean to be as brutish as other men to accomplish your means?" Alenna asked, snapping the words at him.

"Nay." Tynan's fingers did a gentle, exploratory touch along her buttocks. She jerked against him as the tickling sensation zinged through the rest of her body. He was looking at her like he might eat her up in one gulp. "Ye are safe from me."

His fingers slowly pulled up the material of her shift.

Why, the bastard had lied through his teeth. Before she knew it, his hand cupped her bare bottom. She gasped again. She couldn't think of a thing to say, her gaze caught up in his, and the sensation of his hand running over her ass attracting every molecule of her attention. Her nipples tightened, arousal running hot despite her anger. Her breathing came quickly, her heart picking up speed as he kneaded her butt blatantly.

"What do you want from me?" she asked.

A barely there smile touched his lips. "The question should be what ye want from me."

"I don't know why I'm here."

"And I dinnae believe ye. Maybe I will need to find a way to get the truth."

Fear obliterated the sensual surge coursing through her blood. Alenna pushed against his chest with both of her hands.

"No. You told me Elizabet said I was here for a purpose. But not to harm his lordship or you."

"Sometimes beauty is a deceivin' package. I will make ye talk, lass. Ye cannae hide what ye are from me."

"But I don't know what's happening any more than you do," she said, aware that a desperate tone entered her voice. She took a deep breath and tried to hush the alarm galloping through her blood. "I thought you said you wouldn't hurt me?"

"Aye. I would never hurt ye. But if ye dinnae tell me where ye come from and why yer here, I will kiss ye until ye do."

CHAPTER 4

Alenna's mouth opened as she tried to think of a suitable retort or a way to reason with Tynan. Kiss her until she talked? Absurd. How was that supposed to make her talk?

"I told you. I'm from a place called America. I was on an archaeological dig here at the castle. We were digging for artifacts—"

"Huh." He brushed his lips across hers and the sudden movement drew a sharp breath from her. He laughed and the deep, low rumble vibrated through her chest.

"You're right. Your kiss is so repulsive I'll talk just to keep you away from me." Giving him a sarcastic smile, she tried twisting from his arms.

Before she could move again, his lips came down on hers.

Immediately she pushed against his strong chest, anger giving her extra strength. His hold tightened.

Astonished, her mind tumbled with confusion. Tynan held her tight, lest he lose her, but not taut enough to bruise or break.

A wild, fluttering sensation darted through her belly. His lips molded to hers and played over her mouth with ravenous attention. But his lips didn't hurt her...instead they tasted, searched and cajoled in the most exquisite way imaginable.

A strange dizzy sensation filled her head. As he pressed her hips tight against him, his cock went hard and full. Excitement traveled through Alenna's loins. The man was harder than granite. Before she could think much about it, a wild notion came to her.

If this was a dream, maybe she ought to enjoy it.

Suddenly he shifted his grip and lifted her up against his erection. He cupped her bare buttocks and pressed his linen-covered hardness to her naked, tender clit.

When she took a startled breath, his tongue entered her mouth. With deep, languorous thrusts Tynan stroked her tongue, sending a sizzle of warmth traveling across her body. She shouldn't be stunned by the familiarity of the burning caresses considering how he'd tasted and caressed her earlier. Yet the surge of response within her was so strong, she moaned. A deep sound of male satisfaction rumbled from his chest and he increased the passion of his kiss. She met his tongue with her own, tasting him as he tasted her, without boundaries or hesitation.

The kiss went on and on, until the fire throbbing in Alenna threatened to reach ridiculous heights. Before she could contemplate struggling out of his arms, he broke the kiss, setting her back on her feet. She stumbled back a step.

Breathing hard, he clenched his fists at his sides like a man ready to fight. Above flushed cheeks, his eyes glittered with a predatory incandescence.

Mortified she'd let this man paw her and she'd responded to him, Alenna stepped back until she bumped into the table.

"Why did you do that?" she asked, feeling the chill of the room now that he no longer held her within his arms.

"To show ye what happens to cuif women."

"Cuif?"

He shook his head. "Foolish woman."

"I'm not a foolish woman."

Taking a deep breath, as if he had trouble getting oxygen, he said, "Nay...I think ye are."

"But—"

"Do ye need another—" He stepped forward.

"No!" She put her hand out. "What I mean is, I don't let just any man kiss me."

Alenna realized how this sounded as soon as the words came out. This savage man would think she'd enjoyed his kisses, his carnal lovemaking.

God help her. She had more than enjoyed it.

His gaze never leaving hers, he said, "Many men willnae ken that. They'll look at yer beautiful hair and those green eyes and they'll want to taste ye as I have."

He was right. Not about kissing her, but that she walked on dangerous ground if she thought she could move about in the fourteenth century with the freedom she expected in her time.

She nodded. "I...I'm not familiar with your...with this place. I could make mistakes."

The dangerous shimmer in his eyes diminished and was replaced by a twinkle of humor. "I think, lass, ye will be the death of me yet."

The evidence lay in the heavy arousal straining against his trews. She looked away quickly. She couldn't remember a man reacting this strongly and quickly to her. Then again, she couldn't remember responding to any man this way.

Alenna rubbed her fingers against her temples. She had to get back on track. He was a barbaric man of the fourteenth century. How on earth could she be this attracted to a man she barely knew? Insanity had to be the answer, because nothing else made a bit of sense. Perhaps once she'd talked to Elizabet, she would understand more about what was happening to her.

"Could I speak with Elizabet?" she asked.

Tynan tilted his head to the side. "Aye, I suppose ye might. Are ye in need of somethin' only a female can help with?"

Good. Let him think it is a female thing. "Yes."

"Aye."

Trying to stifle a yawn, she put her hand to her mouth.

"Go back to sleep, Alenna. I'll stay in the chair by the fire." He walked to the fire.

"But you'll be cold." She realized immediately it would sound like an offer to let him sleep with her again. She didn't want him getting any ideas. "I mean…take the plaid."

"Nay." He reached for the fur that lay over one chair and settled into the seat by the fire. "This will do for me."

The feeling of tension left the room and fatigue seeped into her limbs like liquid. She sank back onto the pallet. She covered herself with the warm plaid but she didn't expect to sleep. Before she could give another thought to the heat of his kiss and what the morning would bring, she sank into a deep slumber.

* * *

TYNAN GRITTED his teeth and held back a moan. He shifted on the chair and fought against the throb in his loins. The ache subsided with excruciating slowness. Did the strange woman who lay on the pallet have the power to bewitch him? Was she a spy?

A woman had not seized his senses this way since Florie. Since Mary had loved him, then left his soul in tatters. Mary had given him love…something he would never get back. Not from this woman. Not from any woman.

Lust. Aye. 'Tis lust and nothing more.

He closed his eyes, but it was a mistake. Aye, Alenna fit against him in all the right places. Her full breasts and long legs had curved against him as he'd held her. When he'd woken this morning to find her small hand curved around his cock, he'd been unable to resist her. His body reacted, his instincts roaring as he'd kissed her. He couldn't remember the last time a woman had aroused the beast in him without even trying. He had been so close to slipping his cock deep into her warmth. Her response had triggered warring emotions inside him, including the desire to fuck.

Lust slammed through him with a drugging beat as he stood and walked to the pallet.

Covered with the plaid, she looked wee and defenseless. If he'd been like his father, or a goodly portion of the men in the castle, he would have taken her. He could have pushed her against the wall and rutted into her despite her wishes. But the very idea of forcing or hurting her made his stomach roil with disgust. Shame warred with anger inside his head.

Her disregard for her own safety amazed him and put a fire of rage in his blood. Did this wench speak the truth? She didn't look like any woman he'd seen before, and if he believed in evil witchery, he might think she'd been sent as a devil's instrument.

She was taller than most of the women and even some of the men he knew. Her hair lay short over her forehead and the rest hung thick and straight and just touched her shoulders. A strange ripe grain and golden brown, and its scent smelled like flowers. Delicate and pale, her skin seemed unmarred by the ravages of time for a woman her age. What sweet shelter had this wench taken to look so well?

Alenna shifted on the bed. Afraid she would wake and find him staring down at her, he stepped back. She moaned in her sleep, wrinkling her stubborn, wee, freckled nose as if she'd scented something unpleasant. Even the dimple in her chin spelled a willful woman. He wanted to kiss the little dent in the middle of her chin after he finished devouring her mouth.

But two other features made his blood boil like a caldron over a fire. Spiked with long lashes, her green eyes had taunted him, and her sweet, soft lips moved under his with an inferno that might lead to his damnation.

When he'd kissed her, he wanted to show her she was powerless against him or any man who chose to have her. Maybe she'd realize she needed his protection.

Tynan cursed under his breath and knelt by the bed, drawn to her despite all efforts. He lifted his hand to touch her hair and stopped.

A fair idiot he'd been. What on earth had possessed him to take liberties? He was as despicable as the men against whom he had warned her. Even if she was a spy, he could never hurt her.

Kissing her had not brought a confession of guilt to her lips, but had brought an ache to his groin that still begged to be appeased. Nay. Moving in such a direction would lead to his downfall again. Twice before he'd let a woman enchant him with her loveliness and both times had brought them the worst possible fate.

A spike of almost physical pain sharpened in Tynan's soul.

No.

A woman who came to Tynan of MacBrahin's bed was doomed to die.

He couldn't trifle with Alenna. She deserved to be intact and untried when she went to her guidman.

Though past marriageable age, her face and body alone would spur hunger in every type of man, both scoundrel and honorable. Such a woman made danger for those around her. For that reason alone he would have to remain immune to her charms. Especially if she were a spy.

Shoving away rampaging thoughts, he rose from the floor and reached for one of the candles. After lighting the candle, he searched for the strange bag she'd carried. He found the black bag and opened it, running his fingers over the ridged opening with the metal tab. It looked similar to the sealer on her cloak.

Shuffling through the bag, he found a comb made of a hard

substance and in a bright color he'd never seen. He tipped the strange bag over and several other objects fell onto the bed. All were made of an odd material and cut into small rectangles. He could not read a word on them. Most startling, still, was the rectangle with an image of Alenna's face. Even gazing at it now filled him with a sense of awe. This alone did not prove who she was and it heightened his suspicions as he gazed at her image. If this wasn't witchery, what could it be?

Turning away from the bag and its puzzling contents, he picked up the undergarments lying at the foot of the bed.

He traced the lacy edge of the top, touching the round cups. Obviously they covered her—

Tynan gritted his teeth as heat spilled into his groin. He bit back a moan. Tossing the top back onto the bed, he cursed and forced his attention to the bizarre cloak, tunic and trews she'd been wearing when he discovered her. A damn good thing he hadn't been the one to undress her originally. He would have taken liberties that time too. As his cock grew hard, he remembered the hot, tight, wet clasp of her body as his cock had poised at the edge of paradise. One deep stroke and he knew he would have possessed her. Would have fucked her into that wild orgasm she'd enjoyed under the mere touch of his fingers. He shivered.

God help him.

Two questions plagued his mind like a fever.

Was Alenna his savior, meant to protect him from certain death, or bent on destroying Baron MacAulay and all those at the castle?

* * *

ALENNA JOLTED awake as someone tapped on the door. Fear rushed into her senses and she sat upright with a gasp. As she turned toward the door, she heard the knock come again...a distinct rap like a code.

"Fear not," Tynan said, getting up from his chair. He opened the door without hesitation.

As she gathered the plaid tight around her, the young boy named Clandon entered the room. Dressed in the same ragged clothing as yesterday, Clandon's unwashed face and dirty hair gave him the look of a street urchin. Her heart ached for him. Once again wide-eyed, he perused her like a curious puppy.

"She's still alive, sir?"

Tynan tied up the front of his shirt. "Aye. Of course."

"Good morning," she said, smiling tentatively at the boy.

Open-mouthed, the boy simply stared at her.

Tynan ruffled the boy's already messy hair. "Where's yer manners, lad? Have ye forgotten how to address a lady?"

"Lady?" the boy gasped the question softly. "She's a lady, sir?"

Alenna felt the urge to laugh for the first time since she'd been dumped into the past. She let the short bark of amusement escape, then stifled it with her hand.

"She's a woman worthy of respect, lad," Tynan said.

"He can call me Alenna," she said.

Tynan's brows winged together. "He'll call ye by an address of respect."

She sighed. "It's not necessary—"

"Aye, 'tis needed."

Perturbed by his adamant refusal, she crossed her arms. "Fine."

Tynan looked perplexed, but ignored her. He turned the boy about and clasped his shoulders. "Ye'll address her as mistress. She's my cousin come for a short visit. She was set upon by thieves durin' her travel and her guidman was killed. She escaped and found her way here, by the grace of God."

Clandon looked confused. "But sir, she is no yer cousin—"

"Clandon, I dinnae ask ye to think, lad. 'Tis very important ye stay to this story for now. She may be in danger and 'tis our duty as knights to protect her."

For the first time she saw Clandon smile and his lips curved in a way that would, one day, dazzle the maidens.

"Aye, sir. As knights we must protect her."

Tynan knelt down until he was on eye level with the boy. "I need your help again, lad."

Clandon nodded vigorously. "Aye, sir."

"Search the ground outside and see if ye can find a garnet ring. If ye do, bring it here. It belongs to Mistress Carstairs. Also, would ye ask Caithleen to give ye clothes for Mistress Carstairs? Tell her 'tis urgent."

Clandon turned and rushed to the door. "Aye!"

Before Alenna could blink, he was gone.

"Thank you for asking him to look for the ring," she said.

Tynan rose from his crouch and gave her a quick nod. A glower touched his brow and his finely carved lips, and she recalled the moment when he'd rolled on top of her and kissed her. Unbidden feelings of excitement poured back to her. As he continued to stare at her with a penetrating, brooding look, she shook off the memory of his lips touching hers, his cock hard against her, his thigh rubbing her clit into heated enjoyment. His fingers probing her until she flamed in orgasm.

She cleared her throat. "The boy is very loyal to you."

"Aye, he is that."

"Is he your boy?"

His eyebrows speared together. "I dinnae ken your meanin'."

"Is he your son?"

Alenna might have expected a cross word or two. Instead he laughed and the transformation from perturbed Tynan to amused Tynan stunned her. The grin spread over his face and turned his grim expression warm and companionable.

"Nay. Clandon and Caithleen have been at the castle nigh on a year."

"I take it they are very poor."

"Aye. Most are."

"Why does he do everything you tell him?"

"He wants to be a soldier and he believes doin' all that I do will make him so."

Another knock on the door sounded. Tynan went to the narrow window and looked out. "Elizabet and Johanna."

As he opened the door and the two women stepped in the room, her stereotypical expectation of what they might look like shattered. She had imagined Elizabet as a woman with a sharp nose and wrinkled features, a cascade of unruly grey hair on her head.

"Welcome," Tynan said to the petite women. And they were petite. Elizabet wasn't more than five feet tall and Johanna only a bit taller. "I'll give ye privacy. I must go out for a spell."

As he left, Elizabet crossed to Alenna quickly, settling on a chair not far from the pallet.

Elizabet's face was round, but she was thin, and her small stature and angelic face made her look about nineteen. Her crystalline blue eyes held sincere concern and her skin had a translucence that glowed with health. As silver as moonbeams, her fine hair fell in slight waves past her shoulders.

"Are ye well this mornin'?" Elizabet asked, her voice clear and cool, like a soft spring.

"Yes, thank you. Tynan said you took care of me yesterday. Whatever you've done seems to have worked. I feel much better."

The small woman laughed. "Ye are most welcome. It must have been the tea." She pulled out a linen wrapped package and laid it on the table. "Drink one cup every day for a week and ye'll feel to rights soon."

"Thank you."

Elizabet stared at Alenna for so long, Alenna began to

wonder if something was wrong. "Tynan was right about ye. Ye do speak most strangely."

Alenna smiled. "I'm not from here."

Elizabet nodded but didn't comment.

Not eager to plunge immediately into a discussion on trying to return to her own place in time, Alenna said, "Thank you for giving me this dressing gown."

"'Twas Johanna who gave ye the gown. 'Tis hers."

Johanna came to stand by the bed. Alenna guessed the girl might be sixteen. Like her mother, she was pale, but with deeper blue eyes like lapis. Her sharp nose and compressed lips gave her a shrewish appearance that almost outweighed the almost ethereal quality of her looks. Her straight, ash blonde hair fell past her shoulders and down to her waist.

Despite the disapproving look on the young woman's face, Alenna decided to be as pleasant as possible. She needed friends, not enemies. "Thank you, Johanna."

Johanna sniffed and nodded. "Ye are welcome."

Elizabet's gentle expression turned serious. "Tynan has not told us yer true name. When he asked for our help, he said that ye may be the one I spoke of long ago."

"I'm Alenna Carstairs. He told me that you said I would appear to him one day."

"I did. I have many ways of seein' the truth and I saw that ye would arrive from the beyond."

Alenna searched for an easy way to ask her question. "You can see things most people can't?"

With an assessing look, as if uncertain how much to tell, Elizabet nodded. "I have been such since I was but a child. I see things that may be. That have been. When Tynan rescued Johanna and me, I knew he would meet a woman that would change his future. I saw that ye would come and how ye would come."

Alenna leaned forward slightly. "Tynan rescued you?"

Elizabet touched the package of tea on the table, her fingers moving restlessly. "We were set upon by ruffians as we traveled. We had left from Edinburgh with no protector." A glimmer of something akin to pain shone in her expression.

"We left my athair," Johanna said, a hint of animosity in her soft voice. She moved to the fireplace and stared into the flames. From this angle her jaw looked sharp and defiant.

"Athair?" Alenna repeated.

Elizabet threw a sharp look at her daughter. "My guidman. He was cruel. I vowed that I would leave him if he put another hand on Johanna. He hit her."

Sucking in a sharp breath, Alenna felt an ache of sympathy.

"It was good you left," Alenna said.

Johanna turned from the fire and stared out the window. "If athair had been with us, no brigands would have attacked us."

Elizabet dawdled with the tea package and ignored her daughter. "Tynan will take care of ye, Alenna. Ye have no a thing to fash about."

Alenna plunged ahead, eager to understand how she'd gotten here and how she might return to her time. "You said you knew I would appear. Did you know I was coming from the future?"

"Aye. I saw a great many things in my vision. I saw yer life. How the castle has changed in yer world. Wonders that most wouldnae believe."

While her gut told her to trust Elizabet, she was suspicious enough of the world she'd dropped into to be cautious. "What did you see?"

"There are odd ways of transport in your time." Elizabet held her hands out, as if thinking of a way to pantomime what she saw. "Ye have strange wagons that are no pulled by oxen or horse, yet they still move. And there are birds…metal birds that people fly in to go great distances."

If "the wagons are not pulled by horse or oxen" hadn't reinforced Alenna's belief, the mention of planes would have. "You're right."

"How do we ken she's the one?" Johanna said, her tone brimming with disbelief.

"I ken because I saw her face before I met her. 'Twas in my vision."

"I must find a way back to my time," Alenna said, a spike of fear tightening her throat. God forbid, what if she stayed stuck here forever? Every time she thought of it, her heart would pound and panic threatened on the edges.

Elizabet stared at her for several moments. "I dinnae ken if ye can go back, lass."

"You didn't see that in your vision?"

"Nay. I saw only how ye save Tynan."

Alenna recalled the raw power of Tynan's arms. "How could I save Tynan from anything? He's a strong man."

"There are more things to be saved from than those which endanger the body."

Alenna didn't have a chance to ask more. The door burst open and Tynan strode in with Clandon. Clandon held a bundle of clothes under one arm.

Elizabet rose from the chair and glared at Tynan. "Ye fair scared the life out of us. Have ye no mind to comin' in a bit gentle?"

Tynan's answering smile landed on Elizabet and then Alenna. "Why should I? Have ye somethin' to hide from me?"

Elizabet patted his arm, tilting her head back to look at him. "Women's talk. Have ye brought clothes for Alenna, Clandon?"

Clandon nodded and handed the bundle to Alenna with a reverence he might have given a queen. "From Caithleen."

Wondering if Caithleen's clothes could possibly fit her, Alenna said, "Thank you."

He nodded and hurried back to Tynan's side. "I have chores aplenty waitin' for me."

Tynan inclined his head. "Aye, boy. Off with ye." When the boy left, Tynan turned to them and put his hands on his hips. "We saw no ring outside the tower. Mayhap it has already been taken by someone passin' by."

Fear stirred in Alenna's stomach at the thought of never finding the jewelry.

Before she could comment, Tynan said, "So now ye can tell me what ye've been talkin' about."

"I explained the visions I had," Elizabet said.

"And I believe her," Alenna said, bunching the plaid in her hands, feeling the roughness of the material as it scraped her skin. "She's seen things that are in my time that she couldn't have known about otherwise."

"Yer time?" he asked.

Elizabet cleared her throat. "When I said she would come to you through a mist, I left out one thing."

Tynan narrowed his eyes. "What is it?"

"Alenna is from the future."

His mouth opened, then closed. Total incredulity covered his face. "Nay. She cannae be."

"When have ye ever known me to be wrong, Tynan of MacBrahin?" Elizabet asked, crossing her arms.

"Never mind, Elizabet. He's too stubborn to see the truth," Alenna said.

His mouth opened again. "Why, ye little clootie. How dare ye call me—"

"Tynan," Elizabet said, her voice as stern as a mother chastising a recalcitrant child.

A frown marred his good looks as he gazed down at the tiny woman next to him. "Clishmaclaver. 'Tis not possible. She is a spy."

"Nay." Elizabet reached for his arm and pressed gently. "You must listen to me. She is from the future."

"How far?" he asked cautiously. "How far in the future?"

"Two thousand and twenty-four," Alenna said.

His jaw tightened and she could imagine his teeth grinding. "'Tis against nature to travel through time."

The petite woman glared at him. "Tynan, ye cannae believe I'd lie about it."

He crossed his arms and glared back. "Why dinnae ye tell me before? What dinnae ye want me to ken?"

"I feared this from ye. Ye dinnae believe at first that she would even come to ye."

Alenna watched in fascination as Tynan's fierce expression eased until his dark glare melted to warmth. She felt a twinge of something dark and uncomfortable twist her heart. Tynan cared a great deal about Elizabet and somehow that unsettled Alenna. Maybe their relationship went deeper than she'd at first realized.

"If any outside this chamber hear of this, ye'll be branded a spaewife," he said to Elizabet.

Letting forth a small laugh, Elizabet put her small, pale hand on his forearm. "People already think that now."

Johanna cleared her throat daintily. "People shun us for witches. 'Tis a miracle we are still alive."

Tynan turned his attention to Johanna, favoring her with the same warm look he'd given her mother. "Ye are fine women with nothin' to fear. Not as long as I live."

For the first time Alenna saw the crystal ice of Johanna's expression thaw. She favored Tynan with a smile destined to bring a man to his knees in supplication. His answering grin brought a blush to Johanna's young face. Was this man having a sexual relationship with either of these women? Both? Alenna's stomach dropped.

What the hell did he think he was doing, flirting with such a young girl? Alenna gritted her teeth and reminded herself, in this time women often married by the time they reached fourteen. Johanna was probably hunting for a husband and Tynan made excellent prey.

Maybe Tynan was searching for a wife. She tried to imagine what sort of woman could handle a man this barbaric. This... raw and sexual.

"We should go now. Guid day, Alenna," Elizabet said, starting for the door. Johanna followed.

When they'd gone, Alenna felt vulnerable, as if the women had shielded her from the impossibly masculine presence in front of her. She knew they'd kept his devouring gaze at bay and prevented Alenna from giving in to feelings she had no business having for a fourteenth century knight.

CHAPTER 5

"Stay by the fire where 'tis warm," Tynan said to Alenna as he put on his cloak and headed for the door.

Alenna bristled. This was the last straw. Staying cloistered in this cold tower for another day would give her cabin fever. "I need some fresh air. I can't stay in here any longer."

"Ye have been here but two days. Ye'll stay here because I say ye will." His brows knitted together. "Dougald and I are goin' out today. If ye venture out, I wouldnae be here to protect ye."

"I can take care of myself."

He walked toward her, a flicker of anger hardening his mouth. She resolved not to move a muscle.

Stopping within a few inches of her, he said, "Ye'll not go out. I told ye of the dangers."

She sighed and put her hands on her hips. "What do you expect me to do, stay here the rest of my life?"

"If that's what it takes to keep ye safe."

"What about the assembly at the great hall?"

"Nay," he said, stamping on the idea like he was squishing a bug. "Ye no have the proper clothes for the assembly."

Damn the man. For an entire day she had endured his coolness. Silent and surly, he made little conversation. Since his heated kisses he'd become cool, distant and difficult.

"That's lame," she said.

"Eh?"

Alenna looked down at her shabby garments, then perused his less than dapper outfit. "And I suppose you are properly attired?"

Tynan puffed up to his full height. "I will no be there. I have duties this night 'twill keep me away."

He leaned in closer to her and as the warm musk scent of him tickled her nostrils, she wished he stood on the other side of the room. Every time he came near Alenna, her world spun on its axis.

Anger surged within her. "This is crazy. Other women traipse about this castle without escorts."

He lifted a finger and shook it in her face. "If ye dare leave this tower without me, I will skin yer taet doup."

"My what?"

Before she could move a fraction, he swatted her behind.

"Ow! What the hell—"

"Yer little arse," he said, a wide, wicked grin spreading across his face.

Skin her ass.

She had no doubt he could do it, too.

Fuming, she tried to think of a suitable retort, but nothing came to mind. Pent up fury spilled over. "You are such a bastard, you know that?"

His smile widened and he leaned toward her. Her breath caught in her throat, and she leaned back until her rear bumped the table behind her.

"I've got ways of punishin' ye," he whispered, his voice going soft and husky. "Or have ye forgotten?"

Half afraid she knew exactly what he intended, she said

nothing. She shouldn't trust him...didn't want to trust him. Yet every time this man came close, inexplicable excitement coursed through her body and electrified her senses. She prickled with a sense of life she'd never experienced before.

"Don't tempt me, Alenna."

His deep, liquid voice went straight to her middle and filled her stomach with tendrils of heat. Determined to let him see her strength, she straightened. This movement put her even closer to him. His eyes seemed to darken, as if cloaking secrets he'd kept for centuries.

She sensed he was on the edge of doing something he didn't want to do, or that he wanted to do more than anything. Part of her longed to discover more of what lay underneath all that simmering heat and unpredictable exterior. She'd never been driven to tease, test, or torment a man until she'd met Tynan—she never would have pushed a man to do something unexpected and dangerous. Exhilaration rushed over her like a strong wind.

"Tempt you to do what?" she asked, breaking the long silence.

Without answering, Tynan leaned down and kissed her. Touching her nowhere else, he plundered her lips ravenously, thrusting his tongue inside her mouth. Sparks of sweet arousal slammed through her as he took her mouth with heated attention. Before she could think, move or respond, he released her lips, stepping away. His face reflected myriad feelings from surprise to satisfaction.

Taking a deep breath, he said, "Sweet Jesu, do ye have no feelin' for what ye do to me?"

For a moment Alenna was emboldened by the effect she had on him. Startled by feelings of arousal mixed with consternation, she didn't hesitate to answer. "If you think kissing me is going to stop me from doing what I want—"

"Nay!" He made a chopping motion with one hand and then

proceeded to spear his fingers through his hair. "I dinnae ask ye to stay in the tower to imprison ye, Alenna. I do it to keep ye safe. Why can ye no see that?"

"Because I'm not a fragile woman. I can take care of myself, if you just give me a chance."

"God, ye'll be the death of me for certain," he said, turning to the door and opening it with an agitated movement. "Damn silly wench."

Tossing her a disdainful look, he left, slamming the door.

Alenna decided right then she would venture outside. Maybe not to the gathering at the great hall, wherever that was, but she would go outside and see for herself what the fourteenth century was really like. Did the man honestly believe he could make her stay here without placing a guard on her? He must figure his intimidation would be enough. Silly man.

She had to look for the garnet ring and she couldn't do it standing here. The jewelry might have something to do with her travel through time. If so, she must find the ring.

Also, she needed to explore and make certain the past had claimed her. Despite the evidence she'd seen so far, a part of her still believed she would awaken and find this all a nightmare.

After waiting for several minutes to make sure Tynan didn't lurk about the area, she left the tower. Outside, a cold wind whipped at her hair. Glad for her warm cloak, she walked into the crowds milling about doing their daily business.

Immediately Alenna noted a conglomeration of new scents, sights and sounds. Smoke from fires tainted the crisp air. She heard a horse clopping, a cow lowing, the occasional human laugh or shout. Pungent odors, many from unwashed human bodies and cesspools, attacked her nose at every turn. Despite the unpleasantness of the aromas, she wouldn't have missed it for the world. How many other people had the opportunity to view the past in living color?

She passed a ragged man stumping along on a crudely made

crutch, and he glared at her like she'd done something reprehensible. Embarrassed by his hostile scrutiny, she headed toward the barbican, hoping she might glimpse some of the world outside the castle.

Caution kept her alert, but she didn't believe Tynan's assertion that danger lurked in every corner. As time passed and she walked on unmolested, excitement overcame all inhibitions and she enjoyed her freedom. MacAulay Castle had changed considerably.

As she reached the barbican, a guard gave her a curious look but she ignored him. Compelled by curiosity, she stepped through the arch of the gatehouse and onto the drawbridge.

Wind whipped her hair about Alenna's face. When she saw the countryside outside the castle, she drew in a startled breath. If she hadn't believed in time travel before, what she saw now would have cemented it for her.

The muddy brown of the wide moat seemed to jump up at her. In the twenty-first century the castle didn't have a moat. She swayed a little, grasping onto the rock wall to her left. The drawbridge had no railing. Another stiff, cold wind blasted through her hair and cleansed her lungs with the fresh scent of rain. Just beyond the moat the land rolled gently green, thick woodland rising at the top of the hill. To the right, she saw many hut-like structures scattered over a field. She could see a few people moving about, but from this distance they appeared as tiny bugs.

"I'd stay back from there, mistress," a gruff male voice said behind her. Two heavy hands pulled her back into a hard body and she stiffened with fear. She wrinkled her nose. The man stank to high heaven.

"Please," she said, turning her head to see who stood so close behind her. "Release me at once."

The man stepped back and she retreated into the gatehouse a few steps. She watched the man carefully. Though he was tall and powerfully built, she couldn't say how old he was. His face was covered with a dark beard, his collar-length hair black, tangled and greasy looking.

Smiling as if he'd made some great joke, the scruffy man leered. "What's the matter, ye silly wench? Is that the thanks I get for savin' ye from a watery grave?"

Feeling disoriented, Alenna stood her ground and summoned a frown to cover the hard thump of fear in her chest. "Thank you, but I can save myself."

While the sneer didn't leave his large lips, his dark eyes hardened with malice.

Before he could speak, she turned and hurried back through the gatehouse and into the castle. Uncomfortable and certain he would come after her, she continued on at a quicker pace. After a few seconds she realized he hadn't followed her and relief flowed through her body.

As she passed a small group of people listening to minstrels, she recognized one of the instruments as a lute. One man clanged together something like cymbals and another played a small device he held like a flute.

Alenna paused and enjoyed the lilting sounds and wondered if they would play at the gathering at the great hall this evening. Could she slip out this evening without Tynan noticing? It was a tempting thought, but not likely to succeed.

She turned away from the minstrels and wandered over to a group of people huddled among a few tables, which held special wares upon them. As she approached, a few of the people stared at her. Almost all gave her odd looks, either of curiosity or hostility. Did they somehow sense she didn't come from their time? Feeling distinctly uneasy, she veered away. She contemplated what to do.

Staying cloistered in Tynan's chambers wasn't an option. She couldn't huddle by the fire and drink ale all day. She must to do something to get back to her own time.

Her own time.

What if she never made it back?

What did she miss in her own time? All the modern conveniences, certainly. Her friend Demi and the few other people she considered friends. Otherwise, who would even miss her? Her mother and father had become so distant from her, they might consider themselves strangers. She couldn't compare her life here yet. After two days she still had much to learn.

Alenna had noted something within her had altered since she arrived in the past. Her focus had shifted, and she hadn't suffered a panic attack in the entire time she had resided in this new world. Certainly, when she'd first been dumped back in time there had been a solid, tangible reason for fear. Now, with a host of new challenges, her attention turned to survival and to finding a solution for her predicament.

She tried to feel grateful. She could have been plunked down in this time with no one to help her, without food or water, or the comfort of at least a garderobe. She'd convinced Tynan she wanted to clean up this morning and he'd brought her water and Elizabet had provided her with a bar of awful-smelling soap. She'd skipped the soap and accomplished what she could with the water.

Her attention jerked back to the present as a trio of knights completely garbed in chain mail, gauntlets and helms rode by her. Looking at them reminded her of Tynan's occupation.

She thought about the yeoman's tale. At least she knew Tynan was a real person, and he had lived in...did live in the Black Tower. Tynan was destined to die in the year 1318. Alenna winced. Simply the idea of him being harmed or killed sent a deep unease into her heart. Tynan would die fighting the baron for a woman. But who could that woman be?

Elizabet?

Alenna had seen gentleness and sincere affection in his

hooded eyes when he looked at Elizabet. Maybe a man as brawny and uncivilized as Tynan did have a soft spot.

The concept stuck in her craw.

She remembered his kisses, the way his hot mouth and tongue had teased her nipple, the gentle way his fingers had caressed her breasts. Despite his affection for Elizabet, he had no qualms about making love to another woman. Damn his hide anyway.

He'd winked and flirted with Johanna too. Could Johanna possibly be his love? The idea didn't sit well with her for more than one reason...none of it to do with the girl's age. Johanna didn't seem like the right woman for a man like him. She snorted. Whoever tamed Tynan would have to be strong.

A bleating sound alerted her that something was going on behind her. Turning around, she saw a young boy pulling a goat on a crude rope leash. Wearing ragged, threadbare clothes, the boy barely glanced at her, no curiosity gleaming from his pale eyes. He was like a dozen other boys who roamed this gloomy fortress. She watched him, realizing that soon her own eyes might look like his. If she were in this place long enough, would she forget what her century was like?

As she continued to wander the castle grounds, she saw more poverty than she cared to view. Most of the women dressed in kirtles and surcoats of brown and grey, the men in tunics and knee breeches of various browns and dingy grey. Now that Alenna lived among the people of 1318, she had a true appreciation for her own time. The three kirtles and surcoats Clandon had delivered to her had been surprisingly clean. Her bra and panties kept some of the roughness of the dark, scratchy linen away from her most delicate skin.

As she walked, a bitter cold wind lifted her heavy, fur-lined cloak and ate through her garments. Grateful for the cap completely covering the top and back of her hair and sheltering her against the elements, she decided to cut short her walk.

Heavy dark clouds drifted high above the curtain walls. The air grew colder by the minute and her unease in the environment larger by the second.

"Mistress." A hushed whisper hailed her from an embrasure in a wall.

She searched for the source of the voice and saw a young, stunningly beautiful woman standing in the niche, beckoning to her to come forward. Surprised by the woman's gesture, she simply stared. A filmy white veil, held in place by a thick silk band, covered the woman's dark hair. Gold braiding trimmed her purple surcoat made of fine velvet. Flawless pale skin surrounded her almond-shaped cocoa brown eyes. Indeed, these eyes probably melted male hearts faster than butter in a pan. No doubt she was a noblewoman.

"Mistress," the woman whispered again and gestured her forward. "Will ye speak with me?"

Nodding, Alenna went to the woman and stood with her in the shelter of the alcove cut into an inner curtain wall.

The pretty woman smiled. "I'm Caithleen, Clandon's sister. Ye must be Alenna."

How could Caithleen be outfitted like a princess, while Clandon dressed in rags? "How did you know?"

The brunette smiled, showing white, even teeth. "Yer clothes, and Clandon told me what ye looked like."

Alenna smiled. "Of course." She looked down at the almost too short garment and then at Caithleen. Caithleen stood a couple of inches smaller than herself. "It's a good thing we're almost the same height."

Caithleen's laugh was musical, but soft. "A guid thing." She clasped Alenna's wrist gently. "I wanted to speak with ye about somethin' important, but I beg of ye not to speak about this in front of others. Especially now."

"Especially now?"

"Aye." A cloud passed over her youthful face. She hesitated, as if uncertain about revealing something she wanted to say so urgently moments before. "I wished to meet ye and ask ye to give Tynan a message."

Alenna nodded, wondering at the girl's interest in Tynan. "Of course."

"Tell him to meet me at the galley in the gloamin'."

"Meet him?" Alenna asked, a suspicion growing fast in her mind.

Caithleen clasped her hands in front of her and dipped her head, as if ashamed. "'Tis important."

The plot was getting thicker.

An unrepentant disappointment welled within Alenna. Was Tynan dallying with Elizabet, Johanna and maybe even Caithleen? Caithleen appeared no older than Johanna. In this day and age, she realized, it didn't matter. Older men no doubt married and made sport with women far younger then themselves. This knowledge did nothing to remedy her discomfort.

"How old are you, Caithleen, if you don't mind me asking?"

"Seven-and-ten."

Seventeen. Seventeen! "You're so young."

"I'm a woman fair grown for many years, Mistress."

"Please, call me Alenna. Mistress makes me feel like an old crone."

Caithleen laughed and the melodic tones drifted on the air like a sweet fragrance. "Ye do speak most strange, Alenna."

Alenna answered with a smile but didn't comment, happy just to be understood.

"My brother has spoken of ye since ye arrived at the castle. He says Tynan came about ye in a strange way."

"Well, he did help me once he realized my hus...my guidman had been killed."

Caithleen's smile was wry. "Nay. Ye need not hide the truth from me. Clandon told me how Tynan found you in the castle and that ye appeared under Dragon's hooves. From the thin air, Clandon said."

Who else knew about her sudden appearance? "I hope you haven't told anyone else about that."

"Nay. Clandon made me promise to tell no one. Though Tynan would be angry if he had a notion Clandon spoke of it to me." She glanced around, her expression concentrated, almost as if she expected something to happen. "How is it ye go about here in the castle without a protector?"

Alenna thought it ironic Caithleen would ask this when she trundled about without a protector as well. "I've never been in a castle quite like this before. I wanted to explore."

"Have ye no heard the Ruthvens may be comin' soon to fight?"

"I've heard. What is the fight about?"

"Some say Ruthven is but a cruel pagan who has no thought but to do the de'il's work. Others say he wishes to take the castle for his own...in revenge for Ruthven's daughter, Lady Mirabella."

"Revenge?"

Caithleen scanned the area around her again. She lowered her voice. "Lady Mirabella was stolen one day from Ruthven's castle and never returned. 'Twas about ten years hence. Ruthven believes, after all these years, that his daughter was slain by the baron."

"And he's willing to storm an entire castle in order to get revenge?"

"Aye."

"Then what are you doing out here? Aren't you afraid? You have no protector."

Looking guilty, Caithleen said, "I hoped to find Clandon. Have ye seen him about?"

"No."

Distress darkened Caithleen's extraordinary eyes, and she reached up to tug at one sleeve of her gown.

"Is everything all right?" Alenna asked.

"Nothin' has been better in all my life." Her smile glared as bright as a car on high beams. So much so that Alenna knew it wasn't sincere.

Alenna couldn't restrain her curiosity about the young woman's state of dress anymore. "I don't mean to sound rude, Caithleen, but Clandon's clothes are very…in need of repair. How is it your clothing is so regal?"

A soft flush traveled up the creamy expanse of Caithleen's neck and cheeks. Alenna instantly regretted her forwardness.

Caithleen cleared her throat. "I ken how it looks to some. That I am able to dress so well while Clandon has little. But I am helpin' Clandon. I give him some coin."

Chagrined, Alenna shook her head. "I didn't mean to make you feel as if you did something wrong."

"I made clothin' for Baron MacAulay's last mistress. I can spin and weave. 'Tis how I had garments to give ye. But she went on to a new man and I was given some of her garments."

Somehow the explanation seemed out of place, but Alenna couldn't put a name to what made her ill at ease.

Looking distinctly self-conscious, Caithleen gazed around again, as if she expected someone to jump out at any moment. "I must go. I'm expected at the great hall."

Alenna clamped a lid on her inquisitiveness. "Of course. I hope to see you again soon."

Clasping Alenna's hand in both of hers, Caithleen smiled warmly. "Aye."

As Alenna watched the girl walk away, her curiosity burned like the huge torches that illuminated the castle at night.

Suddenly, a cry rent the misty air. "Riders! His lordship comes and the Ruthvens are fast behind him!"

Her heart felt as if it had taken a jagged leap into her throat.

As she moved toward the main gate of the castle and the sound of the cries, she almost tripped over the hem of her kirtle. Gathering up the cumbersome gown, she hurried toward the commotion. Women screamed, and men hurried women and children to places of safety.

She'd barely reached the main gate when several men dressed in chain mail rushed into the two towers near the gatehouse.

A huge white horse galloped through the gatehouse and into the courtyard. The knight upon his back gripped the warhorse with gauntlets splattered red. He wobbled on the horse's back, on the verge of falling from the saddle. Instead of toppling, he straightened and turned his horse about as if he would charge back into the fray.

"The baron!" came a cry from somewhere behind her.

A body was hurled down in front of her, startling a scream from her. An archer lay dead at her feet.

Before she could move or take a breath, another knight charged in on a huge black horse.

Dragon.

Alenna would recognize the beautiful horse anywhere. The man under all the chain mail must be Tynan, but the rounded helm on his head kept her from identifying him.

Tynan put his horse between the other knight and the barbican, lifting his broadsword in one hand.

Another man charged into the castle on a bay horse, his broadsword held above his head. In a split second she noted his attire wasn't that of a MacAulay knight.

The man on the bay horse swung at Tynan, but he blocked the thrust. Immediately the man swung again and dealt Tynan a staggering blow to the side, unseating him.

"Tynan!" Terrified he would be slain before her very eyes, Alenna reacted.

She reached down and snatched the longbow from the lifeless hands of the archer and retrieved an arrow from the quiver strapped to his back. Alenna loved archery, but she used a compound bow.

Just do it. Pull!

She drew back the string but the poundage was far too high to pull back all the way. Arms quivering with the strain, she aimed the best she could. As the knight on the bay jumped from his horse, ready to attack, she aimed at him and released the arrow.

It sailed through the air and hit the man, square in the middle of his helm.

Right between the eyes.

She winced, sickened by the gasping gurgle coming from the man's lips as he staggered and dropped straight back. She may not have killed him, but she'd knocked him unconscious.

"Oh God," she whispered. She'd never attacked anyone before and knowledge of what she had done seemed to envelop her body, paralyzing her.

"Mistress, look out!"

She glanced to her left and saw Clandon a few yards away, kneeling behind a wagon. He peered around the side of the vehicle, his eyes wide with warning.

A sharp sting hit her right arm. Automatically she clamped her left hand to her upper arm, gasping at the pain.

"The archer!" Clandon's voice broke into her daze.

She turned and looked toward the battlements. One of the archers stood at the top of a battlement and pointed his bow and arrow straight at her.

CHAPTER 6

"Alenna!" Tynan's deep voice roared. She looked up and saw Tynan upon Dragon's back once again. "Get down!"

She dropped to the ground as an arrow zinged past her, scarcely missing her side.

"Lower the portcullis!" someone cried. "Draw up the bridge!"

Shouting and screaming mixed with the sounds of the huge chains lowering the portcullis and pulling up the drawbridge.

The sound of horses' hooves pounding the ground sent a surge of strength into her and she pushed herself to her feet, ready to run or be trampled.

"Alenna!"

Before she could blink, a powerful arm grabbed her under her breasts, putting tremendous pressure on her ribs as she was lifted. Jerked onto the saddle in front of a knight, she considered struggling, but the man urged the horse into a gallop.

If she struggled she'd fall and possibly be killed.

"Damned wee taupie!" growled a voice close to her ear.

She'd know that gruff voice anywhere. She turned slightly and scowled at her captor, relief mingling with anger.

"Tynan!"

"Aye, and ye damned well better be glad I'm not one of Ruthven's men!"

He yanked off his helm. His dark brows drew together in a furious scowl, his lips curled in disgust. In the short time she'd known him she'd never seen him so incensed.

"You're hurting me." She turned away from the acid in his glance.

Tynan drew Dragon to an abrupt halt by the Black Tower and dismounted. Adrenaline pounded through her and she felt light-headed as she glared down at him.

"God's blood!" His expression changed drastically to distress. "Ye are wounded!"

Alenna glanced at her right arm and noted her bloodstained cloak and kirtle. "He barely winged me."

He muttered something under his breath she didn't understand and dropped his helm on the ground. He reached up for her and pulled her against him. Before her feet could touch the ground, he lifted her into his arms. "Of all the foolish, silly—"

"Shut up!" She struck out at him with her fist and came up against chain mail. She cursed at the added pain.

He strode into the tower room and promptly dumped her on the pallet. "Don't ye dare do that again! Do ye hear me?"

Tears of fury stung her eyes as she swung her feet off the pallet. "What? Hit you, or save your life?"

He snatched off his coif and his gauntlets, dropping them to the floor. "Ye were supposed to be here! Here in this tower and not dawdlin' about the castle. Are ye cuif?"

Defiant heat rose to her face. "I'm not staying cooped up in this room twenty-four hours a day."

"By God, ye will do it if I tell ye!" Pure venom laced his voice. "If another archer hadnae taken out the man on the battlement, ye might be dead now."

Alenna remembered the real reason she was probably alive. Clandon. "Clandon is out in this—"

"And a damned idiot he is!" He snarled the words. "The pair of ye are both alike!"

Rapidly, Tynan ripped material from a small bolt of cloth Elizabet had left her. He returned and knelt beside her. He said something that sounded like a curse and reached for her arm. He grabbed the top part of the sleeve and ripped the sleeve completely off to reveal a bloody wound. She winced.

"I'll have to pour wine on it," he said.

Great. It's going to sting like hell.

Tynan turned back to the table and grabbed a flagon. He pulled the cork out with his teeth and splashed the liquid onto the wound. Her breath hissed inward as a burning sting lanced her arm. A whimper escaped her lips.

"God, Alenna. I'm sorry, sweet."

Sweet?

The endearment caught her off guard. The man had been shouting at her and now he called her sweet? She stared at him as he tended to her wound. He secured the makeshift bandage around her arm while his dark eyes held the undeniable light of worry. She reached for the flagon of wine and took a deep swallow, coughed and put the vessel down on the floor.

The tight line of his lips softened. "Are ye in pain?"

"Not much," Alenna said softly, realizing the wound wasn't deep. He knotted the bandage but didn't draw it too tightly.

"That will do for ye until Elizabet can bring a poultice."

As he gently brushed her hair back from her face, his gaze dropped to her bodice.

She followed his look and realized when he'd ripped her sleeve he'd torn part of her bodice as well, revealing a healthy portion of skin. The strap of her bra had fallen and one of her breasts peeked from the security of the cup.

A small gasp escaped her as he continued to look at her

naked flesh. She pushed the bra strap back in place, essentially covering his view. When he brought his gaze back to hers, she saw pure male enjoyment in Tynan's eyes.

Before she could block his move, he reached up and pulled the dress and bra down, exposing both of her breasts. He licked his lips and as his gaze devoured her flesh, her nipples tingled and went hard. She drew in a sharp breath. "Tynan…"

"Sweet Jesu." His voice sounded raw and pained. His eyes blazed with admiration. "Temptation of the saints."

She tried to cover her breasts but he caught her hands in his big palms. Then, with as much reverence as he might have for a rare treasure, he leaned forward and circled the tip of one breast with his tongue. Alenna gasped as pleasure sent pinpoints of sensation darting to where his tongue brushed slow, caressing strokes. He kept her hands prisoner, his tongue moving to the next breast. He painted her flesh and she moaned softly as keen pleasure budded to life between her legs. She pulsed, the muscles deep between her legs tightening and releasing in response to Tynan's exquisite teasing.

"This flesh is sweet," he said reverently, his voice velvety to her ears, raw with promise and desire. "Beyond anything I've seen."

That he looked at her breasts, vulnerable and naked, stirred new arousal she couldn't resist. She didn't want to feel this way with him, wished she could resist his masculinity.

When he released her hands and cupped both breasts in his palms, his hot hands gently squeezed and caressed while his tongue tormented. Flick. Lick. He feasted with slow precision, as if he had all day, his attitude reverent and full of concentrated enjoyment. As if a battle hadn't raged around him a short time ago.

Or perhaps, just perhaps, it was because of battle.

Hadn't she read more than once that men sometimes wanted to have sex after surviving a battle? Needed to bleed off the adrenaline. She felt that same urge deep within her body and psyche, demanding a fulfillment with something powerful and life affirming.

She quivered as pleasure drew her higher, deeper into his spell. And finally, finally, he drew her nipple into his mouth and sucked deeply. He clasped one nipple between thumb and forefinger and pinched as his mouth tormented the other. She grasped his head and held him to her, writhing on the delicious torture. He nuzzled her breast, fingers still working the hard bud. Slowly he drew back, then brought her to her feet.

"What are you doing?" she asked, dazed by the amazing feelings he'd aroused inside her.

He turned her around and marched her to the window. His voice, low and husky, still pulsated with arousal. He drew her back against him and his hard cock pressed to her upper buttocks, promising the greatest pleasure if she'd only surrender. Tynan's fingers drew upward over her ribcage until he once again cupped her breasts in his hands. He drew his fingers together, lightly tweaking and twisting her nipples. "See the sky outside? If ye ever want to see it again, ye must make me a promise. Please dinnae put yerself in such danger again."

"I can't..." He pinched her nipples and she gasped. "I can't promise that and you know it."

"There is nothing I can do to convince ye to stay safe within these walls?" He whispered softly into her ear, his hot breath gusting across her neck as he kissed her shoulder. "Nothing?"

Alenna stared outside at the sky, her body fighting with her mind. She could lose her sanity wrapped in his arms, but the last thing she needed was to become his plaything. She wouldn't whore herself for any man, wouldn't pretend she belonged in this ass-backward world where men told women what to do.

Alenna pulled out of his arms and returned to the pallet. "No, Tynan. No."

"Saint George have mercy. I should tie ye to the bed," he said.

A smile touched her lips and she let out a small laugh. She reached for the flagon and took another generous swallow of the sour liquid. "I didn't know you were into kinky sex."

His eyes narrowed. "Eh?"

She sighed. "Never mind."

Still looking baffled, he cupped her face in both his large palms. "Why did ye disobey me, Alenna?"

"You know why. I'm sick of being in this room. When did you plan on letting me out? A month from now?"

One of his dark brows rose sardonically. "It did cross my mind."

Wariness and darkness remained in Tynan's gaze. If anything, she should be thankful he'd taken her away from the brawl outside, but his superior attitude still rankled. Slowly he pulled his hands away and continued to gaze at her.

"What?" she asked, self-conscious of his scrutiny.

He shook his head and rose to his feet. "Ye are a wonder, Alenna. And yer bravery is equal to many a man I've seen in battle. But I willnae have another woman's blood on my hands."

He started for the door.

"What are you talking about?" she asked as she righted her clothes and covered her breasts.

He turned as she started to rise. "Sit down and dinnae move until Elizabet comes."

"I will not," Alenna said, gritting the words out. "I want to know what you mean about having another woman's blood on your hands."

A black cloud hovered over his entire expression. His hands clutched into fists at his sides. "I dinnae need a woman fightin' my battles for me."

It finally dawned on her what his problem was and she put her hands on her hips, sighing in amazement. "Wait a minute. Are you saying you're angry because I saved your life?" She threw her hands up. "And here I thought you might be angry because you were worried about me."

His expression darkened even more and she waited for him to shout. Instead, he turned and reached for the door, his hand resting on it idly.

Without looking at her he said, "I willnae let ye put yer life in danger for me."

She crossed her arms. "Fine. It sounds like I've already done what I was brought here to do. I saved your life. Maybe I can get the hell out of Dodge now."

"Dodge?"

She shrugged. "It's an expression." Alenna sighed and stood. She moved toward him slightly, aware of an increasing need to make him understand. "Now that I've fulfilled Elizabet's prophecy, I can go back home to the future."

"Aye. Now ye can go home."

Closing her eyes, she wondered if when she opened them would she suddenly pop back home the way Dorothy had in Oz. Not really believing that it could be so easy, she opened her eyes. Tynan watched her, his gaze doing a painstaking foray over her body. A shaft of heat melted through her, surprising her with its force.

"I'm still here," she said, smiling at the way his look turned from devouring to puzzled. Without saying another word, he opened the door and started out. Concern pierced her. "Don't go out there, Tynan."

He looked back, his hand on the door. "I must see to the baron. He may need me."

"But it's dangerous—"

"Aye, so ye have seen." He paused again. "Bar this door and let no one in but myself, Dougald, Elizabet or Clandon. If anyone tries to break in, there is a dagger on the table in the next room. Dinnae hesitate to use it."

With that he was gone.

As she barred the door, her hands trembled slightly. Unsteady on her feet, she went into the other room and retrieved the dagger. Holding the hilt tightly in her hand, she sat down on the small stool next to the table. She could still hear shouting and other sounds of battle, so she knew the fight raged on. Fear rose in her again. Fear for the mysterious and infuriating man who had just walked out the door.

* * *

"The wound isnae bad," Elizabet said as she dabbed a concoction of herbs and egg whites across the laceration on Alenna's arm.

"'Tis no bigger than a bug bite, it seems to me," Johanna said as she held back the covering over the window to look out. "I dinnae ken why he sent for ye, mathair."

Elizabet turned an irritated glance on her daughter. "Every wound must be treated, Johanna. Ye ken that as well as I do."

"Why isnae he here?" Johanna asked.

Sighing heavily, Elizabet turned in her chair and paused in her ministrations. "He is tryin' to discover the traitor within the castle."

Johanna looked at her mother. "Traitor?"

"Aye. The man who shot the arrow at Alenna was not one of the baron's soldiers. He might have been sent here to slay the baron."

"He did try to kill Tynan," Alenna said. As Elizabet finished tying the bandage, Alenna stood.

"Ye shouldnae get up." Elizabet grasped Alenna's arm.

"I'm fine." Alenna reached for her goblet of wine and drank deeply. She'd had a full glass of the stuff and planned on having a second glass, despite the taste, to dull the throb in her arm and her anxiety for Tynan and Clandon.

"May I go now, mathair?" Johanna asked petulantly.

Elizabet gave her daughter an exasperated look. "Nay. We are not to leave here until Tynan comes back."

"Did either of you see Clandon when you were on the way here?" Alenna asked.

Both women shook their heads.

"He saved my life, I think," Alenna said.

Elizabet smiled. "He is a guid boy, that one." She paused a moment. "But then, ye saved Tynan's life."

"Just as you predicted," Alenna said, the confirmation of the spaewoman's prophecy tingling along her bones like an electric current. "What I don't understand is why. Why was it so important I come back in time and save him?" The thought of Tynan dying sent alarm through her. She stiffened. "What if Tynan needs me now? What if saving his life this time wasn't the only time I am supposed to help him?"

Elizabet clasped Alenna's hand. "He is no in need of ye now. He is with the baron."

Johanna turned from the window. "Dougald comes."

Johanna opened the door to Dougald. He still wore chain mail, although he had no coif or helm for his head. Grinning he said, "I've come to see how our heroine is."

Johanna beamed at him, and as he winked at her she blushed.

Elizabet stood. "She is fine. Would ye have some wine?"

"Nay. I cannae partake until the assembly tonight. And maybe not even then. We must be on guard for a full attack from the Ruthvens."

"What exactly happened?" Alenna asked.

"A soldier went traitor. Mayhap he thought to slip away with no of us the wiser."

"Why would he want to kill Tynan in particular? Or was that just an accident?"

Dougald sat down in a spindly chair and Alenna heard it creak under his weight. "Tynan was guardin' the baron. 'Twould make sense the archer planned to kill Tynan first and then slay the baron. As was the plan of the knight that chased the baron into the bailey."

"A clever plan," Elizabet said, taking a sip of her own wine.

"Without the brave action of Mistress Carstairs, the plan might have worked," Dougald said, turning his brilliant smile on Alenna.

"I didn't think. I just acted," Alenna said.

"Where did ye learn to use a bow?" Dougald shifted in his chair as if the very idea made him nervous.

"I learned as a child. My father taught me. I use a different bow at home. The one I shot today was difficult for me to draw back."

"He was a wise man, I ken. For where would Tynan be now, if it hadnae been for ye? As it is, I havenae seen a woman able to draw a bow like that," Dougald said.

Johanna sighed dramatically. "Can I go home, mathair?"

Elizabet gave her daughter a stern look. "If it will stop yer whinin' it will be all right with me. Dougald, would ye be so kind as to see to her safety?"

Dougald put his arm out to Johanna. "But of course. 'Twould be my pleasure."

Obviously pleased, Johanna took Dougald's arm.

After they'd left, Elizabet turned back to Alenna. "When Tynan came to me and said ye had been wounded, he was much worried."

Alenna made a sound of contempt. "The man drives me crazy. You certainly didn't see him thanking me for saving his life. Is he jealous? Does he feel since he's a man and a knight he somehow failed?"

A trace of a smile hovered on Elizabet's lips. "Aye. I dinnae ken for sure, but 'tis rare for a woman to fight such as ye did. And that ye kept him from his duty also made him sore."

"Kept him from his duty? How?"

Elizabet sat in the chair Dougald had occupied a short time

ago. "Ye are a woman, Alenna. He feels he must protect ye. Not the other way 'round."

Of course. How could she be so dumb? "His pride is wounded."

"Aye, and more. Ye kept him from doin' his duty because he was worried for ye. He left the baron's side to take care of ye."

Alenna clenched her hands together. "Will he be punished for that?"

"By the baron, I dinnae believe so. By himself...aye." She paused for a long moment before continuing. "He has much sorrow within him, that man. He dinnae like feelin' for ye. He's fair gone in love with ye already."

Alenna almost choked on her wine. Tynan in love with her? "How could that great, lumbering, ugly—"

Elizabet laughed. "Truly you think he is ugly? Most women find him handsome."

Oh, now she was deluding herself. He was far from lumbering and light years from ugly.

"In love with me," Alenna whispered, incredulous.

The idea of his love—no matter how brutish, no matter how crazy—was a wild, robust potion that slid into her bloodstream like a firestorm.

"Aye. Gone from the first he laid eyes on ye," Elizabet said.

"No. He can't be. I don't believe in love at first sight. It's all a chemical thing. You know...hormones."

"Hormones?"

"It's...uh...something from the future. But he can't be in love with me."

"He can and he is. But 'twill take more time for him to ken his feelin's."

Alenna would have spoken, but the door swung wide and Tynan entered, carrying a large bundle under one arm, his shield and his sword. As he slammed the door behind him, he put the weapons and bundle on the bench beside the door. His hair was tousled, a day's growth of beard covered his jaw, and the darkness of fatigue shadowed his eyes.

"Elizabet, thank you for tending Alenna's wound."

"Ye are most welcome," Elizabet said as she stood. "Are ye well?"

"Aye," he said, hastily yanking his cloak off and pulling his stained shirt over his head in another quick jerk.

Alenna let out a gasp when she saw the bruises covering his right side. She rose and walked toward him, her attention fixed on the damage. "When did you get those bruises?"

He glanced at the black and blue skin. "'Tis nothin'."

"Have ye anythin' for those?" Elizabet asked.

"The poultice ye left me two weeks ago."

Elizabet smiled at him, then gave Alenna a conspiratorial smile. "Well, 'tis in a hard place to reach. I suggest ye have Alenna help ye put it on."

"But—" Alenna began to protest.

"I take all is clear and safe now?" Elizabet asked as she walked to the door.

Tynan dropped slowly into the chair Elizabet had vacated. "All is clear. Take care."

After Elizabet left, he stared at the door for several moments, a look of sheer concentration putting tiny lines around his eyes. Curious about what troubled him, Alenna poured him wine and held the goblet out to him. He took it blindly, without speaking.

A niggling annoyance and worry built within her. "Did you get those bruises when you fell off your horse?"

He snapped to attention, as if she'd knocked him out of a stupor. "Nay. I was kicked by one of the men pursuing us today. I fell about twenty lengths over the side of an outcroppin'." He reached out and took her hand, pulling her closer until her legs almost touched his.

"What? Twenty feet—"

"I wasnae hurt that much. How is yer wound? Does it pain ye much?"

It throbbed, but not enough to distract her. Not as much as the barrage of questions Alenna had for him. "No."

"Guid. But ye must never disobey me again and leave the tower without my permission." Stone hard, Tynan's expression was unreadable.

An immediate retort came to her lips and was silenced as he turned her hand over and traced her palm with his index finger. A sweet shiver traced along her body. Lord have mercy. The man had found one of her erogenous zones.

"Ye have such soft hands. The kind of hands a man would die to have on him."

The husky statement sent an additional glimmer of heat over her, setting her pulse into swift beats. Her nipples tightened and a sweet rush of moisture immediately dampened her. *Oh God.*

She pulled her hand away. "Are you worried someone will discover I'm from the future?"

Tynan stood and she stepped back, startled by his sudden movement. He towered over her. All six-foot-five of finely honed, superbly muscled, male creature. As he glared down at her she should have been afraid. Instead she was as exhilarated as if she'd just finished a roller coaster ride.

He smelled of sweat, horseflesh and hard work. Yet despite the tangled hair, dirt on his face, and bruised flesh, he remained the most virile man she'd ever seen. The thought that he might have been seriously injured or killed today gnawed at her and she almost reached out to touch his bruises.

"You're not going to tell me, are you?" she asked.

"Ye could have been killed," he said with a soft hiss.

"But I wasn't. I was sent here to save you, remember?"

"Aye. But no one is free from death. No one." His words, laced with bitterness, ate at her. "And whether you care or no, a woman isnae safe in this castle without her man. Please promise me ye will listen to me."

"You let Elizabet go home with no escort. What makes her different?"

"She is familiar with the castle. And though many respect her, they fear her as well."

It made sense. The superstitious, which would probably include everyone in this case, might think Elizabet could put a hex on them if they dared harm her.

"Promise me ye will listen to me from now on," he said again.

The idea of taking direction in all things from a man grated her nerves. But this was the fourteenth century.

"I can't promise it—"

"Alenna." Tynan cupped her face in his hands. His gaze penetrated something inside her, smoldering and flowing through her like a heady liqueur. "I vow, if ye dinnae obey me, ye'll learn quickly what I'll do."

The threat ignited her in a way she didn't want...shouldn't want. Part of her wished to tell him to go to hell. The other realized letting him kiss her would be surrendering to feelings and emotions she couldn't have. Not for a man from another time. Not for any man in any time. Alenna couldn't allow him to kiss her again.

A grim smile touched his mouth. His fingers drifted down until he touched right above her breasts. "I'll kill any man who hurts ye."

A tiny thrill burned in her center at the declaration. Instead of thanking him, she said, "All right, I'll obey."

"Guid," he said, releasing her and heading slowly to the bundle he'd put on the bench. He unwrapped it and she watched in fascination as a gown not unlike the one Caithleen had worn today was slowly revealed. "Then I will show ye what Caithleen gave ye to wear."

"Another dress," she said, numb.

His smile was tinged with disapproval. "'Twas a present, actually, from his lordship."

The emerald green velvet garment was exquisite in every detail. A matching green silk band for her head and a gossamer thin white veil also nestled within the bundle.

Her gasp of appreciation made him glower. "Put it on now. We have little time to spare before the meal at the great hall."

"But I thought it was reserved for nobility and high born and you said—"

"'Twould be, but there is naught but the knights and the baron and his men who will be there. Yer bravery has taken his attention. He wishes to pay ye homage. And, as yer cousin, I cannae let ye go without an escort."

"I see." Intrigued, she examined the dress.

"And when the baron requests yer presence, then ye must go."

Glancing at Tynan's disheveled state, she gave him a dubious once over. "You're appearing in the great hall like that?"

His sensual lips turned up in the slightest of smiles. "Nay." He reached for the container of poultice. "After ye dress, will ye help me put on the poultice?"

His request made her breath accelerate. The very idea of touching him sent a silly dance of butterflies into her stomach. But if she didn't obey him...

"If you can find me some new shoes." She held up one foot and showed him her ankle-high shoe. "They pinch my feet."

"Those are the biggest I could find."

"I'll just have to wear my own shoes," she said, smiling and knowing she'd do no such thing.

Tynan had spent a considerable time looking at her athletic shoes, totally fascinated by the white nylon and leather and the shoelaces.

"I suppose there might be a man or two with feet as big," he said, straight-faced.

At five-seven-and-a-half, Alenna was hardly an Amazon. She grinned and remembered that Caithleen had expected her to give a message to Tynan. "I almost forgot. Before the siege on the castle I saw Caithleen, and she told me she'd meet you in the galley in the gloaming."

Tynan quirked up one eyebrow. "Did she now?"

He didn't offer any more explanation, but turned to stare into the fire. Although tempted to ask him why Caithleen wanted to meet with him, she doubted she'd get an answer. If he'd planned a liaison with Caithleen, he seemed an honorable enough man not to speak of it in front of others. With a sense of keen disappointment that he might be having an affair with the young girl, she started to change. She knew he wouldn't look at her undressing. He always turned away. The possibility that he could turn and watch her sent a wild, undeniable terror and thrill straight through her.

Tight through the chest, the kirtle and surcoat took some maneuvering. Alenna almost took them off and told Tynan she couldn't wear the garments. After fumbling with them for a short time, she decided they would do. She had no time to wash out her under things, so she left them off.

Taking a deep, nervous breath, she told Tynan he could turn around. Tynan faced away from her, gazing into the fire in the hearth. He turned and his expression went stiff, as if he'd been hit over the head by a hammer.

"Cat got your tongue?" she asked when the silence stretched as far as Death Valley.

A tiny, crooked grin tilted one side of his mouth. He walked slowly toward her until all she could see was his hard, muscled frame and his gaze boring into hers.

"Beautiful," he whispered.

CHAPTER 7

"Beautiful," Tynan said again, softly and with a slight catch in his throat.

Yes, he had seen many beautiful women in his life. But no one compared to Alenna. The vivid hue of the fabric brought a special light to her eyes that enchanted him as much as a sweet muse.

As he walked toward her, her eyes widened. Did she still fear him? Guid. She should be afraid. Seeing her caution gave him back a little of the discipline he'd had before she appeared in his life. No woman had ever released a torrent of emotions within him the way Alenna did. Not Florie. Not even Mary.

"Caithleen is beautiful," Alenna said.

Her words stopped his advance. "She is."

"And very young." Hardness replaced the confusion he saw in her gaze.

"Aye. Young. Too young to—"

He cut himself off in time to avoid revealing anything.

"Too young for what?" she asked.

Alenna would no doubt discover Caithleen's status when she

attended the banquet, so it was useless to hide the truth. "She is the baron's mistress."

Alenna gasped. "Oh my God. That explains her extravagant dress." He watched as she traced her hands down the velvet covering her hips.

God's blood, what he would give to touch her that way again.

A surge of heat poured into his loins, bringing him to instant, painful arousal. He took a deep breath. No. He couldn't give in to the need that ate at his gut like a feeding beast.

"So that is why she is dressed like a queen and Clandon is still in rags," Alenna said.

"Aye." He advanced a few more steps until he stood close enough to inhale her pure scent.

"Why does she do it?" she asked.

"The baron wanted her and she is poor. He gives her jewels and clothin' and food."

A twitch of her lips, a slight curling of disgust marred the shape of her mouth. He'd seen that look before and it intrigued him as much as amused him.

"The baron wanted her," she said again, putting her hands on her hips. "So she just goes off to be his mistress because he wants her? Doesn't she have any scruples?"

Alenna's words baffled him a little. "What is this scruples you speak of? Few women would turn from warm lodgin', plenty to eat, and clothes like ye have on now. And if I think on it, she is a wee bit past marriage age."

She heaved a sigh. "I forgot what century I'm in. Women in my time are not the property of men and rarely marry at seventeen."

Tynan made a sound of disbelief. "Women have no protectors? No men at their hearth?"

A small smile erased the sarcastic tinge from her lips. "Yes, many of them do have husbands. But many don't. In the future women do many of the things only men do in this time." When he said nothing, taking in her words with amazement, she continued. "They are even soldiers."

"Eh? Soldiers? Is that what ye were?"

A soft laugh escaped her. "No. Why would you think that?"

"The way ye fought. I never saw a woman do the things ye did today."

A satisfied gleam came into her expression. "And you were worried about me being able to take care of myself?"

The challenge in her statement, spoken in a honey and smoke voice, did something to his senses. When he stepped closer, Alenna's guarded expression told him his aggressive stance had the effect he wanted. Maybe he would threaten her with kisses to keep her in line, even if it came at the expense of his own sanity.

"Do ye need another taste of the dangers hereabout?" he asked softly, unable to stop himself. He leaned closer, wanting to taste her lips again and hard pressed to keep from taking her in his arms.

He saw the quick intake of her breath as much as he heard it. Her breasts rose slightly as she took another slow, less startled breath. "I've had all the danger I need since I've been here."

"Yet ye defy the very idea of takin' my lead."

"In my time, I have myself to rely on. No one else."

"Ye must ken that everyone in the castle is in danger. Dinnae think these thick walls can keep ye safe if the castle is attacked. Ye must be on yer guard at all times."

Alenna shrank back a little, as if his warning had some effect. Satisfied with her worry and his ability to intimidate her, he eased back.

He took in her prettiness and compared it to other woman he knew. Half her allure came in the bold, often impudent way she talked and presented herself. Her defiance made his blood surge, tossing him from anger to lust with relative ease. His gaze fell to the snug fit of her bodice and he wanted to cup those full breasts in his hands again. To taste the centers and bring them to hard, hot life once more.

What would it be like to smooth his hands down the fabric of her gown and mold her hips to his? He held back a groan when he thought of moving intimately between her legs, of sinking into the hot, tight warmth. His cock ached and hardened. *Jesu.*

Tynan watched her face turn a becoming shade of pink. Her lips parted and he almost leaned down and covered her mouth with his, right then and there. It took all his willpower not to touch her. He cleared his throat.

"And why have ye no guidman?" he asked.

"I was engaged once."

"Engaged?"

Alenna paused, as if searching for the right way to answer. "Betrothed."

"And why are ye no with him now?"

Pain flickered in the depths of her eyes and he regretted that his question served to hurt her.

"He found another woman more to his taste. We worked together. I was a paralegal…a person who assists in the law. We were a day away from our wedding and he…" She swallowed.

"Then what?"

"I found him in bed with another woman. He said he didn't love me anymore, and when I went back to work…I found I couldn't handle it. I got angry and we had an argument in the office. The firm dismissed me from my job. I wanted to get away from him so much I didn't even fight for my career."

"Och, what a sumph. He does no deserve ye."

"Sumph?"

"A man with no brain. Why would he trade a woman like ye for another?" He let his guard down, drinking in the way her lips parted in surprise. Wanting to consume the taste of her as well. He reached out to touch her.

She moved away from him before his hand touched her shoulder.

Tynan took a deep breath and shoved his craving back into the deep well he'd placed it in, after Florie's murder. He doubted this beautiful woman gave her favors lightly.

Alenna reached for the poultice. "I'll put this on your bruises."

The idea of having her hands on him sent a shaft of heat into his gut for what seemed the hundredth time in an hour.

"Nay." He'd live with the ache in his side for a while longer, or he'd have an agony far more powerful in his loins to contend with all night. "I must get ready."

Tynan turned away, wondering how he could continue to withstand this woman in his chambers, so close yet so far away.

* * *

As Alenna advanced into the great hall in the keep of the castle, a feeling of unreality passed over her. Only the sensation of Tynan's hard forearm under her fingers gave her strength. Fortitude she'd bolstered with wine had dissipated the moment Tynan had called her beautiful. The lust-filled, admiring heat in his eyes had unsettled her.

No man had a right to eyes that delved deep into a woman's psyche and plumbed her secret desires. Tynan's eyes were those of a predator, a ravenous beast in need of a healthy snack.

He craved her.

She glanced up at him quickly. He appeared calm and perhaps even bored. Then again, he'd probably attended these repasts numerous times and had escorted woman far more beautiful.

The scent of cooked meat tickled her nostrils and her

stomach growled. Placing a hand over her stomach, she hoped no one could hear. So far today she'd had bread, wine and some stew, and it had worn off a long time ago. Other scents assaulted her—unwashed bodies and a few more aromas as yet unidentifiable.

Alenna gazed at the cathedral-like vaulted roof and its crisscrossed timbers. Two great fireplaces, large enough for a human to stand almost upright within them, were at either side of the hall. Fires burned within them, but she could still see her breath. She shivered, wishing for her fur-lined cloak.

Along a wall halfway between the two fireplaces was the hie burde, the wood platform elevating the high table. Behind the table, in the center, sat a man she could assume was the baron. Above him hung a flag, which Alenna recalled was called a cloth of estate.

Before she could take in more of the room, the baron spied her. From this distance she couldn't identify the shade of his eyes, but he had no compunction about staring. A tumble of light brown hair, thinning on top, curled above his collar. Two dimples creased his narrow face as he gave her a thin, tight smile. He looked about forty years old. Uncertain how to act, she took a wild guess, and lowered her head and gave a slight curtsey.

Tynan leaned down to her slightly. "Are ye sure ye have no done this before?"

"I'm certain." As soon as she said the words, Alenna knew she was lying. Somewhere, at some time, she had entered a great hall, perhaps even this one. For all its feudal harshness, this place had an oddly familiar flavor that she neither understood nor wanted to think too much about. "I guessed a curtsy was in order."

She quickly surveyed the rest of the room as they continued to walk. Next to the main table was a series of trestle tables set in a perpendicular fashion to the baron's dais. Fourteen men sat on benches around the table, some of them in chain mail. Only three people in the room wore velvet.

Herself, Caithleen and the baron.

This made Alenna uncomfortable. In a sense she felt like a slave on display, as the men turned to look at her slow progression.

Caithleen sat to the right of the baron, a smile spreading over her face as she nodded to Alenna.

"She's sitting with the baron," Alenna whispered to Tynan as he led her to the main table.

"Aye. The baron willnae hide his mistresses from sight."

"He has more than one mistress?"

"Caithleen has been his mistress for a short spell...he keeps only one at a time."

"How many has he had?"

"Ten."

"Ten? In the four years you've been here he's had ten?" Her voice almost squeaked in her indignation.

"Nay. He's had but four since I've been here."

Her mouth went on without her brain. "How many have you had?"

"'Tis not yer concern," he said harshly, startling her. "Save your worry for yer speech. Try to sound more like one of us."

"How? It's not like I've been in this country long."

"Try."

She glared at him as they proceeded down the line of tables to the dais.

The baron did not stand, but nodded to them again. Alenna curtsied and Tynan bowed at the waist.

"My lord, this is Alenna, my cousin. Alenna, his lordship Malcomb Leath, Baron MacAulay."

"Mistress Carstairs, I am pleased to make your acquaintance and thank you for Tynan's life. You have given it back to me when all might have been lost. Please, sit at my table." Flavored with cultured English tones, his voice was deep, but sounded rusty, as if his windpipe had been damaged. He gestured to an empty chair to the left of him.

She swallowed hard and tried the best accent she could manage. "Oh no, I couldnae—"

Tynan nudged her slightly with his arm.

"You have saved Tynan's life, Mistress, and perhaps even my own," the baron said. "And for that I would be grateful and have you as my guest tonight. I hear you have acquaintance with Caithleen." He nodded toward Caithleen.

"Aye," Alenna said, hoping this was the right answer. "Both she and her..." she looked for the word she'd heard Caithleen use, "brathair have been most kind to me."

The baron tilted one eyebrow. "Clandon?" He glanced at Caithleen. "He's a mischievous boy, if ever I have seen one."

Mischievous maybe, but a good kid nonetheless. "He's a nice boy."

The baron blinked, as if a bit shocked by her assessment. He gave her a small, rather calculating smile. "He knows how to get into trouble. My steward had him whipped for impudence on more than one occasion."

Alenna's distaste grew in her mouth like mold on bread, but she kept her mouth shut.

Caithleen smiled brightly at her. How could Caithleen sit there and smile, when the baron had just said he'd whipped her brother? Alenna didn't believe Caithleen could be a heartless young lady. There were things Alenna had yet to understand. Unlike the life she'd led before, here in this world she couldn't control much of what happened around her. Sometimes she felt like a duckling swimming on its own in a big, deep sea. Being at this table with the baron made her uncomfortable, as if she were his mistress as well.

Wishing she could rely on Tynan for help with her medieval

etiquette, she kept her gaze on the baron. "I would be delighted to sit at yer table, my lord."

After she was seated, Tynan left the dais area and took a seat on a bench next to Dougald.

A man came into the room and brought a bowl to the baron, then poured water into it out of a pitcher. When the baron and Caithleen washed their hands and took the rough cloth handed to them by the servant, Alenna followed suit.

The baron smiled and his grin showed crooked, yellow teeth. Silver grey, his eyes compelled with a hypnotic lure as potent as a wolf stalking prey. "You are welcome at my table every evening, Mistress Carstairs."

"I usually take meals with my cousin."

"Aye. But I would like to see you here at least twice a fortnight, if not more. Your cousin is a great help to me, Mistress. Like him, you have shown that bravery runs in your family."

Uncomfortable with his regard, she shifted in her chair.

When a manservant set a pewter goblet of wine in front of her, she took a tentative sip, trying not to wrinkle her nose at the taste. Admittedly, it tasted better than the brew Tynan had at the tower.

"Ah," the baron said. "I see you are modest. Such humility is admirable. I like boldness in women. To a point."

Although he'd contradicted himself, she thought she knew what he meant. Spiciness in bed, but meek in all other aspects. "Tynan is brave. I reacted to try and help my beloved cousin."

He leaned his elbow on the table and placed his chin in his hand. As he looked out over the tables filled with men, she hoped he'd keep that keen, penetrating gaze away from her. Unfortunately, he looked at her again.

"Did it occur to you that you might have been saving the enemy?"

The challenging question took her off guard. Her mouth opened, then shut.

The baron chuckled, soft and without remorse. "'Tis not often a woman of your bravery is thus mute."

"I am nae sure I know what ye mean about the enemy."

His lips thinned into an uncompromising line. "Many traitors have been discovered amidst my very own soldiers these many weeks. What if Tynan had been one of those traitors?"

"Are you saying he'd betray ye?" Alenna asked without thinking. A feeling of danger, of looking down into a deep well pumped through her stomach.

"Of course not. Tynan would never betray me. He is my most loyal and powerful knight." Like a chameleon his eyes changed from hard to glowing good humor. "You are indeed a woman of daring and intelligence. How is it that you know of archery?"

"My father taught me when I was a child," she said, wondering if the inquisition had started.

"I see. How very unusual."

"I had a varied upbringing," she said quickly, her heart thumping steadily harder as her discomfort with the situation increased. "I learned many things other girls didnae."

"What other things?"

"Hiking…I mean climbing mountains. Defending myself."

His brow wrinkled. "Defending yourself? Against what, pray tell?"

"Other people."

"Men?"

She looked away from his penetrating gaze. "Aye."

Feeling his scrutiny intensify, she wondered if she'd said too much. Then again, with a man like this, mystery might urge him on rather than repel him. So far her attempt at this particular Scottish accent didn't give her away. In fact, the more she used it, the easier it came to her.

He reached under the table and placed his hand over hers. "I find that extremely exciting, Mistress."

Nausea roiled in her stomach, and she stared at his hand like it was a nasty bug. Momentarily paralyzed, she let him caress her fingers. Fear clogged her throat and she couldn't speak. She sought a glimpse of Tynan and saw him watching them, almost as if he would come to her rescue if she'd ask.

"Don't look so worried, dear. You need not fear I will harm you," the baron said.

Alenna tore her gaze from Tynan's, and slowly she pulled her fingers out from under the baron's wormy touch.

"I am nae worried," she managed to say.

With cool calculation in his expression he put his hand over hers again and said, "I have been told, you see, that you were meant to save Tynan's life. That Elizabet, Tynan's mistress, foresaw your arrival."

For a moment her breath stopped. Not because the baron had revealed he knew her secret. Not because his hot, sticky hand lay over hers.

Elizabet was Tynan's mistress.

CHAPTER 8

*A*lenna felt the blood drain from her face as she stared at the baron's grinning countenance.

Well, she'd suspected Tynan cared for Elizabet. Was that why he wouldn't answer her question about how many mistresses he'd had? Worse yet, did the baron also know Alenna came from the future?

Automatically she looked at Tynan. He watched her, his face granite hard. Did he guess the baron touched her?

"I am sorry, Mistress Carstairs. I have shocked you with my plain speaking. Forgive me," the baron said, removing his hand from hers.

Partial relief swept through her. "There is nothing to forgive, my lord. I suspected they were together."

"Then you are not only beautiful and brave but clever."

"Your lordship is generous with his compliments."

His grin widened, putting grooves in his cheeks. "Nay. I speak nothing but the truth in all matters. My word is my honor."

Trying not to think about Tynan taking the petite Elizabet into his arms and making love to her, she turned her attention full on the baron. "Elizabet told you I would come to save Tynan's life?"

"Nay. She told me naught. But gossip runs rampant among the servants. I was told that you appeared out of a mist, right in front of Tynan's war horse."

A warning tickled the back of her neck, like a chill breeze. She smiled her broadest and feigned a small laugh. "The servant's gossip is a falsehood. I am Tynan's cousin."

He laughed, the sound loud enough to echo around the hall. Many of the men, including Tynan, looked up.

The baron lowered his voice and leaned close to her. She caught a whiff of his unwashed body. "Do not worry yourself, my dear. I see you are an honorable woman. Though you speak with strange words, you are not the Beelzebub's own, come to make mayhem on the people of the castle."

Another disturbing tumble pushed into her stomach. "Do people think I have come here to do harm?"

"Nay. And I shall have anyone who speaks ill of you flogged."

She grabbed his forearm impulsively. "Oh, please, it is nae important enough for such a severe punishment."

He looked down at her hand and she hastily snatched it away. "If I say 'tis important. 'Tis important."

"I apologize, my lord."

His lips curled into a knowing grin. "You are not familiar with our ways here. That gives you much latitude for mistakes. Much."

Damn it. She had to be more careful what she said and did, or soon she'd wind up on the chopping block or hanging from the gallows.

The baron clapped his hands together once and servants came into the room bearing platters of food. "We shall speak no more on it tonight."

Later, after he'd consumed copious amounts of food, he spoke again. "We have fewer at table than I would like."

"Tynan says the nobles wouldnae come here if they believe the Ruthvens will attack the castle at a moment's notice," Alenna said.

His hard eyes told her nothing. "If you mean that they are frightened hens, you are correct. They are afraid. They do not have people such as Tynan of MacBrahin, or Dougald of Douglas here to defend the castle. Without them, as well as my other knights, the castle might fall to the heathens." The baron held up his wine goblet. "To all my good men. Long life and good health, so long as you serve me."

A hardy cheer went up around the room, and Alenna looked at Tynan and Dougald. Dougald smiled and swigged his drink, whereas Tynan took a sip and put his cup down. His frown centered on her and she looked away, conscious of a strange warmth spreading into her chest whenever she caught him gazing at her.

Alenna watched in fascination as servants brought more food into the room. Wooden spoons were provided, though some of the men used knives to eat. The baron, Alenna and Caithleen were given wooden bowls lined with bread and a manservant provided them with beef, venison and chicken from a silver platter.

"I would have you choose our meat for us this night," the baron said to Alenna.

When the manservant held the platter in front of her, she hesitated, feeling slightly nauseated from a night's accumulation of nerves.

"Mistress Carstairs, are you feeling unwell from your wound?" the baron asked, his brows lowering into a frown.

"Mayhap the events of today have distressed ye," Caithleen said, her concern clearly written on her young face.

Alenna was surprised Caithleen had said a thing—she'd been completely silent until this point.

"I am well," Alenna said, and pointed at the chicken.

After the baron took a large portion, he served Alenna and then Caithleen. Once they'd had a blessing, they took more wine while kitchen assistants brought in bread and butter.

The men at the lower tables didn't receive wooden bowls, but trenchers of bread that they shared with another. Tynan and Dougald ate with relish, using their fingers.

As the meal progressed, she followed the examples of those around her. People didn't put their elbows on the table, nor did they spit on the floor, or wipe their mouths on their sleeves. The formality startled her. Somewhere she'd gotten the idea that people in this time didn't care about table manners.

As Alenna ate the chicken, she noted the heavy garlic and pepper seasoning. She wondered if she would ever be able to stomach eating the food in this century. Even sipping the wine didn't take away the bizarre taste. Wondering if the spices covered the flavor of spoiling meat, she put down her spoon. Her stomach did a nasty turn.

As the meal progressed, the din in the room increased as the knights talked. The baron spared few words for Caithleen and concentrated on Alenna. At no time did Caithleen appear angry at being spurned, yet Alenna felt uncomfortable with his attention.

The servants arrived with the washbowls again and afterward served cheese and nuts. Alenna took one look at the additional food and decided if she took another bite, she'd vomit. She pushed aside her bowl.

"You are not eating," the baron said, indignation in every word.

She gave him a feeble smile. She had to have an excuse for not eating or he would be insulted, and right now she did feel nauseated. "I fear I am unwell, my lord."

"She does look most pale," Caithleen said, looking around the baron. "Perhaps you should take your leave and rest, Alenna."

Grateful for Caithleen's suggestion, she said, "Thank you."

"My apologies," he said, his tone changing to sympathetic.

Deciding it was better for him to assume the arrow wound was the problem and not the food, she nodded. "My wound does pain me. I am tired. It has been a long day."

"Then we shall not keep you longer at table. Tomorrow, if you are well, you may dine with us and stay long enough to hear the minstrels play."

"Thank you, my lord."

As she stood a wave of dizziness came over her and she grabbed the table edge. Hoping she could stop the twirling sensation, she closed her eyes and tightened her hold.

"Alenna," a deep, concerned voice said at her elbow. She opened her eyes as Tynan put his arm around her waist. "I will take care of her, my lord."

"Tynan shall see you safely to your chambers," the baron said. He nodded and smiled as they left.

Once out of the great hall, Tynan pulled her to his chest. His expression was thunderous, as if she'd committed a great transgression.

Before he could speak she said, "You can wipe that glower off your face, Tynan. I can't help it if I don't eat rotten meat every day."

"Meat in yer time is better?"

"It's preserved by freezing."

His eyebrows went up. "Then ye have only guid meat in the winter?"

His comical expression temporarily took her mind off the muddle in her intestines and she smiled. "No. We have a way to keep it frozen year round."

Cocking his head to the side slightly, he said, "I've much to learn of yer time, Alenna."

In contrast to the glares he'd given her all evening, his gaze grew soft and concerned. Without hesitation he lifted her in his arms.

"Tynan, you don't have to carry me."

He strode through the castle. "But I will. I'm takin' ye home."

Home.

A strange word for him to use.

He shifted her in his arms as if to get a better grip. "I'll have Elizabet put together a tea for ye."

At the mention of the woman's name, a twinge of consternation added to the conflict in her stomach. "The baron was very talkative tonight."

"Aye. I could see that. He likes yer company too much."

The sour quality to his tone surprised her. "Why too much?"

"When it comes to women, I dinnae trust him."

"Because he's had ten mistresses?"

Tynan looked down at her, and in the flickering light of one of the torches, she noted the tightness about his mouth. A sure sign of his disapproval, if ever there was one.

"A man with mistresses is often foolish. He doesnae think with his mind."

She smiled. "I see. You mean you're afraid he won't make good decisions if he's distracted by a woman."

"Aye."

Alenna let out a laugh. "Do you know this from personal experience?"

"Aye. If a man places a woman's welfare above his duties, above the trust other people have in him, he is fair ruined."

Startled by his statement and by how it made her feel, Alenna said, "So a man in love is stupid?"

His nodded firmly. "He is."

"You think the baron can't perform his duties correctly when he has a mistress?"

"If he dare fall in love with her." As they came to the Black Tower, Tynan sat her on her feet.

"Is he in love with Caithleen?"

"Nay. But if he were to take ye as his mistress, I ken it wouldnae be long before he were a mad man."

Indignation stirred her as he opened the door and they went into the room. "Are you saying I would make him crazy?"

Shaking his head as if she couldn't possibly understand, he leaned in close. "Ye might, at that."

"I don't know whether to be insulted or flattered," she said weakly.

"He finds ye comely, as any man with two eyes must."

Suddenly the warmth and special attention in Tynan's gaze was immediate. Too intimate.

Do you find me comely, Tynan?

He jerked back and for a moment Alenna thought she'd asked the question aloud. Feeling tired, she sat on the pallet. Immediately he went to work on starting a fire in the hearth.

"The baron will want ye for his mistress before long."

"What?"

"I watched ye together. Dougald even noticed it."

"If you mean that he was rude to ignore Caithleen, then you're right—"

"'Tis not just that. 'Tis in his eyes. I saw it before he took Caithleen as his mistress. If a man looks close, he can see what another man is plottin'. 'Tis not a hard thing to do."

"You had me fooled. I thought you were staring at me and yet you were watching the baron."

He cocked an eyebrow and grinned. "I was starin' at ye part of the time."

The little devil on her shoulder wanted to know why. "Oh?"

He stood. "I wanted to see if ye wished for his attentions."

"Of course not. He touched me," she said.

His spine stiffened. "He touched ye?"

"On the hand. Several times."

He swallowed hard. "He should nae have done that."

"Well, he seems like the type of man who does whatever he wants, whenever he wants."

Tynan's face hardened again. "Aye."

Even in that moment, when he frowned, she knew the essence of what made Tynan a powerful man. When he looked at a woman he saw her. Beyond a woman's fetching face, or fancy clothing, Tynan looked into the soul.

Somehow his watchfulness was deeper than sexual, though as disquieting as any lustful gaze. As he continued to stare, she felt devoured, yet somehow protected at the same time.

Alenna drank in the sight of him like a thirsty woman. In that moment she understood why women admired him and yet feared the primal man hovering under the surface.

"God's blood," he said, his voice rumbling deep. "How does any man resist ye? How do I resist ye?" He shook his head. "I'll get Elizabet for ye."

Seconds later he was out the door, leaving her more confused about the man than ever.

* * *

"Drink this."

Elizabet handed Alenna a goblet filled with a substance that looked like weak coffee. "What is it?"

Elizabet sat in a chair next to the table. "Southernwood. 'Tis a weak herb tea I've put together for the cramps. Cures most that ails a poor stomach. Though ye must not have more than one cup, for beyond that 'tis most unhealthy."

Skeptical, Alenna tested the drink and found the flavor similar to chamomile tea. "Toxic?"

"I dinnae ken that word."

Alenna took another healthy swallow and found the taste better the second time around. "Harmful."

"Aye. But dinnae fash yerself. I wouldnae give ye that much."

Smiling, Alenna ignored the continuing tumble in her stomach for something else plaguing her mind. "Did Tynan go back to the great hall?"

Elizabet rose from her chair and checked the makeshift bandage on Alenna's arm. "Yer wound looks much better even now." For a moment she appeared unwilling to speak about Tynan, but then continued with, "He dinnae say where he was goin', only that it would be awhile and I should stay with ye until he returns."

Decidedly weary, Alenna said, "You don't have to stay."

"Tynan would be angry with me if I left ye here alone."

Alenna sighed. "Do you always do what he says?"

Elizabet smiled. She held her hands out to the roaring fire. "He is used to my stubborn ways, if that is what ye mean."

The answer seemed designed to obscure rather than clarify and Alenna wanted to ask the petite woman if she was Tynan's mistress. But despite the need, she managed to rein it in for fear of alienating Elizabet. She appeared to be a woman with a kind heart. Alenna already considered her a friend.

"Then he shouldn't have trouble getting used to me," Alenna said finally.

"Ye have softened his hardened soul. But 'tis no a bad thing."

Alenna rose gingerly from the pallet and discovered her stomach already felt better. "He thinks the baron wants me for his mistress. But he said the baron only keeps one at a time... and there is Caithleen."

The tiny woman retreated from the fire to stand closer to Alenna. "The baron takes women when and where he will."

"What about married women—"

"Oh, nay. Nay, he chooses them carefully. 'Twas barely a day after he banished his last mistress when he had Caithleen move into his chambers. I saw what he was about long before that."

"What do you mean?"

"'Twas plain he meant to be rid of his other mistress. She

was gettin' nigh on five-and-twenty years old and her looks were goin'."

"Twenty-five? Terribly old."

A grin tilted Elizabet's lips. "In your time, I take it this is very young."

"Adult. But still young." The idea relieved Alenna somewhat. "If I'm nine-and-twenty, he shouldn't want anything to do with me."

"But ye are fine lookin' and unmarked for someone of yer age."

Speculating on Elizabet's age again, Alenna finally gave up and asked. "You're a beautiful woman. How old are you?"

"I am three decades old."

Alenna knew her mouth hung open. "But your daughter is so—"

"Six and ten. I gave birth to her when I was but four-and-ten."

"How is that Tynan has reached his age without a wife and child?" Alenna asked without thinking. "He's old by the standards of this time. Even that scar on his forehead doesn't take away his looks."

"Aye. Tynan is a braw man. Make no mistake, the women hereabouts think very well of him. Many a young woman, and some not so young, have pined for him. Mathairs have oft set to make their girls available in marriage to him."

"Well, you were wrong to say he's in love with me, Elizabet. He told me tonight a man in love is stupid and distracted from his duty."

"He does fine work of pretendin' that which he doesnae feel."

The wistful tone in Elizabet's voice led Alenna to believe the baron was right. Elizabet was Tynan's mistress, but maybe she wanted his love.

Elizabet went to the window. The bright moon illuminated her finely drawn features. Did Elizabet want Tynan with her now? Alenna recalled his meeting with Caithleen. Annoyance moved through her like writhing worms. Screw him. She didn't care if it was the fourteenth century. He couldn't play with the hearts of these women. Elizabet and Caithleen deserved men that would love them with all their heart and soul.

"I suppose he has more than one woman at a time?" Alenna asked, fiddling with the plaid on the pallet.

Elizabet turned her gaze from the window, her brows pinched together in a frown. "No."

Yet Elizabet said he loved her. If Elizabet was his mistress, why would Elizabet believe him in love with another woman? Deep in her heart Alenna felt Tynan couldn't hurt someone he cared about. Could he?

"Has the tea helped ye?" Elizabet asked as she returned to sit at the table.

Either the tea or the conversation had helped, because the discomfort had reduced. "I do feel better. Thank you."

* * *

TYNAN MOVED through the semi-darkness of the castle, working his way toward Dougald's chambers in the west tower. As he walked, he inhaled a deep draught of the night, scented the clean air that washed away more of the earthy aromas of the day.

All around him though, he sensed an unsettled wave of discontent and malaise, increasing with each passing day. The people of the castle were loyal to the baron. But with what he had learned tonight from Caithleen, he wasn't certain how much longer he could remain a faithful attendant to his lordship. It wounded his soul to think all this time he might have placed his trust in someone who did not deserve it.

In four years he'd found refuge from the heartache that had trailed him from Glenfinnan, and he'd encountered much to be thankful for in his lordship's service. Strong in body and spirit as he may be, Tynan didn't know if he could withstand anything more. It seemed the last few years had been nothing but blow after blow…disappointment after disappointment. Such was the life of a sinner, and it may be his iniquity had been too great to atone for. Too great to stamp out with good deeds or intentions.

Shoving aside self-pity, he thought of Alenna and hoped she felt better. Although he'd wanted to remain at her side earlier in the evening, what he'd seen at the meal had assured him that a visit with Caithleen was necessary. The baron planned something involving Alenna and Tynan had to know what.

A fierce rush of protective instinct entered his soul. By God, no man—not even his lordship—had better lay a hand on her again.

He would kill them.

CHAPTER 9

When Alenna awoke late in the night, the room was silent and cold. Nothing of the fire remained.

Tynan hadn't returned yet from his trip to see Caithleen.

She rose from the pallet and looked out the window. She saw nothing but the darkest black night. No one seemed up and about.

A niggling of worry for his safety started within her. She shouldn't worry, though. If he was snug in Caithleen's bed…

That's right. If he is snug in another woman's bed, I shouldn't give a damn.

Intuition poked her and said something was wrong. She had a feeling that even if he'd visited with Caithleen for a liaison, he wouldn't have stayed the whole night with her.

Perhaps Tynan had stayed away from Alenna because of anger. As the biggest, strongest man in the whole damned castle, he probably believed he could do fine without her.

She smiled. His male ego had splintered when a mere woman had saved his life. At the moment she didn't feel at all macho.

She hadn't spent one night alone in this alien world. She'd found restless snatches of sleep, stolen from the few moments her ears didn't detect the sounds of night.

Restlessness continued to annoy her. What if Tynan was hurt, lying somewhere in need of help? Fright went straight through her like a cold sword. The idea of him lying dead terrified her. She wrung her hands and tried to regain her wits. Determined not to give in to a fresh spate of unreasonable panic, she shoved her feet into her shoes and set about making a fire. Even this simple duty couldn't keep her mind off Tynan's whereabouts.

Maybe he was safe. Maybe he was in Caithleen's bed, damn him.

She poked at the fire, stabbing as if it were Tynan's face. The image startled her and she stopped at mid-thrust. She wouldn't have peace until she knew he was all right, even if she found him in a woman's bed. She went to the other room and located the dagger Tynan had left for her use.

For several minutes she stood by the fire contemplating her plan to leave the tower. Tynan had to be all right. Besides, what could she do for him? The fire snapped, reminding her she had saved his life once.

Perhaps her purpose in coming back in time was to be his permanent guard.

Absurd.

What would be the sense in that?

Nerves fraying at the edges like unraveling cloth, she made a decision. Intuition told her to seek him out—there must be a good reason for her being here.

After changing her clothes, she went out into the night. Shivering under her cloak, she hurried out the door toward the tower where she knew Dougald and several other knights resided.

As she moved along, her suspicious streak and Tynan's advice to be wary kept her alert. Her eyes slowly adjusted to the darkness. Moonlight slanted along the ground, unnerving her with shadows against the castle walls.

The guards standing at the entrance to the castle barely glanced her way as she rushed by them.

"Mistress," someone whispered from an alcove in the curtain wall.

Alenna started as she turned about. Nestled in the alcove, Clandon grinned at her, beckoning her toward him. In the gloom he looked like a little ghost from a Dicken's tale. A forlorn, flea-bitten, hungry child.

"Clandon, what are you doing here? It's late." She stepped close to the ragged boy and kept her voice low. His thin shirt and hole-ridden trousers couldn't conceal the trembling in his limbs. "It's freezing out here."

Clandon's eyes widened, a clear sense of urgency in the way he clutched her arm. "Mistress, what are ye doin'? Ye could be set upon by ruffians—"

"Enough, Clandon." Thoroughly tired of being told she couldn't make a move without a man by her side, she continued, "I can take care of myself, no matter what Tynan says. I don't see him worrying about your protection."

His face screwed up in confusion. Despite the high pitch of his voice, the boy managed to sound vaguely authoritative. He'd been watching Tynan's tactics for too long. "But I'm almost a man, Mistress, while you are only—"

"A woman. I know." Alenna heaved a sigh. "Have you seen Tynan?"

"Nay."

Annoyance and apprehension sharpened her tone. "When did you last see him?"

"With Dougald, Mistress. He's been there most all the night."

"Dougald. Not with Caithleen?"

Once again his slim face registered mystification. "Nay. Though he did say he was meetin' her tonight."

"Where?"

"They have a secret hidin' place not far from here."

Secret hiding place.

She tried unsuccessfully to jam back a torrent of jealousy. She took two deep breaths. Maybe it would be better if she turned away now and went back to the Black Tower. What Tynan did in his spare time wasn't her business.

Clandon took the decision away from her. "Come with me, Mistress. I bet ye a half-penny I can find him."

He held out his grubby hand.

Alenna smiled. Little beggar. "After you find him, you'll get the half-penny."

With a sense of urgency, she followed the boy. Again, she imagined Caithleen and Tynan in an embrace and it made her nuts. She didn't think she could stand the sight of them together as a couple. Secondary to that irritation was her concern about what would happen if the baron discovered Caithleen had a lover. Would he hurt Caithleen and Tynan? Visions of Caithleen being executed and Tynan thrown in the dungeon or hanged hurried her forward. Either scenario made her stomach tumble and fear raced like tiny bursts of energy over her body.

Clandon led her past a square tower dominating the west wall. They'd barely gone past when three men stepped out of an alcove right in front of Clandon. With a gasp Clandon stepped back and into Alenna. She grabbed his shoulders.

"Well now, what have we here?" one of the men asked, his voice a viper's hiss.

All three men wore dark hoods with holes for their eyes, noses and mouths. Ghosts in a motley parade, they immediately surrounded her and Clandon. Like the alarm in a fire station, her mind blared for her to get the hell out before the real blaze started. Her feet remained rooted to the ground.

"Let us pass," Clandon said, stepping from her grip to face the tallest, biggest man.

"I dinnae think so, lad," the man said, reaching out and shoving him violently to the side.

Clandon growled at his attacker as he fell. "Ow! Bluidy swine!"

Alenna gasped. "How dare you touch him—"

"Shut up," the man said as she reached for Clandon.

One of the men grabbed her from behind before she could assist the boy. "Where ye goin', bonnie wench?"

She struggled against the man's hard grip, yanking forward. Pain sheered through her arms as his fingers tightened cruelly.

The man who had pushed Clandon down lashed out, his palm landing squarely on her cheek. Sharp, stinging pain spread across her skin as she fell back into the other man's arms. Instinct sent adrenaline straight into her blood and she kicked back, landing a solid blow on her captor's shins.

All hell broke loose.

Clandon launched himself at the man who had hit Alenna, landing on the brute's back.

As the third man reached for her, she ducked under his arm. With a twist and a kick she booted him in the butt and sent him flailing. He stumbled but didn't fall.

"Clandon, get out of here!" Alenna yelled.

The boy beat at the man's back, ignoring her.

"Get off me, ye bluidy fool. I'll rip ye to pieces and feed ye to the hounds!" the man said.

She would have run if she'd been alone. Ready to cry out for help, she backed up and ran straight into the big man she'd just booted in the behind.

Before she could let out more than a squeak, the man spun

her to face him, bringing her flush against him. She gagged on his heavy stench of liquor, sweat and urine.

"I've got somethin' for ye, wee bitch," the man said. "Wanna taste?"

Nausea pitched her stomach as if she were in a ship tossed on a sea. "You make me sick!"

Violently Alenna twisted and stamped on his foot. He cuffed her across the face again and pain rocketed through her head, dizziness weakening her knees. She sagged in his grip.

Suddenly, the man's arms released her and she fell to her side on hard stone. She heard the angry roar of a man's voice and saw her captor being yanked backward and thrown to the ground. Shaking her head to clear the fog hovering over her vision, she saw a figure looming over her attacker.

"Tynan," she whispered.

If he heard her he made no indication. Instead he held his broadsword high and glared down at the man, as if ready to slice him to pieces.

"Ye stinkin' piece of filth." Tynan lifted his sword higher. "How dare ye touch her."

Instead of raising his voice, Tynan spoke each word slowly and precisely. Each assertion made the man at his feet sink lower, as if he sensed the deadly power Tynan could unleash.

The quiet lasted for all of thirty seconds.

The man who originally had gripped Alenna from behind launched himself at Tynan.

"Look out!" Alenna screamed.

Tynan turned with a lightning move, his sword catching the man across the throat. Alenna winced as the blade cut through flesh, and in the moonlight she saw the dark stain of the man's life force spray and spread down the front of his shirt. He staggered and fell dead, an expression of utter surprise in his cold dark eyes.

The momentary distraction gave the man on the ground time to kick Tynan in the midsection.

"No!" Alenna ran forward.

Clandon grabbed her arm. "Nay, ye'll be killed."

The man who had slapped her grabbed for a piece of wood and swung it at Tynan's head. He missed as Tynan ducked and landed a blow to the man's belly with the sword. The man moved quickly enough and the blade barely split his flesh. Surging forward, he rushed at Tynan once more.

The man who had hit Tynan in the stomach lifted the huge piece of wood and aimed for Tynan's head. Alenna's cry of warning came too late. The wood came down on Tynan's head with a sickening thud. He fell flat on his face.

"No!" Alenna ran toward Tynan, dropping down next to him and reaching for his sword. She lifted the heavy sword with both hands, grunting. As she stood, she staggered under the weight.

"Don't come any closer," she said, panting for breath.

The big man laughed, and the man who bled from his stomach gave her a gap-toothed smile, even as he grimaced in pain.

"And what do ye plan to do with that, wench?" the big man asked.

"Kill you," she said, not even taking a chance to look down at Tynan and see if he might be alive.

Oh God, Tynan. Please, please be all right.

Alenna fought back the fright turning her legs to mush, her head spinning with dizziness. Her arms weakened as the heavy metal of the sword dragged at her arms.

The big man stepped forward, but she held the sword in front of her. "Don't touch him. I swear I'll kill you."

"Now, little lass, why dinnae ye drop the blade and we will let ye go. All we want is this here—"

In her peripheral vision, she saw the second man lunge at her. As her heart leapt into her mouth, she turned the sword to the left and lifted it toward the oncoming man. He barely had time to hold himself back and prevent himself from being impaled.

Anger gave her strength. "Get back! I swear, I'll kill you."

"Back away, ye stinkin' curs," a voice said from the darkness. Dougald marched out of the shadows with four other soldiers, his sword at the ready. "Back away. If she doesnae kill ye, I will."

The men moved away, and Dougald signaled two of the four soldiers to take care of the brigands. Within moments, the bloodied men were hauled to the dungeon.

Trembling, Alenna felt her arms give way and she dropped the sword and fell to her knees beside Tynan.

Dougald put his arm around her as he knelt beside her. "Are ye harmed, Mistress?"

"I'm fine. Oh God, Tynan," she whispered searching for a pulse in his neck. Anxiety hammered in her throbbing head and throughout her sore body. "Dougald, help me."

Dougald rolled him over as she found a pulse. She sighed in relief and tears ran from her eyes like rain. "He's alive." In the semi-darkness she couldn't see the wound to his head. "We have to help him."

Dougald gestured for the remaining two soldiers to assist. "We'll take him to the west tower."

As the two soldiers lifted Tynan and started away, Alenna began to follow.

Dougald put a hand out and stopped her. "I'm sorry, but women are no allowed in that tower."

"Why?" she asked, incredulous.

"'Tis the weaponry inside and lodgin' for soldiers."

"I don't care."

His hand remained firm on her shoulder. "'Tis Tynan's own rule. He would skin me alive if he heard ye had been inside."

"I can't believe this. That's ridiculous." She clenched her hands into fists at her sides.

Dougald ignored her and nodded at Clandon. "Take her home."

Clandon latched onto her arm.

"But how will I know whether he's all right?" Alenna asked as Dougald started to walk away.

"He'll be all right, Mistress. His head is as hard as stone, take my word for it."

"But—"

"I'll have Clandon bring word to ye."

Dougald left and Alenna allowed Clandon to guide her to the Black Tower. All the way back, Clandon endured her mutterings about men and stupid rules, and stupid men and rules.

* * *

MORNING LIGHT STREAMED into the Black Tower and Alenna paced, the sound of her feet over the stone chafing her already taut nerves.

Exactly two hours had passed since Clandon had left to see how Tynan fared. Just enough time for every imaginable horrible scenario to play out in her mind.

Tynan's life was slipping away at that very moment.

Tynan had already died.

"No," she whispered, putting her hands to her bruised face.

Tynan must be all right.

Stupid fool. The man was nothing more than a savage Highlander, with the brute strength of an elephant. Why should she worry about his tough hide?

"Worthless rules anyway," Alenna muttered to the empty room and continued to pace. "Leave it to a man—"

A solid knock on the door made her heart jump. She'd been

as twitchy as a skittish colt since she'd returned to the tower. She opened the door and Clandon stood at the threshold.

"Mistress, I have guid news of Tynan."

A ripple of relief softened the tight knots in her stomach. "How is he?"

A smile lit his pale face. "He is well. 'Twould hardly ken he was in a fight. He's askin' for ye."

"Asking for me?" she said in surprise. "But I thought I couldn't enter that tower—"

"Dougald told him to loosen the rules for ye," Clandon said as he started away.

Ignoring the need for a cloak, Alenna rushed with him through the castle, bumping into several people as she trotted to keep up with Clandon's pace.

As they arrived at the tower, Clandon solicited permission to enter from the guard lounging indolently against the wall near the entrance. As she glanced in the first room next to the stairs, she noted a large, poorly lit room that held armor and weapons of battle.

The spiral stairs were slimy with dampness and more than once she almost slipped. At the top of the stairs, Clandon entered a bright room, Alenna following close behind.

"Here she is, sir. I found her pacin' the floor, just as ye said," Clandon said to Dougald.

"Fine work, lad. Now be gone with ye," Dougald said.

Clandon left as she entered the austere room. A large table at the center of the room sported chain mail and a helm. A pallet and one chair graced the other side of the room and a frayed tapestry hung from one wall. A smoky fire and stale ale gave the room the lingering reek of a pool hall.

Tynan sat in a chair, a bandage wrapped around his right forearm, a large bruise rising on his forehead over his scar. He held a goblet in his left hand.

"Guid day, Mistress," Dougald said, beaming a smile in her

direction as if he hadn't spoken with her two hours ago. "'Tis a fine day out."

"Fine?" she asked, ignoring his grin and pinning them both with a glare. "I've been wondering for two hours if Tynan was all right, or if he'd died and no one was going to tell me." She gestured to Tynan, anger wiping her worry for him straight out of her system. "And you! Making an absurd rule about women not being allowed into this tower."

Tynan glared right back. "What are ye bleatin' about, woman?"

His condescending tone lit her like a match. Heat rose in her face and she couldn't stop the words spewing forth. "Bleating? I am not a sheep, and stop calling me woman."

Tynan gave Dougald a bemused look and Dougald shrugged.

"Well, ye are a woman, make no mistake," Dougald said, his smile a gleam of masculine assurance.

"You stay out of this," she said sharply.

Dougald's eyebrows speared upward, practically disappearing in the shaggy bangs across his forehead.

When she said nothing more, Tynan gave her a hard, lingering stare. "She's no happy to see me, Dougald, that much is for certain."

Dougald cleared his throat and started for the door.

"I'll be in the arms room," he said. He paused at the doorway and gave Tynan a long-suffering look. "Tell me Caithleen doesnae have a temper like this wench does, Tynan?"

"Nay, Dougald. I think this one is the hottest of them all. 'Tis a great wonder I have if she's as hot to bed."

Throwing back his head, Dougald gave a bark of laughter.

She gasped, and the implication of Tynan's words made her entire body flair with heat. Inhaling another indignant breath, she watched as Dougald beat a hasty retreat, the echo of his continuing laughter lingering in the room. Alenna felt her temper raise another notch.

"How dare you?" she asked as she turned on Tynan, placing her hands on her hips. "I have half a mind to smack that smirk off your ugly face."

Instead of growling at her as she expected, he laughed. Liquid sloshed out of his goblet. As he placed the cup down on the table, she stepped up to his chair within easy reach. She might decide to belt him one.

"Aye. I'm ugly at that. Are ye just now takin' notice of it, lass?" he asked.

"No," she ground out. "I noticed it the first time I laid eyes on you."

Tynan laughed again and then gasped, a flicker of pain darting over his features.

She put her hand on his broad shoulder then gently turned his face toward her. She inspected the wound on his forehead. "Elizabet should look at this. Have you cleaned it?"

"Aye. Dougald took care of me. He was about to put a wrap on it." He twitched an eyebrow. "Would ye like to wrap it for me, sweet?"

If he hadn't let a soft, almost sexy smile cross his lips, she might really have taken a swing at him. The man had obviously consumed too much wine. Spouting endearments. Humph.

"Don't call me sweet. Where else are you hurt?"

"I've naught but some small cuts and such. The rotten, carrion-eatin' swine barely put a dent in me." He passed a hand over his chin.

"A dent! They practically killed you!"

Anger deepened his eyes to onyx. "The other one's lucky I took mercy on him and cut him in a way that he still lives." His face went grim and tight, the bloodlust of battle clearly etched on his features.

"You could have been killed," she whispered, her voice almost strangling.

"Nay. I am well nigh invincible." He cupped her cheek gently in his big palm. "Yer poor, wee face. Does it hurt ye much?"

"No."

Tynan traced a finger gently along her jaw. "Now ye see why ye must never go out alone."

She sighed, half from the sensation of his calloused, warm hand on her face and half over the continuing lecture about her safety. When his hand dropped from her face, she wished he wouldn't have moved.

"You hadn't come back to the tower. When I woke up it was late and I thought…"

"What did ye think?" His fingers gently touched the bruise on her cheek.

Alenna shook her head and didn't answer. She couldn't tell him she'd gone in search of him and Caithleen, intent on nosing into his personal life.

"The two that attacked me are in the dungeon, waitin' out whatever punishment the baron sees fit to give." He shifted in his seat, a flicker of pain crossing his face again.

Curiosity still moved her to discover where Tynan had been most of the night. "I suppose you were coming back to the Black Tower after seeing Caithleen safely home?"

Tynan's brow furrowed and he dropped his hand away from her face. "I was."

As she stood, she felt at odds with herself. Walking out would show him she didn't care about him, or at the very least show him how much his impertinence and teasing perturbed her. Why was she so mad at him?

The answer pained her because she didn't want it to be true.

She *was* jealous.

Plainly, simply, unequivocally jealous.

"Are you messing with that young woman's heart?" she asked suddenly.

"Eh?" His frown deepened.

"You know what I mean. Are you…are you sleeping with her?" When this wording received a perplexed look, she practically yelled at him. "Are you Caithleen's lover?"

He opened his mouth then closed it.

"Never mind," she snapped, turning to go.

Alenna let out a squeak of surprise as he grabbed her hand and swung her about, tugging so that she fell directly into his lap.

CHAPTER 10

Tynan settled Alenna's butt tight against him and wrapped his arms around her. One glance at his face said his time for teasing had ended. His dark-as-soot eyes melted her insides like chocolate and penetrated her guard, pulling her as close as his handhold. She stiffened against him and at that moment felt his cock harden beneath her. His strong arms tightened and that feral look entered his eyes that indicated only one thing.

This man, whether he wanted to or not, was thinking about sex.

"Do ye always walk away when a person is speakin' to ye?" he asked.

"No. Only big, obnoxious, dumb—"

"Are ye callin' me a fool then? I ought to—"

"What are you going to do? Hmm? Throw me in the dungeon? Feed me to the wolves?"

"Nay," he whispered, leaning over her. "I've got other plans for ye."

He gently kissed her forehead.

A startled gasp left her throat as the burn of his lips zinged through her sensitive skin. The light touch set sparklers of need exploding deep in her belly and the heat went straight to her core. Involuntarily, she squirmed and he groaned softly when her butt rubbed against the growing length of his cock.

"Let me go," she said.

"I'll let ye go when ye tell me why you think Caithleen and I are lovers."

"You were meeting her alone last night. I just assumed—"

Tynan let out a growl and gritted his teeth. "Woman, I swear by all that's holy, ye were sent not to save me but to fling me into my grave."

"Huh. I won't get so lucky. Maybe some more henchmen will beat me to it. They'll catch you next time and beat you into a soup. All you brave, braw macho types are like that, aren't you? You think no one can bring you down. Well, you're wrong." On a roll, feeling a rise of lust and distress, she pushed forward, letting the words flow without thinking. "Or maybe the blow to the head has scrambled your brains even more than they already were—"

"Enough!" Tynan's face reddened, cheeks tinged with unmistakable resentment.

He looked like a madman for the space of a second and she went rigid as a board in his arms, pushing against his chest. The rock solid feel of his muscles, his masculine scent and feral attention, heightened her awareness of him as a man. His eyes blazed with a smoldering intent she couldn't deny.

"I dinnae ken why yer whinin' and yammerin' like a hound from hell's gate. I'm here. I'm alive. What in the blazzin' infernos of Beelzebub—"

"Shut up."

"Eh?"

Tears welled in Alenna's eyes and she crammed a sob back into her throat. God, since when had she turned into a complete ninny? Why was she overreacting?

"I'm sorry." Sighing, she relaxed in his tight grip and deliberately softened her expression. "I was...I think it's because I—"

"Ye were afraid to be alone at night," he said, as matter-of-fact as if he'd announced that clouds produce rain and snow. A mighty grin punctuated his words.

"No—"

He laughed again and she frowned.

"Dinnae worry, lass. I never fight unless I have to." His voice softened. "When I saw those bastards hurtin' ye, it made my blood boil. Do ye call me mad for protectin' ye, goin' off to get myself beaten to a bluidy soup?"

When she didn't answer, he let out a sigh.

"Is that what ye want, lass?" he asked softly. "First ye act as if I'm a madman and that I've done somethin' wrong, yet ye act as if ye might care for me." He shook his head. "Nay, that couldnae be."

Once more his embrace tightened and the liquid heat in his gaze warmed her entire body. A sizzle of sexual need burned low in her belly as her fingers drifted over his broad shoulder. Damn his eyes. Damn his deep, dark, sexy eyes. She cared about the thick-as-a-plank, fierce, insolent—

"Would ye like to see me dead?" he asked. "For that is the look in yer eye."

"No. Of course not...I...you..."

"Aye? Why the burr under yer saddle, then?"

Alenna clutched at his torn shirt. "I understand this is your time, but I hate to see women used by men like livestock. Like chattel traded from man to man, at a whim or pleasure."

"Who is tradin' women from man to man?"

She flung out a hand. "The baron, for one. Elizabet explained to me that his last mistress was only twenty-five and that she was thrown aside when he tired of her, and then a while later he replaced her with another woman."

"Aye." His granite features hardened. "But she wasnae traded."

"How do you know?"

"Her name was Florie. I came to know her well." He moistened his lips. "A fine, fair woman with light hair and brown eyes. There was nothin' old nor ugly about her. I dinnae ken why he put her aside, other than he tired of her."

"You knew her well?" She leaned back against his arms but he held her firm. "The baron gave her to you as a present, didn't he? For a job well done?"

"Aye. But 'tis no what ye are thinkin'."

"Well, how else could it be?"

"The baron said he was given' her to me because he dinnae like her ways. She spoke with spice and fire. Like ye—"

She rapped him on the chest lightly. "Get on with the story."

"There's more. She was goin' to have a babe. The baron's babe. She asked Elizabet for somethin' to get rid of the babe, but I said that she could have the child and I'd take care of it with her."

Her heart squeezed in her chest. "You were going to marry her?"

He flinched slightly. "Nay. I dinnae wish to marry her. But I could have kept her from harm until she found another man to take her. She was a free woman. But she chose to stay with me and after a month we became lovers. I bought her clothes and she stayed with me at the Black Tower."

A tight knot formed in her throat and threatened to choke her. "And?"

"She took a likin' to Dougald and I thought he might make her his mistress."

Alenna recalled the conversation between Dougald and Tynan on the first day she'd arrived back in time. "He didn't?"

He shook his head and his hair fell over his shoulders. Temptation almost lured her to reach up and brush it away from the hard planes of his rugged face. "Nay. She was gone one mornin' when I awoke and when I found her—" He inhaled a deep, harsh breath and her own air supply seemed suspended as she waited. "She was dead, lass. Someone had cut her in the belly."

"Oh, Tynan," Alenna said, her throat aching with unshed tears. "How awful. No one tried to find out who killed her?"

"Dougald and I tried but found nothin' to prove who did the horrible deed. Mayhap if she had still been with the baron…he may have looked for her murderer." His gaze was hot and determined. "I did ask him, but he refused."

"Caithleen was already with him then?"

"Nay. Florie was dead two years before Cathleen became his mistress. She has only been his mistress a year. There was another woman during that time."

A pause stretched like a canyon between them as Alenna took in his solemn face. Shame rolled over her in a great wave. She'd acted like a fool.

"Why did you want to help her with her child when it wasn't yours and she wasn't your wife?" she asked, certain that his answer would explain so much about him. "Many men wouldn't."

Tynan tenderly traced the side of her neck with his index finger. A shiver of pleasure darted across her skin. He drew her closer yet, his body a cocoon of safety, of genuine caring mixed with deep, heady need.

"Florie was a fine woman. She'd had but two lovers. The baron and myself. She thought the baron loved her. When she told him she was havin' his babe, he tossed her out with the rubbish."

New anger toiled within her breast. "He's a rotten bastard."

"Aye. But perhaps no more rotten than I."

"What do you mean?"

His voice grew ragged. "If ye knew what I was…if ye knew

what I had done in my life, ye wouldnae allow me to hold ye now."

At one time she would have believed him. But she had witnessed his honor and his integrity. Certainly, he was a bit of a savage. But he couldn't have done anything so bad to warrant this self-loathing.

Tynan slipped his hands up to the cap that held her hair, pushing it off with one sweep. She reached up to trap his fingers. Trying to distract herself away from the sensuous touch, she asked, "But how could you work for him…how could you like—"

"I dinnae say I like him. I pay homage to him because…"

"Yes?"

He closed his eyes tightly and for a moment she wondered if the ugly bruise on his forehead hurt. The sensation of his fingers pushing through her hair, caressing the tresses like a lover, sent her heart drumming in overtime. His hand slipped deep into her hair to cup the back of her neck.

"When I tell of the horrors in this castle, I am no tellin' ye to have my foot on yer neck. Ask me and I will take ye wherever ye wish. I will protect ye with my life. Just dinnae go about this cursed place without me."

His heat enveloped Alenna, warming her from the inside out as his lips descended and he kissed her forehead again. She drank in his handsome, battered features and tried to control her budding tumble of emotions.

"You'll protect me with your life because you know I was sent here to save *your* life," she said cynically. He didn't answer and her heart did the inevitable jump back to reality. "I see."

"Nay. Ye dinnae know everythin' about me."

She almost moved out of his arms, tired of the verbal battle and sickened by Florie's tragic story.

"Why do ye look at me that way?" he asked.

She shook her head. Giving him a mock laugh, she said, "You

are a mess, Tynan of MacBrahin. Only a mother could love your face."

A grin moved slow and silky over his lips, setting off a chain reaction in her that dissolved every nasty word, every abuse she'd wanted to hurl at his head.

He cupped her cheek for a moment in his rough palm. He gently massaged his fingers against her scalp like a caress. Her pulse pounded and her breath quickened.

Although all her anger didn't drain away, her defenses felt plundered. Brought down as easily as he might have besieged a castle wall.

"Ye are a bonnie woman, Alenna. Did I ever tell ye that?" he asked softly. His gaze went to her lips.

"Please..." she said, moving slightly so that he dropped his hand away from her face.

"Please what?" he said as he lowered his lips until they almost touched hers.

God, she wanted him to kiss her. Wanted it so much she couldn't stand the wait.

"Don't." He moved, nuzzling her ear gently with his lips. Electric tingles danced over her and she gasped. "Tynan, what will Elizabet think if she saw you like this with me?"

He didn't flinch, didn't move...just continued that maddening trace of his lips over her ear. Alenna's body reacted with a vengeance. Her breasts felt full and achy, brushing against the material across her bodice until she wanted to beg him to touch her there. All this time, sitting on his lap with his big cock prodding her butt, she'd become wet between the legs. She needed to accept his cock, his fingers, whatever he would give her to remove this staggering need.

He dipped down to her neck and pressed a lingering kiss to the pulse hammering at the base of her throat. His fingers traced over her neck where his lips had touched. She shivered.

"Ah, Alenna, I cannae take this fire. I have to put it out."

With a slow, determined movement, he boldly cupped her breast. Alenna gasped in surprise, captured in the animal hunger she saw within him.

His fingers traced over the sensitive mound, swept over the nipple so that tingles of exquisite pleasure darted all along her body.

He placed a kiss to her lips, barely touching his mouth to hers…lingering…drawing her closer until Alenna allowed her lips to part. Deepening his caress, he tasted her with a hungry fervor. His tongue surged inside, thrusting with a heady rhythm. A message of primal need…a staggering, erotic sensuality pulsed through her blood.

Alenna felt the heat of his caresses in every part of her. Her body betrayed her as her nipples stiffened, her pussy tightening…clenching. Needing his cock burrowing high and hard inside her.

Tynan released her lips.

"Please," she murmured again, a gasp escaping her as he placed a tender kiss to her cheek and trailed toward her lips again.

"Please not want ye so badly I ache?" he said with a husky murmur that sent her arms about his neck.

Before she could answer, his mouth covered hers. Tynan's lips took hers in a shimmering, delightful way that didn't force or demand. His kiss asked. It appealed to her for comfort.

And Lord help her, she wanted to give it to him.

Over and over his kisses lingered like soft flutters, touching then retreating. Maddening and gentle, they drove her wild with need. Alenna lost all touch with time, all need for anything but his arms around her.

He tore his lips from hers and buried his face in her neck, breathing hard. When he touched her breast again she gasped, aroused by the intimate caress. She welcomed his soft touch as he circled around and around her nipple, brushing lightly with his index finger.

Tynan plucked her nipple and she moaned into his mouth. Hot waves of need moved through her in all directions. She ached with longing. She writhed as his hands caressed her rib cage, over her waist, then traveled to her hips. When his fingers drew up the material of her garment, his fingers lingered over her stocking-clad calf then homed in on her naked thigh. Anticipation built inside as she waited while his hand cupped the outside of her thigh. His hand felt big, intimidating, but oh so gentle.

He broke from the carnal kiss to whisper against her lips, "God, sweets. Yer so soft. So…" His fingers urged her thighs to part just enough and then oh…oh… He made a soft, pleased sound in his throat. "Wet."

She gasped as he touched her mound, locating the slick heat. He traced the wetness, gliding over plush folds. "Tynan. Oh God."

Her head tilted back and she kept her eyes closed as he slipped one finger, then two into her hot center. Her hips surged upward as he pushed them deep. Immediately he withdrew, then circled her clit.

She couldn't stop the gasps, the groans that issued from her throat as he stimulated her with short strokes of his middle finger over her bud, then a deep stroke of his fingers.

Clutching at the thick mane of his hair, she gloried in the silky texture, enjoying the feeling of something forbidden and wanton. Then, in a move vastly bold for her that demonstrated her arousal more than anything, Alenna pulled his head up so she could place a soft kiss on his lips.

"Jesu, but yer a beautiful wench," he said hoarsely.

"Don't call me wench," she said.

"Woman."

"Don't—"

His mouth smothered hers again, his lips prying her mouth open so he could dip inside, stroking her tongue repeatedly until she moaned and moved in a torment of excitement. No man had ever kissed her quite this way. Not her ex-fiancé, not any man. The insistent stroking over her clit and his persistent kiss made her writhe in his arms, her breath panting, her heartbeat pounding. Screaming arousal scalded Alenna until she couldn't keep the maddening sounds of her excitement contained. Repeatedly he teased her, his tongue in her mouth, his fingers buried in her, his thumb now taking command of her clit as he stroked…stroked her into maddening oblivion and climax broke.

She threw her head back and shivered, racked with blistering ecstasy as orgasm tore through her like lightning. He stayed buried inside her, his thumb on her clit, and her feminine walls tightened and released in waves over his fingers.

When he released her mouth, he breathed, "God's blood, yer sweet."

His fingers left her warmth and she sighed in a sensual satisfaction she couldn't deny. His big hands circled her waist and he drew her up with his strength.

"What—" she gasped in surprise. Before she knew it, she straddled his lap.

The hard bulge of his erection pressed against her. His mouth teased her ear, his voice harsh with sexual need. "Take me inside you, sweet Alenna. I want to be deep inside ye when ye find your pleasure."

His rough, no-holds-barred statement sent a shock of hot desire rocketing through her like a flare. In the pit of her stomach, she surrendered. Her senses rioted with the need for more. More of his kisses, his hands, his body freeing the woman inside to the ultimate pleasure.

He reached down and within seconds freed his cock. His nostrils flared, his breath coming harshly between his lips as his chest rose and fell. Tynan's eyes were bright with passion, his expression fierce. A wild, uninhibited desire demanded attention inside her. Now was the time to make a decision. Free her passion for him, or keep it locked up as surely as if she wore a chastity belt.

"Take me inside," he said, his voice raw and hot.

"I..."

Shaking her head, confusion battering, she shifted on his lap. Her gaze landed irrevocably on his cock. He held the proud erection in his hand and began to stroke over the impressive flesh. His lips parted and he groaned.

Oh. My. God.

He was the most beautiful thing she'd ever seen. Hard, thick and long, his cock looked so big in his hand. Oh, yes. She wanted it. Wanted it so badly. With long, languorous strokes, his hand pumped.

"Yes." The word came out feathery, a barely there entreaty, a final admittance she couldn't resist him any more.

She lifted her hips, ready to slide down on his cock. Be damned with consequences. Be damned to them all.

A grunt of surprise from the doorway sent Alenna out of Tynan's lap and his arms in one swift move. Embarrassed, she put several paces between herself and Tynan just as Dougald came in the room. Tynan didn't even try to put his cock back in his pants.

Dougald bowed slightly. "I dinnae think ye would still be here, Mistress. Then again, I could see ye were tendin' his wounds."

Another wave of mortification swept her as her insides tumbled with a combination of arousal and pain. "Dougald, did anyone ever tell you you're a pain in the neck?"

"Aye. Tynan tells me daily."

"Wipe that grin from yer face," Tynan said to Dougald. Tynan grimaced as he stuffed his cock back into his pants.

She started toward the door. "I'll return to the tower."

Tynan sprang up from his chair. "Yer not goin' there without me."

Ignoring his order, she made her way gingerly down the steps. Back into the morning air, she picked up her pace. Tynan rushed to catch her.

"I dinnae mean for that to happen," he said as he walked alongside of her.

"For Dougald to catch us, or for you to…?" What could she call it?

"To take advantage of ye. It wounds yer reputation to be caught so."

Alenna let out a chuckle that sounded more like a snort. "Is that all you're concerned about? My reputation? What about your reputation?" She stopped walking and turned to him. "You didn't take advantage. I could have told you to stop."

His smile was colored with a mingling of gravity and indulgence. "As a man, I dinnae fash myself about reputation."

"What do you mean?"

"I mean that bein' seen touchin' and kissin' ye gathers respect to me. It wouldnae hurt my reputation to be caught fuckin' ye. Now, ye savin' my hide twice in two days, that hurts my reputation."

He was right. Double standard was approved here in the world of 1318. Her forehead was stamped with a big 'W' for woman and no one let her forget it for a minute.

"Are you saying your ego is hurt because I helped you?" she asked.

"Ego?"

"Your pride."

"'Tis not yer place to fight men. 'Tis a man's place to defend women and children."

"It's not always like that in my time."

When she looked at him he frowned. "Ye keep speakin' of

yer world and yer time. Well, that isnae how it's done here." He stopped abruptly and grabbed her arm. "Jesu, ye really dinnae ken. What would have happened to ye if I hadnae come along?"

Alenna didn't want to admit she needed Tynan's protection. So she stared at him stubbornly and he stared back until it became a game of who would look away first. Finally, she jerked away and stomped off.

He followed. "I would ask ye not to speak of what I told ye. About Florie."

She almost stumbled over a root in the ground and he reached out to grab her arm. Shaking off his hold, she asked, "Doesn't everyone know about Florie?"

"Nay. Caithleen has heard the story, as well as Dougald and Elizabet."

"That is practically everyone."

"Nay. Only those I trust."

Warm feelings stirred in her heart. "You trust me?"

He stopped and turned her so his hands lay on her upper arms, gripping her firmly but not cruelly. "Aye. I trust ye. Though damned if I ken why."

In that moment she almost hugged him…almost went back into his arms to give him a sense of solace and understanding.

She couldn't walk a mile in his shoes, but she understood this was a man who didn't trust often and when he did, it meant something beyond simple words. She nodded and they continued walking.

What about Caithleen and Elizabet? In her heart she couldn't deny she'd felt tremendous pleasure in his arms, but she couldn't be with a man who toyed with other women. She picked up the pace to get as far away from him as possible. He continued to walk by her side until they reached the Black Tower.

When they entered the tower, he turned to her and asked,

"Are ye about to suffer female problems? You seemed...hot." His gaze heated as well. "Very ready when I touched you."

"Female problems," she said in complete surprise. It was true—she did become horny right around the time of her period, but that wasn't the problem. "No. That wasn't it."

Then she realized she'd admitted to getting turned on by him regardless of hormonal enhancement.

His grin was all knowing. When she glared at him he gave a laugh reminiscent of Dougald's. "I'm sorry. Do women still have 'female problems' in yer century? Or is that somethin' you've been able to fix, too?"

The sheer cockiness in his question made her smile. "We still have 'female' situations."

He sighed. "'Tis a bad thing, to be sure. Men still put up with yer moods—"

"I'll give you a mood in a moment if you don't stop."

"Aye. Best I should, lest ye decide to lop my head off with my own sword while I sleep."

"You've got that right," she said as he went out the door.

She came to a rapid-fire conclusion. Men in 1318 were different from their male counterparts in the twenty-first century in dress, vocabulary and battle skills. And she was too different to fit into this alien world. Her life belonged to the future...her life belonged to her and no one else.

Her modern outlooks were turned aside even by those who seemed to have her interest at heart.

Alenna sank down in a chair and pondered. What other tricks did this century have in store for her?

CHAPTER 11

Wind battered the castle and Alenna wondered if the approaching storm would be a heavy deluge. She settled into her chair with a disconsolate sigh and sipped wine from a goblet.

Maybe the heavy atmosphere of the clouds depressed her. No. If she admitted it to herself, it all came back to one source.

One thoroughly, most completely, most maddening man.

Tynan.

Certainly he managed civility and he threw an occasional smile her way. Something, though, was missing in the way he spoke to her. To admit she had a longing for the type of conversation they'd had back in Dougald's room would be to admit she wanted his good regard and another taste of his physical needs. She had no intention of admitting to anyone, least of all herself, that being close to him excited her.

Since his tender, plundering kisses and the way he'd brought her to orgasm, she had forced away the nagging yearning threatening to overrule her sense. Craving more of his attention...desiring it...would lead to disaster.

Certainly she couldn't deny was a handsome man, but he

was stubborn, impossible, chauvinistic and about seven hundred years old.

A pounding on the tower door made Alenna drop the goblet she held and she simply stared at the mess on the table for a moment before asking, "Who is it?"

"Message from the baron."

She didn't recognize the voice, but stepped to the door and opened it anyway. A short man dressed in the lowly garb of a servant stood at the door.

"His lordship requires yer presence in the great hall," he said.

Apprehension hit her, but she could hardly refuse baron's summons. She followed the servant, heading through the great hall and up the stairs that brought her to the vast area of the baron's living quarters. The servant stopped inside the doorway and gestured for her to proceed ahead of him.

"His lordship will await ye here," he said, and left so quickly he might have been a puff of smoke.

Reluctant to sit in one of the hard chairs circling the large, crude wood table in the center of the huge room, Alenna stayed at the door.

A gust of air blew her kirtle to the side and she half expected to see the baron materialize at the door on the opposite side of the chamber. Instead, the breeze ruffled cold through the room and a shiver glided along her skin. Foreboding emanated from the room, as sure as the skin of a snake embraced its owner.

A scent filtered in—the cloying odor teased her nostrils, adding to her unease. The word for it popped into her head without warning.

Evil.

Shivering, she crossed her arms for warmth. A short time ago Alenna would have laughed at the notion of evil, of knowing this room had seen terror, death and destruction. Perhaps the decor might be responsible for how she felt.

Lancet windows, barely larger than arrow slits, gave the

room a gloomy atmosphere. Rushes covered portions of the floor. Her footsteps were muffled by the fibers as she forced herself to walk forward onto the crude mats.

Huge tapestries, all of them in nice condition, hung on three sides of the room. On one wall stood a fireplace and next to it resided a large, ornate table and chair.

Somehow this space managed to feel less a home, less a comfort than the far more modest lodgings she shared with Tynan in the Black Tower.

Alenna stepped farther into the room and noted the doorway opposite led to another spiral staircase. Perhaps these stairs lead to the baron's bedchamber, which he shared with Caithleen.

Time marched on and she wondered if the baron would ever appear. Maybe she could leave now and plead later that she thought he wasn't coming. No. That was risky business. Better play by the rules.

Footsteps sounded on the staircase and she turned to see the baron standing in the doorway. She advanced to the center of the room, her heart beating fast and her pulse racing. The baron looked older today, as if something weighed on his mind. Hardness tinged his mouth, giving him a grim countenance.

He bowed over her hand and said, "Welcome. I am pleased to see you."

Alenna curtsied and murmured, "Thank you, my lord."

"Please," he said. "Sit at the table. Would you take some wine?"

As she settled into one of the hard chairs, she knew that it would be impolite to refuse, so she accepted a goblet. He remained standing, his position of authority marked.

He cleared his throat. "You are wondering, of course, why I asked you here."

"Aye."

The baron's face retained its implacable line. "I have an offer from which I feel you will benefit and which would give me great pleasure."

Alenna felt her insides jumble. She didn't know what to say. Was he going to ask her to be his mistress?

"As you may know, I have extra chambers for those nobles that may visit."

She nodded but said nothing. He couldn't be offering her rooms here. He couldn't be.

"'Tis my wish that you take the chambers above my own on the fourth floor." He waited, staring at her with assurance.

He didn't expect her to refuse.

"I have fine chambers with Tynan."

"Aye. They are better lodgings than most knights who are not of noble birth can boast. You must understand, 'tis with gratitude I offer these lodgings. You did save my best knight's life and this is a small way I can repay you. And you are Tynan's cousin. Such gifts are not given lightly."

"Of course not." Nervous knots tightened her throat. "It is just that your offer is so generous. But unnecessary."

Once again, a cool, tolerant smile crossed his lips. "'Tis not seemly for a young, unmarried woman to live with a man without marriage. That he is your cousin matters not." He reached for the pitcher of ale and poured another portion for himself.

"My lord, I am quite safe with Tynan. He's an honorable man."

"Aye, that he is. But appearances, my dear, are most important. Have you any hopes to marry while you are here?"

"Marry?"

"One of the men about the castle. Perhaps your cousin?"

Startled, Alenna put her goblet down. "I have no plans to marry."

The baron advanced on her with a stride as smooth as a

panther on the hunt. Stopping much too close in front of her, he forced her to look up at him.

"Caithleen thought it might be of great help to you both if you could act as her companion." He hesitated, then leaned slightly forward. "Unless, of course, I ask too much. Perhaps you are offended by the idea of being a companion to one such as Caithleen."

Anger for Caithleen welled in her, but she shoved it down.

"Nay," she said hastily. "Caithleen is kind and a fine woman."

"Then you will accept?"

Leaving her place with Tynan would mean she no longer had his protection. But it would also mean she could come and go as she pleased. Even with no modern conveniences, she'd find the chambers in this tower more comfortable and the food and drink better.

That alone should be enough.

A vision of Caithleen in Tynan's arms forced her decision. Despite her vow not to care, she could discover the nature of the relationship between Caithleen and Tynan if she took the baron's offer. Also, without Tynan so near, she might concentrate on finding a way out of this time trap.

Without another hesitation she said, "I accept."

The baron's smile widened. "'Tis settled then. You shall move in immediately."

"But—"

"I shall send someone with you to gather your things."

"My lord, do we need to be so hasty? I need to tell Tynan."

He cocked one eyebrow. "Of course, but I would have you move your things into the room now. You will dine with us this night and I shall invite Tynan. You may tell him your intentions then."

His words radiated no-nonsense confidence, sending a chill over Alenna. She wondered if she did the right thing.

"Caithleen shall be so pleased and you will be more comfortable. 'Tis a cold day and your new chamber has a large hearth and warm wraps to stave off cold."

Moments later, he sent for a guard to take her back to her room. As her escort followed her to the Black Tower, a hollow feeling grew within her chest. For a moment it felt this walk would end at the executioner's block.

* * *

TYNAN SAW ALENNA coming out of the donjon with a guard in tow and every muscle went on alert. Had the baron summoned her, or had the cuif woman gone to him uninvited? If she'd appeared to the baron without a summons, the baron would see the visit as an invitation.

Bluidy hell. What did he care? She irritated him like a winter illness, lingering and never quite leaving his thoughts. Women of the future were far too forward and independent for his tastes.

After he'd held her in his lap and brought her to pleasure, he'd put distance between them. He wanted to take her so badly that even now the thought hardened his cock, and if that damned Dougald hadn't walked in on them, he would have taken her. Hard. Deep. Until she'd never forget him, and he'd spilled his seed in her womb and marked her as his. He clenched his fists together. Besides the fact she wanted to leave his time, Tynan had other reasons to keep his distance. After she'd challenged him about his confrontation with the three thugs, he knew she cared for him a little. There had been tears in her eyes and she'd responded to his kisses.

But even if she cared about him, he could not do what his body clamored to do every single night. Every pore screamed to make love to her…see the fire in her eyes as he gave her more of the ultimate pleasure.

As Alenna disappeared out of sight around the corner, Tynan hurried to catch up. Not wanting her to know he followed, he immediately slowed down. When she went back to the Black Tower and the guard went inside with her, a fierce surge of protective instinct hit him in the gut. He ran the rest of the way to the tower and slammed inside without hesitation, ready to break the guard into tiny pieces if he'd so much as laid a hand on her.

Tynan thundered into the room. Alenna stood by the pallet, which was laden with a bundle of surcoats and kirtles. The guard stood too close. Far too close.

When he saw Tynan, the man pulled his sword from the sheath. Alenna gasped, her hand going to her mouth as she stumbled away from him.

Tynan's muscles tightened and he clenched his fists at his sides, his feet planted ready. The guard, a mere boy, lunged for him. Alenna let out a startled cry.

Tynan dodged the sudden movement, grabbed the lad's sword arm and wrenched the weapon away. He tossed the weapon in the corner as he gripped the guard by the neck and slammed him against the wall.

The guard gasped as he lost his breath, his eyes wide and fearful. Tynan pressed his forearm against the guard's windpipe. Enough to hold him, but not to kill.

"I should pull yer limbs from yer body, one by one," Tynan growled.

"Tynan, no! Release him at once!" Alenna clutched Tynan's shoulder and yanked. "You're hurting him!"

He didn't release the boy. Instead he glared at her in disbelief, a heavy surge of anger adding to his fighting instinct. Couldn't she see he wanted to protect her?

"Damn it," she hissed and pulled on his arm again. "Let go of him. He's one of the baron's guards."

"I can see that. He was in here with ye. Alone."

She dropped her grip on his shoulder and arm. "The baron sent him as an escort."

Anger made his voice loud. "Ye have my protection and that is enough. I'll no have another man sniffin' around ye like ye was a bitch in heat."

Alenna's face flamed, her eyes filled with fury.

"He's here to help me pack up my things," she said coldly.

Slowly he released his grip on the boy, the initial thrust of anger shrinking away. He snapped his attention back to the limp guard, who stayed against the wall, his gaze darting back and forth as if looking for escape.

"I beg yer forgiveness," the young guard said. "I wouldnae have drawn my sword, but ye scared me, sir."

Alenna glared at Tynan. "You should be glad he was so quick to defend me. If you hadn't come barreling in like a lumbering beast, he wouldn't have drawn his sword."

Tynan took a deep breath. He looked at the guard. "Get outside."

"Nay. If I disobey his lordship—"

Tynan took a step forward and the boy shrank against the wall again. "I could break yer neck like a chicken, lad, and it would be over so fast ye wouldnae ken what hit ye. And all I would have to tell the baron was that I found ye touchin' her. He would no blink an eye to hear that I had killed ye. Go outside and wait 'til I say."

The boy nodded and inched his way to the door. Without attempting to retrieve his sword, he quickly went outside, slamming the door.

Alenna walked up, her mouth a tight line, her ever-changing eyes darting blue and green sparks of animosity. "You big, hairy oaf!"

"What did ye call me?"

"A big, hairy oaf. Why did you come charging in here before you knew what was going on?" Comprehension came over her features. "How did you know the guard was with me anyway?"

"I saw ye come out of the baron's tower."

"Fabulous. So now you're stalking me."

"Stalkin'?"

"Never mind. You practically scared the poor kid to death. He was only doing what he was told. Why are you so overprotective? Are you trying to control me? Are you one of those men who gets off on power?"

Alenna stood practically nose-to-nose with him, her hands on her hips. He took a deep breath to slow his galloping heart. Fury plunged through him at the way she disregarded her own safety. He had half a mind to let her venture where she would and the consequences be damned.

"What are you staring at?" she asked.

"In battle, ye no give a man a chance to explain himself. When he pulled his sword I thought he intended to harm ye. If I hadnae reacted, he could have run ye through before ye could say clishmaclaver."

For a moment Tynan thought he'd reached Alenna, but her expression hardened almost instantly. "You know I can take care of myself. I've already saved your life twice. In my world you—"

"I am not of yer world, Alenna. And I never will be."

Her face flushed a light pink. "No. No, you're not."

Tynan had a tremendous urge to yank her into his arms and hold her. Hold her tight and tell her it didn't matter where she came from, or that she had dropped into his world from the future. Pride held him back. Pride and the realization that she spoke the truth. She had saved his life twice.

Her earlier words penetrated his brain and an apprehension filled him. "Why are ye gatherin' yer clothes?"

"The baron has asked me to live in the tower as Caithleen's companion. As a gesture for saving your life."

He shook his head firmly. "Nay. Nay, I'll not allow it. I'll never let ye live with the baron."

Alenna should have been angry with Tynan. She thought about this a second more, but something else bugged her and kept her from being completely incensed.

Tynan's protective actions when he thought the guard intended to hurt her stirred an equally primal response within her.

That he'd kill for her…that he'd kill to defend her startled and amazed her. Yes, he had shielded her before. But she'd never seen such fierceness in his face, such overwhelming male determination.

Like a wolf defending his mate.

Damn it, but it stirred a part of her she didn't understand. Sexual urges so inappropriate they stung her with the force.

Alenna's mouth opened and closed and then she put her hands on her hips. "I'm to be Caithleen's companion. What harm can there be in that?"

Tynan stood stiffly, his arms crossed, his feet planted apart in an arrogant stance. "Because I said yer no goin'."

That did it.

She gathered together her bundle. "Excuse me, but we've talked about this before. I'm not a child and you are not my father. But I can see your social training is too ingrained in you to change. You're right, Tynan. You're not from my world and I'm not from yours. So we'd better part ways."

He shifted, dropping his arms to his sides. "Ye said ye would obey me. Ye lied to me."

Tears surged into her eyes. "So I'm a liar and you shouldn't want anything to do with me. Now if you'll excuse me—"

"Ye cannae do this."

"Tynan, why are you so sure there are ghosts around every corner? You seem to think every man is out there to hurt me."

He shook his head. "Not every man."

"Then why are you so opposed to me moving out?"

"Ye just cannae do it."

"That's not an explanation."

When he said nothing she relented. "You don't mind me being in Dougald's company."

"Nay. He wouldnae harm ye. The baron may be different."

"Are you saying the baron has hurt Caithleen?"

Tynan took a deep breath and walked to the hearth. He leaned a hand against the stone mantle.

"He has interestin' needs."

Nausea crawled in her stomach. "You mean he does things that Caithleen does not like?"

Tynan nodded. "Aye. That is the way of it."

Caithleen had felt comfortable enough to tell Tynan about the baron's sexual appetites? "Caithleen must trust you very much to tell you something so personal."

"She cannae tell Clandon. He would try and avenge her if he knew."

"But he's a boy."

"Aye. But a strong boy, at that. Willful, he is."

"He'd be killed."

Tynan turned toward her and even with the table between them, she felt his power and his resoluteness as a palatable force. "I'm tellin' ye this so ye'll not go."

"You fear the baron will attempt these…to do these things to me as well?"

"Aye. I wouldnae have ye sullied by his needs. A man's needs are sometimes cruel."

Bemused by the hoarseness in his voice, she watched as sadness passed over his face. So many of his emotions sat on the surface, yet she sensed that deep within him dwelled a thousand other feelings. At that moment, a yearning to know every one of those feelings made her speak.

"Have you lost a woman to another man's cruelty, Tynan?" Alenna asked softly.

He jerked his gaze to her and she saw his pain disappear under a mantle of coolness. "I have lost no one."

Disappointment made her regret her words. "If what you say about Caithleen is true than she needs me as a companion. I can help her deal with whatever is happening. Maybe I can even stop the baron from harming her more than he has already."

Tynan came around the table so fast, she almost fell backward onto the pallet. He grabbed her shoulders.

"Why do ye have to help her?"

"Because she's asked for me. The baron won't expect me to help her. If he's anything like the rest of the men around here, he won't believe I'm capable of doing anything."

"Huh," he said, squeezing her shoulders. She knew she'd hit a sore spot, but she didn't care. "He's no a stupid man, Alenna. If he thought ye might be able to help her, do ye think he'd let ye live in the donjon?"

He had a point, but she couldn't abandon Caithleen. "I *must* help her."

His hands tightened on Alenna's shoulders again. "Ye are determined to be killed, are ye?"

"No. I don't want to die. I want to go back to my time and live my life. I want another chance to start fresh. Instead I'm stuck in this barbaric, cruel, confusing world."

"Ye cannae change this world," he said, his jaw jutting slightly in irritation. "Dinna try."

"How do you know? In my world I can make a little difference here and there. Maybe not much, but some. Revolutions have been fought because somebody finally believed in change."

Alenna regarded him. He was a symbol of this world's realities. The scars on his forehead, hands and chest stood as badges of proof. Tokens of the battles he'd fought for his beliefs. He might be an honorable man, but he was still a primal male animal of his time. Expecting him to understand or change on a dime pushed reality's limits.

"What if I am trapped in this world forever?" she asked, the idea a deep ache in her chest and throat. "Do you think I'd settle for playing someone's wife and staying at home and cooking and cleaning and having babies? In my world I don't have to do that unless I choose. And I don't want to do that here.

"For the last few months of my life I've been running from my problems. I've looked at the world through a fog of hurt. When I came to Scotland I was worried about getting my life under control." She made a sound of disgust. "Well, my life here is insane enough, without letting everything that happens lead me around by the nose. At least while I'm here I'll help Caithleen. Like you, I fight for my beliefs."

Tynan's features transformed with the gradual movement of a man contemplating. Maybe she could reach his intelligence and common sense. Perhaps he could understand how helping Caithleen gave her a purpose. A reason to keep on going in this strange place.

"Ye have no told me much of yer life in the future. About the man ye almost wed. About these...these things ye call a panic attack. The place called the United States."

"You haven't asked. You're usually scolding me for venturing out alone or ordering me around. I assumed you didn't care."

He said nothing, staring blankly at the wall for several seconds. He reached for his dagger in a leather scabbard. After he handed it to her, he said, "Then take this with ye and keep it close."

The tightness in Alenna's throat welled, threatening to choke her. "Thank you, Tynan."

"Is there nothin' I can say or do to keep ye here?"

She thought about it—her mind raced from wild idea to wild idea. *Kiss me again. Tell me you want me to stay because you care for me. Not because of some need to protect a woman. Any woman. But because you feel something for me.*

These thoughts swam inside her like a rolling current, rushing in and rushing out, leaving her aching with staggering desires she couldn't and wouldn't express. Any sign to him that she wanted his approval or needed his attention would be an advantage to him. She couldn't afford to care more than she already did.

"There's nothing you can do to stop me, Tynan. Besides, even if I wanted to stay, would you have me defy the baron?"

She saw him shift gears, his mind working frantically for another lead...anything to alter the course.

"I could talk to him in your stead. Explain ye were so overtaken by his offer, ye dinnae think." He paused. "I could tell him we're to be married."

Alenna thought her heart would stop. She inhaled a ragged breath. "What?"

"Marriage. If we were married—"

"No." She waved a dismissing hand. "He'd never believe a fake marriage."

"We'd no fake it."

She couldn't believe her own ears. She gave him a tattered laugh. "You really are a knight in shining armor."

"Eh? My armor doesnae shine."

Despite the gravity clutching at her emotions, she managed a small smile. "Never mind. I can't do it, Tynan. I can't marry you to avoid the baron. I could never live with myself if I abandoned Caithleen."

"I wouldnae have ye forsake her. We'd find a way together."

"It wouldn't be fair, to me or to you. Someday...someday you'll find a woman you really do want to marry and—"

"Nay!" he said harshly. "I willnae."

"There isn't anything you could do to make me marry you," she said abruptly.

He flinched as if she'd hit him. For a moment she regretted her strong words. Then he stepped back and gestured to the door.

"Then be gone with ye. I'll have no more time to waste with ye."

The coldness of his tone struck at her heart like an icy needle. Surprised that his words hurt, but determined to push passed the pain, she took her bundle and headed for the door without a backward glance. When Alenna closed the door it sounded like a gate had sealed forever in her heart.

CHAPTER 12

"*M*istress, is somethin' wrong? Ye seem unhappy," Caithleen said, as she helped Alenna put her clothing away in a heavy wood trunk.

Alenna smiled at the young woman and gazed around the chamber. A fire roared in the large hearth. "Nothing is wrong. This is a beautiful room."

She'd never seen a more comfortable and pretty room in the fourteenth century. Four times the magnitude of Tynan's chambers, the high ceiling gave the illusion of an even larger space. Narrow windows limited the view and the light.

She walked over to the large table in the center of the room and traced her hand over the somewhat uneven surface of the wood. A large pitcher with four pewter goblets and two heavy candlesticks lay in the middle of the table. She strolled to the bed and sat on the edge. Several plaids graced the large frame bed and a tapestry hung at the head of the bed and afforded some protection against drafts.

Caithleen sat down beside her. "Are ye sure ye will be comfortable here?"

"What's not to like?"

Caithleen's pretty eyes sparkled with good humor. With small, delicate hands, almost childlike in their structure, she smoothed her blue kirtle and surcoat. Though tall, Caithleen somehow managed to appear frail and this brought out a protective instinct in Alenna. More than once she had to remind herself that in this century, Caithleen was considered a grown woman.

While she made sure to add accent to her words when she talked with Caithleen, she realized her speech had already been inconsistent. She couldn't keep up with the deception on the accent. She'd spoken one way with Clandon, Tynan, Elizabet and Johanna. They'd all heard her American accent. When she'd given a Scottish accent her best shot speaking with the baron, she realized her mistake. Now she'd have to switch back and forth and never be caught in the same room with the baron and another person who'd heard her use a different accent. She'd been very stupid.

"I am so happy ye have decided to be my companion." Caithleen's smile faded even as she said the words. "I dinnae think the baron would let ye come. And I dinnae think Tynan would let ye go."

"He didn't want me to come here. I told him to buzz off."

Caithleen's face screwed up. "Buzz off?"

"Sorry. It's a way of saying he should leave me alone."

"Tynan is a guid man. Why do ye hate him?"

"I don't hate him. But I knew you needed help and he was trying to prevent me coming to live here."

An impish gleam popped into Caithleen's eyes. "A man like him...well, a woman could do far worse. Yet ye dinnae set yer cap for him."

"No," Alenna said swiftly. "I...I'm not in love with him." The speculative glance Caithleen sent her way said she doubted Alenna's assertion. "Are you in love with the baron?"

Caithleen started as if she'd been jabbed with a cattle prod.

Standing swiftly, she walked to the table and clasped the back of one chair with both hands.

"Nay," she said breathlessly. "I could never be in love with him. Never. There is someone else in my heart."

Alenna had to know. "Tynan?"

Caithleen turned, her lips softened with a gentle smile. "Tynan is a braw man. But another has stolen my heart. I dinnae ken if the man knows what I feel."

"Caithleen, you can trust me. You can tell me anything at any time. And not just about who you love."

Hesitating like a baby venturing to crawl for the first time, Caithleen said, "Tynan told me ye are a guid woman."

Alenna sucked in a surprised breath. "He said that?"

"Aye. He much admires ye. Dinnae ye feel it? Why, I can see it in his eyes when he talks of ye."

A sweet, tingling pleasure centered in Alenna's body, blossoming outward until she had to admit to herself the revelation pleased her. "I...he hasn't told me. Most of the time he thinks I'm too bold."

Caithleen giggled. "Aye, he does think ye are bold. But it seems he's a man that admires that."

Alenna's throat tightened with emotion. Not seeing Tynan often anymore would be good for her. Yet she already missed him. "You're clever. We've managed to get the subject off your secret love."

Caithleen smiled. "I did try." Clasping her hands in front of her, she said, "I am in love with Dougald of Douglas."

"Oh," Alenna said, the syllable popping out in surprise.

A frown creased Caithleen's forehead. "We've known each other for ever so long and when I see him, I get these strange feelin's. I can hardly tell ye about them." She knelt down on the floor in front of Alenna and sat back on her heels. "I've never felt this burnin' in my breast. This hungry need for any man. Have ye ever felt that way?"

Immediately an image of Tynan came to Alenna's mind. Ruthlessly she shoved it away and remembered her ex-fiancé.

"I...I thought I did once. My betrothed, long ago. But it wasn't right. He didn't love me."

Caithleen's eyes saddened, the ache of despair etching lines in the smooth skin of her face. Alenna's heart ached for Caithleen's ruined innocence and for the suffering she'd endured at the baron's hands.

"Do you and Dougald see each other often?" Alenna asked.

"Nay. But when he does see me, he smiles and is very gallant." She looked down at her hands. "He has never addressed me with affection."

"There is hope," Alenna said, already concocting an idea to get them together. Caithleen needed another ally in her corner. A male protector might assist her when the time came to escape the baron.

"Aye, there is always hope." Caithleen's smile returned, rejuvenating the natural glow that seemed a part of her nature.

Alenna wondered how to ease her into a conversation about the baron's behavior, and knew no easy way around the subject. She had to jump in headfirst.

"Caithleen, Tynan told me of your...problems with the baron."

The young woman started, her hand fluttering to her mouth. "He told ye?"

Leaning forward to clasp her arm, Alenna said, "I'm sure Tynan didn't mean to break a confidence. He said he told me because he worried that it would happen to me, as well. That is part of the reason I agreed to the baron's suggestion I stay here. I couldn't refuse his order and I knew I could help you."

"Nay. He...I cannae tell ye. If the baron ever found out—"

"He won't. You must tell me, if I'm to help you."

"There is nothin' ye can do."

Nothing you can do.

Her words rang together with Tynan's. Like a litany Alenna thought of the time right after her breakup with her ex-fiancé. She'd felt helpless and out of control. Lack of control had helped her lose her job and lack of control had sent her into Tynan's arms. No matter what, Caithleen couldn't be allowed to sink deeper into an abyss. There must be a way to release her.

"We can do something, if you'll let me help you," Alenna said.

Caithleen wrinkled her nose, apparently incredulous. "I dinnae ken. Of course I must do what he wants. He's my...he is my keeper. I am his mistress."

"I know you're afraid, but if you continue to live this way you'll die. Your heart, your soul, your physical body will be destroyed."

Caithleen shook her head. "I need the coin for Clandon. 'Tis not me I do this for. Nay, I wouldnae have fallen to this sin if we had enough to eat. But 'tis my coin that keeps Clandon alive. I fear someday the baron will realize I give Clandon money."

Tears spilled like a waterfall over Caithleen's lashes. She covered her face with her hands and a small sob broke from her lips.

Mortification and empathy gripped Alenna. She sank to her knees in front of Caithleen and the cold stone floor penetrated her clothing, freezing through to the bone. An icy, horrible portent clutched at Alenna's soul. She must assist Caithleen before time ran out. Gently she clasped Alenna's shoulders.

"I'm so sorry. I didn't mean to hurt you, or bring back bad memories."

Sucking in a shuddering breath, Caithleen dropped her hands from her face. Swimming with moisture and sadness, her eyes glazed with despair.

"Caithleen, please tell me so I might help you."

"How can ye help me? No one can."

"How do you know unless you tell me what the baron has done?"

"I am ashamed."

"You mustn't be. Whatever horrid things he does, it is his fault alone and not yours."

Caithleen's bottom lip trembled. As she clasped her hands tightly in her lap, the tears fell one by one onto the backs of her hands. "He...he likes to do things to my body. I had always imagined a man's touch...the things a man likes to do with a woman would be beautiful. He...the baron was my first. He took my virtue." She looked up at Alenna. "It hurt. It was horrible."

Alenna bit her lip. "Did he strike you?"

"Not the first time. But he has hit me many times since. When he thinks I am bletherin'. Or...for no reason other than he wants to hit me."

"Bastard." Alenna dropped her hold on Caithleen's shoulders. "I wish I could strangle him."

"Shhh." Caithleen looked around the rooms as if she expected the baron's guards to crash into the room. "We must be careful what we say. If he sees that ye know...if he thinks anyone knows, he'll kill me."

Rage roared in Alenna's blood and she could feel the heat rising in her like a furnace. "Don't worry. He won't find out. At least not until it is too late."

"What do ye mean?"

"We must make a plan for you to escape, so you don't have to be his mistress anymore."

Caithleen clasped Alenna's hands in hers. "Oh, Alenna, would that were true. I would try anythin'." She looked down at their hands. "Yer hands are cold. We can stoke up the fire and talk."

As they placed another log on the fire, Alenna suggested they pull two chairs over closer to the hearth.

She thought of the times she'd sat by the fire in the Black Tower, and she wondered what Tynan did at that moment. Did he ever think about her? His last words as he'd gestured for her to leave his chambers echoed in her mind, like a ghost haunting a house. Sadness filled her if she thought of the cold way he'd dismissed her. She brushed aside thoughts of him with difficulty and set about explaining her plan to extract Caithleen out of her predicament.

* * *

ALENNA HEARD the sound as she first drifted to sleep that night. On the edges of her consciousness the creaking noise invaded, a lingering image on the rim of a dream. At first she thought the wind battered the walls of the castle and sent rain down with lashes of fury. Another night sound to ignore.

Shuffling. The sound of stealthy feet moving over the floor.

Coming fully alert, she stiffened.

She turned onto her back. Opening her eyes, she looked about. The heavy mantle of night choked everything in a devil's darkness. Looking toward the door, she thought she saw a crack of light. As if someone opened the door, passed through and barely pushed the door to.

She knew it as surely as she knew her own name. Someone was in the room.

"Caithleen?" she whispered softly. "Is that you?"

Silence.

A vision of a mouse or other vermin rushing over the floor made her stomach lurch.

Another shifting sound, barely on the edge of her hearing, kept her immobile in the bed. For what seemed forever she lay without a sound, half-afraid to breathe.

Straining to hear any noise, she waited. Waited.

Swiftly her heart pounded, the tempo increasing in every pulse point in her body. As sweat dampened her palms, her limbs became cold. Rigid with fright, she couldn't even call out.

A stab of terror hit her center, striking like a cobra. Without warning the panic grew to a perilous height she hadn't experienced in months. Like a child she feared the night once again, trembling with uncontrollable desperation.

God, help me.

Help me.

I am going to die.

Alenna panted for every breath and as the strangling sensation overwhelmed her, she cried out. The small shriek set her free and she reached frantically for a candle at her bedside. A clatter sounded as she knocked the candlestick off the small table and it rolled to the floor.

Any second, she expected to feel the cold hand of death about her neck.

Suddenly, the sound of footsteps retreated as the intruder moved away from her. The door to her chamber swung wide and she saw a tall silhouette run through the door. She leapt from the bed and hustled to the door, slamming it with a force that surely would wake the dead. Securing the lock again, she leaned against the door for a full minute. Her heart hammered, her legs trembled, threatening to tumble her to the cold floor. When she could move, she shoved a chair under the door handle, realizing it wouldn't stop someone who wanted to get in badly enough.

At least it afforded a small measure of comfort.

As Alenna sank onto her bed, she let the tremors of receding fear prickle her skin and shake her body.

Who had been in her room?

* * *

As Tynan strode through the castle bailey, his thoughts turned to the one person he couldn't forget. Battle plans against the Ruthvens, possible border war skirmishes, even piecing together new chain mail before he left the castle later today couldn't remove Alenna from his mind. Only a few days had passed since Alenna had moved into the donjon, but it felt like months to him.

No occupation, no sword play, no food or drink abolished the wicked grip Alenna had on his thoughts.

He'd seen her in the company of Caithleen and one of the baron's guards. He'd seen her at his weekly visit to the baron's evening meal. Perhaps four times he'd spotted her from a distance and she'd spoken to him briefly, her words cool and polite. And she wouldn't look into his eyes, damn her.

Each time she wore a different dress. It seemed the baron kept her in fine clothing. Tynan shouldn't have cared. He was done with her. Didn't give a clishmaclaver if the silly woman stayed in the donjon forever.

But damn it, he did give a damn.

Every morning he woke to an empty room. How he missed her smooth laughter and quick wit. Nothing was the same. Visions of her shiny hair, bonnie features and her tempting mouth made his insides clench with need.

Her mouth. If he closed his eyes, he could almost remember the carnal pleasure as he'd feasted on her lips, and the softness of her breast in his hand, the lushness of her nipple in his mouth. And, oh, fuck, the sensation of thrusting his fingers into her wet heat.

"Bluidy well watch where ye be goin'," one of the merchants said as Tynan bumped into his cart of goods.

Tynan swung about and landed a glare on the small man. The man realized whom he'd chastised and his face turned white.

"Oh, beggin' yer forgiveness. I dinnae know it was ye, sir," the merchant said hoarsely.

Tynan took in the man's expression and noted he'd frightened the man with a mere look. Sometimes he forgot his reputation as a hardened combatant garnered more than respect.

"Nay. 'Tis I that must beg forgiveness, for I have acted the knave. Have I damaged yer cart?"

The man's color returned as he gave Tynan a tentative smile. "Aye. I mean, nay. No harm done."

Tynan smiled and tossed the man a coin. "For any damage ye might find later."

Surprise popped into the man's eyes. "But...I cannae take this...ye havenae bought anythin'. 'Twould be wrong."

"What is yer name?"

"Willem."

"Willem, then I will look at yer wares. Mayhap there's a trinket that would make a lady feel special."

Any token he gave Alenna would be paltry in comparison to what the baron could provide. The idea didn't stop him as he looked at the merchant's supplies. Cloaks of fine wool lined with fur lay arranged on the merchant's cart. Tynan recalled that Alenna's threadbare cloak wouldn't last much longer. As the days grew shorter and the nights longer, the cold would advance as well.

He lifted a heavy cloak in a dark shade of blue. It was about the right size for a woman Alenna's build and height.

"I'll take this one," he said.

"Aye, sir. Will keep yer lady warm, this one."

As Tynan took the cloak and draped it over his arm, he wished down deep in his gut that *he* could keep Alenna warm. In more ways than one. Sliding inside her so deeply until she screamed and heat flushed her body. He wanted her to himself, until her cries of pleasure echoed loudly into the night.

Moments later, he caught sight of Johanna walking with Elizabet and he hurried forward to greet them.

"Guid day, ladies. 'Tis a fine day for a stroll."

Both of them smiled, Johanna's grin particularly bright and happy. She curtsied as he bowed.

"'Tis a bright day. What brings ye this way?" Johanna asked.

"Business for his lordship. I was on my way to see him."

"What a beautiful cloak." Elizabet glanced at the garment in his hands and reached out to touch the fabric.

"'Tis for Alenna."

He saw Johanna's frown as he mentioned Alenna's name and wondered why the chit was so jealous of Alenna.

"Why, we were goin' to see Alenna. Would ye like us to take this to her?" Elizabet asked.

Torn between wanting to see Alenna and not wishing for the baron to know he brought the cloak to her, he hesitated. Anger came on him, irritating like scratchy wool. He had no business seeing Alenna. She wanted nothing to do with him.

"Aye," he said finally. "I have business with the baron that cannae wait."

He handed Elizabet the cloak and they made their way onward to the tower. He half wished he'd never run into them. Seeing Alenna would have been a sweet agony indeed.

* * *

ALENNA TOUCHED the cloak lying on the table in front of her. "It's beautiful."

"The wool is fancy and the fur new and clean," Caithleen said, brushing her hands over the soft fur with reverence. "'Tis better than any I have."

"'Tis better than all of us have," Johanna said, settling into a chair around the table. Her lips pursed with displeasure.

Alenna ignored her. "Elizabet, I can't take this from you. It must have cost a fortune. Where on earth did you find it?"

A gentle smile crossed Elizabet's small mouth. "I dinnae find it. Tynan bought it for ye."

Alenna felt her knees turn mushy under her. She sank into a chair and stared at the three women in front of her. "What?"

Caithleen's light laugh drifted through the room like a sweet melody. "I've told her time and again he's partial to her, Elizabet. This proves it."

"'Tis a sign of a much deeper sickness, I'm thinkin'," Elizabet said.

"Sickness?" Alenna asked. "What are you talking about?"

"The man is heart-sick. A man dinnae buy this for just any woman."

"This proves nothing," Alenna said, pushing out of her chair and crossing to one of the tiny windows. A draft came in, affording her a little fresh air to clear the cobwebs in her mind. "I won't take it."

Elizabet sighed. "Would ye have us insult him, then?"

Alenna turned toward her. "Insult him? Of course not—"

"'Tis like a slur. Ye should accept it, Alenna. If ye dinnae feel anything for him ye could give it back. But I don't believe ye want to do that," Elizabet said.

Embarrassment reddened Alenna's face. "You're saying because he bought something expensive for me, he's in love with me?"

"Aye," Johanna said, her voice like a discordant and indignant sound in the choir. "Dinnae be a taupie."

"Johanna!" Elizabet snapped around to look at her daughter. "That was rude. Apologize."

Alenna looked at the young girl, and Johanna's eyes were flat with anger. "I am sorry, Mistress Carstairs. 'Twas rude of me."

Alenna wanted to smack the impudent teenager. "Apology accepted."

"Why else would he buy this for ye?" Elizabet strolled up and placed her hand on Alenna's shoulder. "Ye needed a new cloak. The one ye have is not fit for the dead."

Alenna turned to her friend. "I can't take his present." She gestured to the room around her. "I have all this and you and Johanna have so little. You need it far worse than I."

"They cannae take it," Caithleen said, advancing toward her a few steps. "Tynan would be angry."

Alenna threw up her hands in exasperation. "Why does everyone care about what Tynan thinks? You would think the man was God."

"Aye, he is to some," Elizabet said. "The people here revere him. They have great respect for a man so strong and a respect for a man who treats them well. There never is a cross word to be heard about him, from anyone I know."

"Yes. He's a regular gingerbread boy," Alenna said wryly.

"Eh?" The chorus of three feminine voices came at once.

Alenna sighed. That he'd given her anything at all surprised her beyond measure. Did he think he could entice her back to his lodgings with presents? Well, if that's what the damn rogue thought, he could suck eggs.

"I'm not going to take it. I don't care if Tynan comes in here and puts it on me himself."

"Aye, that sounds like a mighty challenge," said a deep, husky voice from the doorway.

CHAPTER 13

"**B**y God! Zounds!" Caithleen twirled at the sound, almost knocking over a chair.

Alenna knew the whiskey and velvet, sexy voice at once. Every fiber within her came alive at the sight of Tynan. Tingles like static electricity ignited within her belly.

The bump on his forehead had disappeared and the gleam in his eyes was voracious as ever. Danger lurked in those dark depths. Danger that she understood but didn't want to acknowledge. Once she admitted he mattered to her, she'd never be out of his hold.

Anticipation rushed through her, as if her body couldn't help responding to him on a deep level. "Tynan, what are you doing here?"

His gave her a sarcastic smile. "Aye, and 'tis pleasant to see ye too."

"Welcome, Tynan," Caithleen said. "Would ye take some wine?"

"Nay, I cannae stay for long. But I would have time alone with Alenna."

Alenna opened her mouth to protest. "But—"

"Johanna, Caithleen, let us take the air. A brisk walk, I'm thinkin', to keep our minds fresh." Elizabet clasped each of their arms and gave Alenna a conspiratorial smile.

The women exited without a backward glance. Even the usually obstinate Johanna didn't protest.

Tynan proceeded to walk toward her. The urge to escape came strong, but Alenna held her ground. She wasn't afraid of him. No, what she felt didn't match anything she'd experienced with anyone before. As he advanced, the tingling in her lower stomach increased. The sensation spread into a heavy warmth in her chest. Until this moment, she had been sure she could put him out of her mind. Instead he appeared and all bets were off.

Despite Alenna's frazzled state, she noticed his shirt had come untied in the front and his hair was tangled about his head in disarray. His black attire gave him a menacing air.

"Why do you do that?" she asked impulsively.

"What?"

"Dress all in black."

He tossed his head like a stallion might in defiance of the bit. "Suits me." He continued toward her. "I came to see how ye like yer chambers." He glanced around the room, his expression unreadable. When he came to a stop in front of her and she'd said nothing, he touched the cloak on the table. "Do ye like the cloak?"

"Yes. But I can't take it, Tynan."

His gaze darkened like a thundercloud ready to burst. "Why?"

"Because it's too expensive. You can't afford it."

"Humph." The sound was caustic. "I say what I can afford. I dinnae buy it to have ye toss it back in my face."

"I'm trying to be pleasant about this."

He moved until less than a foot separated them. His smile laced with cocky assurance set her hackles on end.

She retrieved the cloak and handed it to him. "I thought you had business with the baron."

"Aye. I did. Then I came here." Tynan opened the cloak wide, then swirled the folds across her shoulders in one quick movement, mantling her in the garment's warmth. Keeping her gaze trapped within his, he tugged the cloak closed and held it together with his hands. He pulled her nearer until she almost leaned against him.

Why was he doing this? Did he realize that this close to him her pulse raced? Is that why he hovered over her, coming so close to touching her?

"Tynan, I can't take this." Too late she realized her statement might be taken another way.

"What are ye afraid of?"

"I'm afraid the baron won't like you giving me gifts."

"Pah. He thinks I'm yer cousin. I can give ye anythin' I wish as family, and he will have no say about it."

She supposed he was right. Still…

"You said you wanted nothing more to do with me."

Tynan released his grip on the cloak, but he didn't ease back from her. She slipped the cloak from her shoulders and placed it on the table nearby.

She saw regret enter his eyes. "I did say that. 'Twas foolish of me, Alenna. 'Twould be seen as strange if I dinnae wish to be with ye. As yer family, of course. The baron would wonder what had happened."

"Why is it important he think we're close family?"

"I dinnae want him to think our ties are broken and that ye are under his power. Ye are still under my protection. If he tried to harm ye, I would come to yer aid."

That Tynan wanted to keep tabs on her after everything she'd said to him surprised Alenna. With his pride and sense of honor, something about Tynan's behavior didn't make sense to her.

"How can you be his knight knowing what you do about him? He's a horrid man."

He gave her a sardonic grin. "I fight for the most pay. No one will offer me as much coin as the baron. And I have my other reasons."

She rubbed her forehead. No matter which way she looked at things, Tynan could be in danger because she'd chosen to help Caithleen. "If you tried to come to my aid couldn't he just have you killed?"

He nodded. "He could at that. But I'm his best knight. Without me leadin' the men-at-arms he's in fair trouble in a siege. Dougald could take my place, but it wouldnae be the same."

His words sounded firm and certain, but without a hint of arrogance. Tynan knew his strengths. His assurances gave her a little comfort. The longer Alenna remained in this world, the more paranoid she became. Dangers lurked around every corner. She recalled the strange night someone had crept into her room and a slight shudder went through her.

She couldn't tell him she kept a chair against her door at night to alert her if anyone entered. If she did tell him he'd insist she leave the baron's household.

"Tynan, you have to keep away from me," she said suddenly.

His eyebrows shot up. "Am I that repulsive to ye, lass?"

"No, no. You could never be repulsive—" She stopped, confusion building in her heart. "It's just that you're in danger coming here. If the baron thought you were a threat, he might hurt or kill you. I can't have that on my mind if I'm to help Caithleen."

His expression turned hard. "I see. Ye worry ye might feel the least bit guilty if somethin' happened to me?"

"Of course I'd feel guilty. But it's not that so much as…"

Alenna gritted her teeth and resisted the urge to bonk him

over the head. Why did this man twist her in knots so easily? She spun out of control whenever he came near her.

"Aye? Ye were sayin'?" When she didn't offer to complete her sentence, Tynan crossed his arms and glared down at her. "Ye care more about what happens to Caithleen then ye do me. And that's fine. She's defenseless, where I am not."

"She's not defenseless. She's a strong girl but she doesn't realize it."

Nodding his head in an all-knowing manner, he said, "And yer goin' to make her realize it?"

"Yes. She's already feeling more confident. She's told me several times how much safer she feels with me here. Caithleen says the baron hasn't even touched her since I moved in. Maybe he'll leave her alone from now on."

The barest of nods moved his head. "Mayhap he tires of her already."

"If he does, that's great. When he throws her out, she can go back with her brother."

"It may not be so easy."

"What do you mean?"

Within the large room, Tynan's silence seemed deep and fraught with meaning.

"If he tires of her, then he must be lookin' for another to replace her," he said finally. "He is testin' the waters. He's tryin' to see what ye are really like. By keepin' ye close, he can observe ye."

His meaning came clear. "You still think he'll want me for his mistress."

"I dinnae think. I know."

Then she had to act quickly and decisively. "If that's what he's planned, I must get Caithleen out of the baron's grasp. I must get her away from here."

A tiny muscle in his jaw twitched. "If she runs away, she might survive. No other plan would work."

Putting her hands on her hips, she said, "With an attitude like that, you would never have survived all these years in battle."

"I am a warrior. Caithleen is not."

"Caithleen and I talked about it. But we need your help and Dougald's. Especially Dougald's."

Tynan regarded her for a full minute, until his stare unnerved her. Finally, he uncrossed his arms and reached for a chair. He turned it around and straddled the seat, then he put his arms on the back of the chair. "Tell me what ye plan to do."

Under his scrutiny Alenna felt like a lowly soldier presenting a battle plan to a skeptical general. She considered getting Caithleen out of the baron's clutches without Tynan's help. But he stared at her, daring her to clam up. Knowing him, he'd badger her until she told him. He wouldn't like the plan, she knew as sure as she knew her mother's first name.

"Caithleen tells me the baron wants to have a party in the great hall two nights from now," she said.

"Aye."

Alenna's discomfort increased as she thought about the activities the baron had planned for the party. "She also told me about the strange game he has in mind to play during the party."

"The baron told me. I'm no likin' it."

She kept her expression closed. "I would think you'd enjoy a chance to play games with the ladies."

He leaned his chin on his forearm and scowled at her. "Aye, and why would ye think that?"

Searching for a word to describe the risqué spectacle the baron had planned, she sat on the edge of a chair. "It sounds like an excuse for men to…to pick bed partners for the night. I would think most everyone would be opposed to it. Except for men who are on the prowl."

When her gaze flicked to his, his eyes crinkled at the corners with amusement. "On the prowl. Well, when ye put it like that, it could be a fine time, lass. There's to be many a bonnie woman there, I will be bound."

Though his tone came out teasing, annoyance roiled in Alenna's mind. Well, he could take any woman he wanted. As long as the plan worked, it wouldn't matter. Caithleen would be on her way to freedom.

"Caithleen said that if a man claims a woman on that night, she is to be his for a fortnight."

"Aye." His voice went husky…a hungry sound that made her even more aware of him as a man. "And every night she must submit to his passion."

Oh God. Images of submitting to Tynan's passion, to experiencing his long, hard cock sliding into her—

Clearing her throat she said, "We must arrange for Dougald to choose Caithleen."

Tynan laughed. The booming sound bounced around the room.

"What's so funny?"

"It willnae work, Alenna."

"Why not?"

"Yer thinkin' that if Dougald claims her, the baron won't want her any more?"

"Well, yes. It's likely, isn't it?"

"The baron is no worried about sharin' a woman with another man. He would have to care for a woman to be jealous and he doesnae have enough of a heart for that. But he would demand her back at the end of a fortnight. She's his property."

As Tynan said, a cold bastard like the baron didn't care enough about any woman, he'd proven that. He hadn't been concerned enough about Florie and his child to keep them with him, nor to catch Florie's murderer.

Shifting her thoughts back to the present, she said, "That doesn't entirely ruin our plan. If Dougald pretends to take Caithleen as his own during the game, then they can get to know each other and she'll be safe from the baron's advances for a fortnight."

Tynan stood, smiling as he walked to a window and put his hands against the stone on either side of the tiny aperture. He peered out. "Ye ken Dougald could no last a fortnight without takin' Caithleen?"

Alenna nodded. "Well, I'd thought of that..." She gasped. "You don't mean he'd rape—"

He turned swiftly. "Nay! Dougald is a man of honor. But he has a way with wenches that turn them into a puddle of porridge. They dinnae have any resistance to him. She'll no defy him."

Alenna smiled. "That's ridiculous. He certainly hasn't tried anything with me and even if he did, I certainly wouldn't turn to porridge over him."

His brows went up. "Aye. But 'tis more that he is my friend, and as he thinks yer my cousin he has respect for ye. That is the only reason he dinnae try anythin'."

"Maybe. Elizabet let him escort Johanna home one night. If he's so charming you'd think Johanna would have..."

She didn't want to think of the young girl succumbing to a man's desires. Or that Dougald would stoop to seduction of one so young.

"He respects Elizabet as well, so he wouldnae try anythin' with Johanna. No matter that Johanna is a silly wench and comely. She flirts with every man she sees. Elizabet knows Dougald can keep Johanna safe. But with Caithleen, everythin' is different. I've seen the way he looks at her. The man is fair tempted."

"How does he look at her?"

Tynan grunted. "A bit like he's been hit over the head. Dazed. Out of his bluidy mind, more like."

Alenna sprang from her chair and went to stand by him. "That's what I'm talking about. Caithleen cares for Dougald and from what you've said just now, Dougald has at least a little special feeling for her. If Dougald got to know her, he might—"

"Ye think he'd marry her and then she'd be sheltered from the baron?" he asked incredulously. "Are ye out of yer mind? In a fortnight, ye expect Dougald of Douglas to fall in love with Caithleen and marry her?"

Alenna took a deep breath. "Well, yes."

He laughed again. Anger pushed from somewhere deep within her and flowed over like lava. "Damn it, Tynan, would you stop it?"

Her harsh words stopped his guffaw. "Lass, yer cartin' a load of clishmaclaver around if ye think he'd marry."

"I see. Because he's just like you?"

"In that sense he is. He's no goin' to marry, so ye can get that plan out of yer head."

Alenna's frustration simmered below the surface, steaming like a volcano vent. She was getting mighty tired of hearing she couldn't do things. Mighty damn tired.

"Well, at least if Dougald was good to her for two weeks and he didn't hurt her the way the baron does, she'd know a little happiness. Even if it was *only* for two weeks." Sinking down onto the bed, she speared him with a withering look. "I'm sick of you, the baron and every other idiot man in this stupid century. You'll turn your back on common decency because of your misplaced loyalty to the baron, Tynan of MacBrahin. Get out of my room."

Stiffening in indignation, he moved away from the window and towered over her. "I willnae. I am not finished with ye."

"Well, I'm finished with you. Get out before I scream."

"Ye wouldnae dare—"

Alenna opened her mouth, but before she could take a breath he marched her out of the room and into a small anteroom nearby. He released her, turned toward the door and shut it.

"Now we'll have more privacy in case anyone decides to come in," he said. Then he stomped forward until he towered over her once again.

Eyes blazing, he said tightly, "Are ye crazy, woman? Now ye listen, I have had about enough of yer wailin' about men. Do women in yer time clap their hands and men come runnin'? Ye have got to understand the way of things here. The baron doesnae give a fishmonger's arse about ye, lass. He has never loved a woman in all his life. And mark my words, if ye do anythin' at all to anger him, he may kill ye on the spot. Yer plan is no goin' to work. All it will serve is to bring the baron's wrath down on Dougald and Caithleen if they were to marry. And, as I told ye, there is nothin' that could make Dougald marry her."

Tynan yanked her close, both of his arms secure around her.

She licked her dry lips nervously and saw his gaze follow the movement. A burgeoning heat ignited in his eyes. Intense and devouring, it told her she'd pay and pay dearly right that moment.

"Not even if he were to fall in love with her?" she asked.

"Nay," he said softly, his voice so husky and deep. "He wouldnae love her."

His mouth came down on hers with swift, undeniable, voracious need.

CHAPTER 14

Alenna remained rigid in Tynan's arms until the pressure of his lips lessened, barely touching hers with featherlight tenderness. He seduced her mouth with sweet, seductive tastes, kissing her over and over, each meeting of their mouths thrilling her more than the last.

Every part of Alenna craved his touch, melting her resistance inch by inch until she might have done anything he asked. Her lips yielded, softened, and his tongue stroked and explored until the desire in her loins heightened, heated. Her arms went about his neck and she pressed against him, relishing the hard contours of his body. Groaning deep in his throat, he increased his passion, tracing his hands over her shoulders, her back, until he could cup her buttocks. Relenting, she kissed him back.

As Tynan's tongue stroked into her mouth continuously, her excitement overtook any reservations and she clutched at his shoulders and arched her hips. When he touched her neck and trailed slowly down to her breast, she felt her nipples tighten unbearably. Nothing in her life prepared her for a passion this mindless and all consuming.

She wanted him to touch her. She wanted—

He pulled away from her suddenly and she stumbled back a step and almost fell. He breathed heavily, clutching his hands into fists at his sides. She couldn't deny the hot, obvious desire raging in his gaze. Suddenly Tynan closed his eyes and took a deep breath.

"Jesu, I cannae take this any more."

Anticipation sent a wild thrill inside her. Before she could speak, he cupped her face in one hand and kissed her hungrily, his tongue plunging deeply. Without any regard to their vulnerability, the fact they might be found out, he drew one of her hands to his cock. She gasped into his mouth as she felt the hard evidence. His cock pushed against her fingers and she caressed the ridge of thick male flesh. A few seconds later, she felt him wrestling at the waistband of his trews as he opened them. When he urged her to clasp his naked cock, she moaned softly in pure enjoyment. Oh, she remembered this. *Oh God, yes.*

With a quick decision, she drew her hand up and down the burgeoning length of his cock. He jerked under her touch and bit back a groan, his head falling back and eyes closing. She felt an answering sensation low in her belly, her body hot at the idea of taking him here. Now. He literally shook with excitement as she caressed him with faster strokes. He'd been fully erect when he'd released his naked cock from his trews, but now he literally throbbed in her hand.

She was frantic to give Tynan the full measure of pleasure. Insensible with desire, she pumped him rapidly, pre-cum making it easy. He stared down at her hand encompassing his cock. His lips parted, his breathing harsh as his eyes glazed with fiery excitement. She could tell he wouldn't last long. She knew exactly what he needed and wanted to give it to him more than she'd wanted anything in a long time. She had just enough room in the alcove to get on her knees.

"Alenna," he whispered, his tone rough. His fingers buried in her hair. "You dinnae— You dinnae have to—"

She held his cock and fed it straight into her mouth. He tasted hot, a tiny bit salty and musky. Oh, so delicious and big.

As her mouth covered him, Tynan's hips pushed forward and he moaned. "Ah shite, shite that's so guid."

After that, his gasps of pleasure filled her ears as she pumped him with her hand and mouth until his entire body shook. She didn't back away when he stiffened and a rough growl left his throat. Hot semen spurted into her mouth, shooting deep into her throat as she swallowed and licked and sucked in wild enjoyment. When he stopped shaking, she released his cock and stood. She licked her lips and then dared to look at him.

A smile covered his mouth, his eyes glazed with passion, his chest still rising and falling rapidly. He refastened his trews and then cupped her face. "Alenna, fair one, that was...I dinnae think I can describe it." He shook his head. "I thought ye hated me and then you—" He brought her hands up to his lips and kissed the tips of her fingers. Her own breath came quickly and her heartbeat hadn't stopped slamming in her chest. "You are bluidy wonderful. So women in the twenty-first century ken how to pleasure a man like that?"

She couldn't help put smile. "Some do."

She didn't want to think too much about why and how she'd come unglued and gone from anger to a raging desire to pleasure him.

The way his arms tightened about her should have warned her, but part of Alenna wanted his embrace. Wanted it and craved it like a drug. So when his mouth lowered to within an inch of hers, she allowed her eyelids to flutter shut.

A sound at the doorway stopped them. Before she could yelp in surprise, he dragged her toward a large wooden freestanding wardrobe. Opening the door, he urged her inside. Swiftly he followed her and clicked the door closed. They had little room to maneuver and he drew her back against him, his arms tight about her waist.

His mouth pressed to her ear. "Shhh."

She wriggled but he gripped her harder. She wanted to shake him off, but she could see through the wooden slats that she'd better not make one tiny sound. One of the dark-haired workmen stood with a red-headed maid in his arms, their mouths mating hungrily. The young couple's faces showed clear arousal, both of them panted, chests heaving as they rubbed, pressed together. She recognized the couple as people who worked in the donjon. Yet she couldn't believe they took this chance that someone might find them.

Right. She'd given Tynan head not long ago and these people could have walked in on them. Anyone could have.

The man urged the woman toward the middle of the room. He lifted her onto the table, then tossed her skirts up. The man groaned low in his throat and the woman smiled.

Alenna's lower belly clenched in response. She moved the slightest bit and felt Tynan's cock harden to granite. With one hand he slowly pulled the skirt of her dress upward until he could reach her naked buttocks. He squeezed gently and she wanted to squirm, to wriggle against the tickling sensation. Instead, she kept her body still, afraid the other couple would hear them.

Alenna couldn't look away as the man bared the female's privates. Pink and wet with arousal, the women's pussy showed how much she wanted the dark-haired man.

The woman groaned, and Alenna's eyes widened as the man went down on his knees between the women's legs and started feasting. Hot, long, plundering licks devoured the woman. The woman gasped then covered her own mouth with her hand as if to hold back a scream.

Alenna drew in a sharp breath as Tynan worked open the front of her bodice. Before she could move or cover her breasts, Tynan brushed her nipple with light, feather touches. She ached high up in her pussy as he tweaked, caressed, stimulated her flesh. His other hand worked up the fabric of her dress and found her naked belly. He caressed, tantalizing her with slow, tempting brushes of his big palm just above her mons and the rhythmic twist and pluck of her nipple. When he drew his finger over her clit, she held back a strangled gasp, pressing her lips together in an agony of pleasure. Tynan's fingers teased her, slicking her moisture along the tender flesh. All the while, his touch brushed over and over her nipples. When he stopped caressing her clit, she almost forced his hand to return to the job.

Outside, on the table, the man sucked at the women's folds and clit. The woman lay back on the table, arching her back.

"Nay," the woman said. "Now. Before anyone comes. Now."

"So be it," the man said.

The man drew her off the table, turned her around and shoved up the maid's skirts. From the side angle, Alenna could see the man free his cock from his pants. It was average as cocks went and reminded her that few men had a cock as large as Tynan's. The thought of Tynan's hardness stirred a frantic need inside Alenna.

The man aimed and with one ramming thrust, he plunged deep into the maid's body.

Alenna shivered, feeling dirty and aroused and everything in between as she watched the uninhibited scene. She quaked, wanting Tynan with a power so fierce she knew nothing would stop her from throwing away every caution to get it.

Be damned with his belief that every woman he made love to would suffer some doom. She made a decision. She reached behind her and stroked over Tynan's cloth-covered erection. He jerked in reaction, then pulled her hand away.

Alenna wanted to moan as Tynan slipped his hands up to cup her bare breasts. His fingers plucked and twisted her nipples, just hard enough to sting delightfully. Alenna shuddered under his attention, scared out of her mind they'd be discovered, yet oddly aroused by the possibility and her voyeur status.

As the man and woman fucked in slow, agonizing detail, she thought she'd never seen anything so erotic. The woman threw her head back and moaned softly as the man gripped her shoulder and one hip. From the side view, Alenna could see the man slow his thrusting. Glistening with the woman's arousal, the man's cock slid in and out. The man panted, his breath coming hard as he suddenly shortened his strokes and reamed the woman's pussy. The woman gasped and squirmed. Ecstasy outlined on the woman's face, her eyes closed and lips parted. Alenna couldn't close her eyes, too captivated by the sight.

Alenna held her breath as her own arousal heightened in response. Her breath quickened.

She couldn't stand it. Tynan's breath panted in her ear as his tongue came out to tease her earlobe. He drew her dress up in back and she felt Tynan's naked cock pressed between her pussy lips. He teased her, slipping the head along her folds, probing and easing an inch inside.

No more waiting.

She barely had time to take a breath before she took the option away from him and arched backward, impaling herself halfway on his cock. She held back a cry. Despite her arousal, he felt like a pillar of hard, hot stone burrowing up inside her. Tynan eased his hips back, then pushed a tiny increment into her channel. She twisted in his hold, so aroused she didn't think she could take it much longer. She pushed into his thrust and Tynan sank deep, pressing, spreading her walls. Alenna almost cried out, but stifled the sound in time. Tynan stilled and she absorbed the sensations of them locked together in total intimacy. His body quivered against hers and his hot breath tickled her ear.

Watching the other couple continue their erotic dance, Alenna savored the thickness spreading her wide and deep.

Swallowed in the luscious sensation, she closed her eyes. Tynan didn't move and she clenched in unbearable agony, wanting him to thrust. She started to move her hips, just enough to slid his cock over one spot high up inside her. Pleasure escalated and she bit back a sound of bliss. God, he reached places inside her she'd never realized she had. Tynan strummed her nipples, and his hips moved with her.

She clenched hard on Tynan's cock and their tender, slow lovemaking picked up pace. Tynan didn't have much room to move and neither did she, but they couldn't afford to make one single sound.

Desire exploded within her until she became nothing more than a physical being tortured and thrilled by the clandestine quality of their mating. She'd never imagined making love with him like this, thinking if they ever came together it would be in a slow mating in an appropriate bed, a mild counterpoint to this feral union.

But *oh*, what a glorious mating it was.

Nothing tender, nothing sweet, only the raw, blatant coming together of two people in the most intimate act of all.

Each firm but slow thrust drew her closer to climax. When a small sound escaped her throat, her eyes flew open in fear. What if they were heard? What if they were found? To her amazement, the idea created a wild buildup inside her. She strained to keep her excitement tamped down.

Her gaze found the other couple and realized they fucked hard, their restrained cries gathering volume and speed. It fueled Alenna's desire until it seemed the other couple's pace became a counterpoint to the excruciatingly slow movement of Tynan deep in her body.

The man's hips rammed into the woman's, and suddenly the woman cried out and the man grunted. The man stiffened, then shivered hard.

The couple quickly pulled apart and the woman turned

around. They panted, their smiles happy as the man took her hand and they left without another word and closed the door behind them.

Now the couple had disappeared, more of Alenna's inhibitions shattered. She pushed back into Tynan's next thrust, the movement demanding. "Tynan."

The word came out as a whimper and he seemed to read her mind. She spread her legs wider.

"Jesu," he said, panting into her ear. "Alenna. That's it."

His command thrilled her and the pulsating in her lower body rose higher by the second. One of his hands slipped under her skirts to discover her clit. As his fingers touched her and his cock continued its relentless movement inside her, Alenna bucked in his hold and the pleasure became too much. She dissolved in pure, melting ecstasy. She choked back a scream, trembling from the inside out as her pussy clenched on his cock. He continued his movements, pushing hard through the last few thrusts as he started to shudder against her and his last thrust sent a new, harder orgasm blasting through her. She yelped, unable to hold back the bliss. He growled low and soft and as he shoved one last time, she felt his cock throbbing inside her and the hot flood of semen.

They held still in the aftermath, and the ecstasy of what happened mixed with one realization.

He'd come inside her.

Without any protection.

Her passion disappeared as surely as it had come. She could be pregnant soon. *Oh God.* Trembling with the thought, she drew away from him, shoved open the closet door and stumbled outside. She hastily righted her clothes to cover her breasts.

He pulled up his trews, his gaze intense with spent passion. He stepped from the closet. "What is wrong, Alenna?"

She gulped. "We…you were inside me when you…released."

His grin was, to put it bluntly, pure male shit-eating satisfaction. "Aye."

When she stared at him in disbelief at his cavalier attitude, his eyes narrowed. He took her hands in his and kissed them, lingering over her fingers in a way that almost sent her straight back into his arms and begging him to take her again.

She withdrew her hands from his. "You must leave now. We shouldn't have...we took too big a risk."

He smiled again. "Aye. We could have been caught."

She couldn't admit out loud that he could have just impregnated her, nor could she acknowledge to herself that the thought honestly stirred her desires once more. The thought sent a hot flush to her face.

He frowned. "Ye were naught a maiden, but ye still gave me a part of ye. I will take yer gift with me to my grave. And you must be careful from now on."

Rattled, she managed to take her own steadying breath. Tears stung her eyes. "Don't say that. I can't stand it. You aren't going to die and I'm not cursed because we made love."

"Then you will do as I say? You'll no try this cuif plan to make Dougald rescue Caithleen."

That he could switch gears so easily ticked her off. Determined to continue with the plan, despite his opposition, she decided she'd let him think he'd won. This time.

"I feel very sorry for Dougald. For you," Alenna said, moved from the intimacy of what they'd done to cold, stark facts. "If you never love at least once in your life, you have nothing. Even if you lose it."

A deep well of hurt seemed to drown the passion in his eyes and his lips hardened into a frown. The sight of such pain startled her, and for a second she regretted her words. He turned away and walked to the door. Once there he paused and looked back at her.

"I have loved a woman once in my life. And it wasnae worth the pain of losin' her."

Seconds later the door closed behind him. Stunned by his admission, Alenna stared at the floor. Within her breast grew an ache so abysmal, a sadness so thick it filled her throat and threatened to choke her. He was right.

She'd fallen in love once, and when she'd dumped her two-timing fiancé before the wedding, she knew the love had been hollow. It hadn't been worth what she'd gone through the last few months. And now Tynan made her feel things she didn't want to feel. Made a passion boil inside her so intensely, she knew if anything happened to him, she would never recover. She knew he'd given her the most exciting, most beautiful moments in her life.

Any anger she had with Tynan dissipated, and without warning tears trailed down her face in a slow, steady rain.

* * *

A DECISIVE KNOCK on Alenna's door the next afternoon brought her out of a deep sleep. Groggy from the lengthy nap, she sat up slowly.

"Who is it?"

No answer. Letting out an exasperated groan, she pushed off the bed and walked wearily to the door. Suspicious, she called through the door again. "Who is it?"

"Baron MacAulay."

At the sound of his voice, her stomach muscles clenched with tension. In the time since she'd moved into the donjon, he'd spent little time with her, and then always in the presence of others. Perhaps this time he brought Caithleen with him.

When she opened the door, though, he was alone. Nervous knots tightened her stomach. Automatically, she dropped into a curtsy.

"Guid afternoon, my lord."

He nodded and bowed. "A splendid afternoon. You are well?"

"Aye." She stepped back to let him in.

He advanced into the room, putting a long walking stick and a large wood box down on the table. As if he'd been through a stiff wind, his hair stood up in spikes on his head. Quickly he ran his hand through his hair, but pushing his thick fingers through the unruly strands disordered his hair even more. If she didn't know that the man had a stone-cold heart, she'd think he was nervous. As a precaution, she kept the door open.

"I hope I am not intruding," the baron said.

"Nay."

"Splendid. I wanted to give you this before the party tomorrow night."

He retrieved the box and walked toward her, as if he had all the time in the world.

Apprehension skittered up her spine but Alenna managed to plant a smile on her face. "What is it, my lord?"

He held the box out in front of her. "A little trinket to express my admiration."

Inside the lined box lay a large necklace made of gold, the long strand dotted with pearls and what looked to be emeralds and garnets. In the center nestled a huge square-cut garnet.

"Oh my," she gasped.

He laughed, the sound echoing glacial and soft in the room like a ghost's cackle. His cheeks creased as he smiled, the grey of his eyes like two cold nickels. "I had hoped you would like it."

Alenna almost reached out to touch the stones, but restrained the urge. Instead she schooled her face into a serious mask. "I cannae take this."

She'd never seen a scowl form on a man's face so quickly, not even Tynan's. "Why do you refuse it?"

"Because it would be unseemly to take such a gift from anyone other than a…a husband or a betrothed."

The baron shut the box with such a loud clack that she jumped. "Yet you took a present from your cousin and he is neither husband or betrothed." He paused and lifted one eyebrow. "Was that not unseemly?"

Her mind raced for a plausible answer. "He is family. He gave me the cloak because he feared the one I have wouldnae be sufficient. Jewelry is an intimate gift."

"While you are my guest you have only to ask and you shall be provided with every accommodation," he said, conveniently ignoring her statement on intimacy. He placed the box back on the table.

Alenna clamored for something to say to placate him. She reached out and touched the box gingerly.

"I wouldnae presume that I might ask for anything I wanted, my lord. It would be ill-bred and equally unseemly."

He twisted his lips into something that might be called a smile to some, or a grimace to others. Either way, it made her quake inside. Without breaking the smile, he reached into the box and retrieved the necklace.

"You are quite different than Caithleen, are you not?"

His change in subject startled her, but she managed a reply. "We are very different."

He took the necklace out of the box and examined the gems sparkling in his fingers. "She has little patience for the appearances one must have as a man of my stature. The little wench is so artless. You, however, are very mature. Age, of course, has much to do with this. But I think 'tis not all."

"I have been married, my lord. And I have seen more of life all together."

"Aye. No doubt. But she has received anything she asks of me. I refuse her little."

Except her freedom from your cruelty.

With a tone somehow intimate and detached at the same time, he said, "You are a very extraordinary woman, Alenna.

Indeed, you are different from any woman I have ever met. 'Tis something I find fascinating."

Alenna didn't want his fascination or his necklace. When he stepped in front of her and looped the jewelry around her neck, the cold of the metal made her skin prickle with goose bumps. His smell repulsed her, and the way he let his gaze drift over her face and body told her exactly what he had in mind.

Letting his fingers slide between the necklace and her dress, the baron managed to caress her collarbone. Thank goodness for high necklines, she thought. Simply the thought of his bare skin touching hers again left a nasty taste in her mouth.

"Doubtless you have been admired by many men," he said as he let his fingers lay against her.

"Nay."

"Then I shall take your reluctance as a sign of modesty, rather than of distaste and defiance. You would not defy me?"

Affronted by his haughtiness, but realizing she didn't have much choice in how she acted around him, she said, "Certainly not, my lord."

Even though Alenna hated it, she decided playing an insipid woman, or at least someone stupid, would keep him off guard. Let him think she hadn't a clue what he planned. Then again, she wasn't entirely sure what he was up to.

Was this necklace, something she might have expected for him to buy for Caithleen or a wife, a sign he wished to banish Caithleen for certain?

"I was sheltered by my parents," she said. "And then I was sheltered by my guidman. I have little understanding of a man such as yourself, my lord."

Smiling with that caricature of a grin, the baron released the necklace. The strand felt hot through the material of her dress. Despite the beauty of the necklace, she'd never wanted anything off her so quickly.

"Innocence becomes a woman," he said softly, as if he might

be talking to a child. He put his hand on her shoulder and the press of his fingers felt like hard, cold metal. "With a beauty such as yourself, purity of heart is particularly becoming."

If he'd been anyone other than the baron, the words might have sounded smarmy. Instead his grave, heavy tone took on a frightening significance. She sensed malice and hate deep within the man and knew she treaded dangerous waters.

The baron moved away and she took a deep breath, releasing the tension.

"You will take the necklace and wear it to the party tomorrow night. As a sign of my affection…as a sign of your meaning to me."

Without another word, he bowed and left the room.

Quickly Alenna took the necklace off and put it in the box. She stared at the dazzling jewelry for a long, long moment. She never would have imagined something so beautiful could be so ugly.

CHAPTER 15

Wounded and desperate, the cry came out of the darkness and penetrated Alenna's deep sleep.

At first the fog of sleep convinced her she'd imagined the sound. Night lay heavy, like a smothering blanket on the room. She couldn't see anything. The fire in the hearth had burned down hours ago.

Wind created a high-pitched whistle that screeched around the tower like a banshee. Perhaps she'd heard the wind and nothing else. She lay back in bed, the veil of sleep luring her under the warm coverings.

The next cry came like a muffled sob. She sat straight up in bed, listening intently. Caithleen?

Could the baron be hurting her?

If the swine hurt Caithleen, Alenna would kill him.

Enraged, she jumped out of bed. With trembling fingers she lit a candle and quickly put on shoes. After removing the chair from in front of the door, she cautiously peered out. She half expected one of Clandon's clooties to jump her.

Her candle made a token dent in the blackness. A tiny quiver of rage centered her determination and banished her fear. She stepped into the hall. Shutting the door behind her, she headed down the spiral stairs to the third floor where Caithleen shared chambers with the baron. Gingerly she stepped down, never taking her eyes off the dark stairs as one by one they were revealed to her by the candlelight.

Halfway down the stairs she heard another scream, and this time it wasn't a whimper of despair but an agonized call for relief. The desperation of someone under torture. Galvanized, she rushed down the stairs. Almost at the bottom, she slipped on the damp stairs and fell forward. Involuntarily she cried out and cursed, dropping the candle as she threw out her hands to break the fall.

Alenna gasped in pain as her elbow hit a step. Reaching out for a handhold, she tried to slow her descent. Each blow as her body hit the steps caused her teeth to jar together. Pain raced through her as her head hit something hard. Pinpoints of light danced behind her closed eyes and everything went dark.

When she came to she was resting on the cold third floor landing. Her head hurt, as well as her elbow and her hip, and for a moment she wondered if she'd done serious damage. All because she'd been stupidly impetuous in her dash down the stairs.

The door next to her opened and she felt the rush of cold air and saw the light through her closed lids. "Good God."

The baron.

Behind him she heard Caithleen sobbing. Caithleen's welfare impelled her to forget her own aches and pains and she pulled herself into sitting position. Pain crashed through her head.

"What has happened here?" the baron asked sharply, kneeling next to her.

Alenna put her hand to her forehead and attempted a weak smile. She couldn't let him know she'd heard Caithleen, or he might do something drastic. "I'm sorry, my lord. I'm afraid I slipped."

Light fell on his face from the open door. "What were you doing here at this time of night?"

She had to have an explanation. "I heard strange noises in the hall. I thought there might be an intruder in the donjon."

"Bah! Nonsense. The guards assure no one enters who does not belong here. You were dreaming."

Slowly she pushed herself into standing position, feeling every bruise and ache. "Of course. If you'll excuse me—" He grabbed her arm and the sudden movement made her head swim. "What types of noises did you hear?"

Think quickly, Alenna.

"It was as I said. I heard strange noises. Perhaps it was the wind."

He released her arm. She tried to read the expression in his eyes and saw cold, dark suspicion.

"The wind."

"No doubt, my lord. If you will excuse me, I would like to nurse my bumps and bruises."

Looking unconvinced but not worried, he nodded and backed away. With a full sweep, he took in her mode of dress. His gaze centered on her breasts through the fine linen of her nightdress, and without thinking she crossed her arms over her chest. Another whimper came from behind him. The sound hit her heart full force. How could she stand here and pretend indifference?

"Is Caithleen well, my lord?"

"Aye."

"But I hear her crying."

He stepped forward again and she backed herself against the wall. She smelled his breath and repressed a shudder.

"What you hear coming from my room is none of your concern, Alenna."

Alenna stiffened, wishing he would back away. Half tempted to kick him in the nuts and run, she quelled the urge.

"Is she ill?"

Mistrust danced in his eyes. "She is distressed because she's learned of her brathair's plight."

Fear shot through her belly. "Clandon? What has happened?"

"I'm afraid he tried to steal food from my kitchens."

"Stealing? But he would not—"

"He was stealing from me. This is a serious offense. I have had him thrown in the dungeon."

Fury climbed into her throat but she held back words that she knew she'd regret later. Alenna recalled the horrifying feelings she'd encountered while visiting the dungeons. She had to get Clandon out of there.

"When did this happen?" she asked.

"A few hours ago. After our evening meal."

"He is only a boy, my lord. Maybe the scare you've put into him is sufficient. When will you release him?"

The baron's lips curled in a cruel smile. "A thief is a thief. He shall remain there until I have thought of a more suitable punishment."

God, he didn't mean to execute the boy?

"Suitable punishment?"

"A few lashes might do, or if I see fit, something far worse."

"What do you mean by worse?"

He made an exasperated sound deep in his throat. "'Tis not for you to ask. Do you think I need your approval of such things? Surely you do not condone thievery?"

"Nay. But he has very little. And as a boy he wouldnae understand the seriousness of such an offense. Perhaps he was hungry—"

His hand came up and clamped around her throat.

She'd gone too far.

"Enough! 'Tis not your place to meddle in such matters."

"Wait," she rasped.

His hand pressed and she gasped for air.

Panic struck her and she kicked out, landing a blow to his knee. He added his other hand to the pressure on her throat. If she didn't do something, she might die right here, right now.

She didn't want to die, damn it.

Not in this Godforsaken time. Not in this way.

As her lungs ached for air and tiny black dots danced across her vision, she thought of Tynan.

The thought of him gave her strength and she twisted in the baron's grip, kicking out again. As he jerked back with a curse, Alenna plastered herself against the wall and pulled deep breaths into her deprived lungs. She lunged up two stairs and then her knees collapsed. Pain slammed through her as she fell against the steps.

"I suggest you get back to your room and stay there," the baron said harshly from behind her. "No matter what you hear, for your own safety, you will not creep the halls at night. You had a mild accident this evening. Who knows what could happen if you don't mind your own counsel?"

Alenna turned and looked at him. He gazed at her balefully. Tingles of dread raced along her skin. The man was evil. Pure, unadulterated depravity.

"Do not defy me again, Alenna," he said quietly as if he were making casual conversation.

The baron went into his chamber without a backward glance, leaving her in the darkness. On trembling legs she ascended the stairs, relying on her sense of touch.

Anger and shock gripped her and by the time she reached her room and slammed the door, she ached in every muscle. She quickly lit as many candles as she could. Her limbs trembled with cold as she climbed into bed. Huddling under her bedcovers, she tried to absorb what she had learned about Clandon and the baron's violence. Down deep, Alenna knew the baron had no intention of releasing the boy.

Did he intend to manipulate Caithleen into doing what he

wanted by threatening Clandon? Could the baron have another reason for his cruelty? No. The man was colder than a corpse and had a sadistic streak a mile wide. He didn't need any reason for his actions.

He'd almost snuffed out her life tonight. Yet he'd stopped.

Playing with fire could get her killed, but so might doing nothing.

A relentless throb pounded at her skull and her throat ached. She touched the rising bump on her forehead.

She had to do something about Clandon. Images of the boy, frightened and huddled in one corner of a damp, freezing cell, caused a swell of panic to rise into her bruised throat.

"No," she said, taking a shuddering breath to calm down the insistent fear. She couldn't allow fear to rule her. Clandon's safety came first and foremost. With a semblance of calm and determination, Alenna left her bed and dressed immediately.

* * *

ALENNA KNOCKED on the door of the Black Tower and waited for a response. When she received no answer, she rapped on the door a little harder. Abruptly the door swung open. Silhouetted by the dim light behind him, Tynan stood shirtless, his hair dripping wet.

"Alenna," Tynan said, looking surprised to see her. "What brings ye here so late? 'Tis dangerous—"

She swallowed, her mouth dry and her throat throbbing. "I must speak to you. May I come in?"

He let her in and closed the door.

"Did you know that Clandon has been thrown in the dungeon?" she asked. "The baron claims he stole food from the kitchens."

Tynan glowered. "Eh? Where did you hear this?"

"The baron told me, tonight. We must free Clandon."

Instead of answering, he brushed her hair back from her forehead. "Alenna, what happened to ye?" He touched her throat and she winced. "There is a bruise on yer head and more on your neck. God's bluid!"

"It's nothing." Her experience with the baron threatened to catch up with her. Tears created a logjam in her throat as she realized how easily the baron might have ended her life.

"Dinnae tell me 'tis nothin'," he whispered huskily, his eyes filled with concern. "Did the baron do this to ye?"

"Yes." Alenna explained how she fell down the stairs after hearing the noises.

"Fell down the stairs?" he said a bit louder. "Ye could have been killed."

"Well I wasn't. What would you have me do? Lie there in bed and listen to him hurt her?"

Tynan put his hands on his hips. "Nay. I know ye too well. That doesnae explain the bruises on yer throat."

When she explained about her conversation with the baron and how he had throttled her, Tynan's faced flushed with rage.

"God knows what the baron did to Caithleen. Either she was terrified because of what he'd said he'd do to Clandon, or…or he was hurting her," Alenna said.

With a disgusted sound, Tynan grabbed his shirt from the back of a chair and yanked it over his head. "Damn the filthy swine!"

"That's too good a word for him."

He grasped her shoulders gently. "I'd like to yell at ye until yer ears ring for puttin' yerself in the baron's path, but ye wouldnae listen."

Alenna gave him the barest of smiles. "No, I wouldn't."

He pushed the hair away from her forehead again and looked closely at the lump. His gaze traced her entire face, as if searching for another wound. His lips tightened. It wouldn't surprise her if he went in search of the baron and beat the man to a pulp.

"Are ye hurt anywhere else?" he asked, his voice hoarse. "By God...if he touched ye..." He sucked in a breath. "Did he try—"

"No."

He muttered something that she guessed might be a curse and closed his eyes for a moment.

Impatient, she asked, "What are we going to do about Clandon?"

He prowled the floor in thought, raking his hands through his hair several times in an agitated movement.

"I thought of at least going to the dungeons to see how he is being treated," she said. He stopped pacing and faced her. Before he could speak she continued. "Don't even think of telling me not to go."

"Ye'll no go there alone."

"I hadn't planned on it, unless you refused to come with me."

A grim smile curved his mouth. "Do ye think I could let ye go in that wretched place alone?"

"I wondered how you might react. Remember, I refused the cloak."

"Ye are wearin' it now."

She touched the warm wool. "I didn't thank you properly. It really was a nice thing to—"

"Thank me later." He turned and reached for his own cloak. "When and if we get Clandon out of this mess."

* * *

AS ALENNA DESCENDED the steps leading into the dungeon, the first prickling of dread roamed along her skin like a thousand ants. Like a monster in a horror story, the dungeon lay before her. Waiting. Waiting to swallow her up.

Cold created goose bumps on her arms as she looked into

the dimness below. While torches threw flickering light onto the damp walls, they barely penetrated the murky hell.

A place of nightmares.

A putrid stench rolled up from the bowels of this abode of the damned and sounds of moaning came heavy to her ears.

God, please don't let one of those moans be coming from Clandon.

In her haste to reach the boy, she had dismissed her earlier fear of the dungeon. Now it came back to claim her with a vengeance.

Alenna stopped her descent as if she'd walked into a brick wall.

Tynan turned to look back up at her. "What is it?"

"Nothing," she said on a strangled breath. She took another step, but her apprehension leapt another notch, pounding in her chest and ears like an overeager heartbeat.

"It cannae be nothin'." He took the stairs two at a time until he reached her. Clasping her arm, he started up the stairs again.

"No," she said. "I want to help Clandon."

"Aye, I ken that ye do. But ye dinnae look well and like as not ye will scare the boy."

"Thank you very much."

"Upstairs, sweet. The stench below makes the strongest of men feel a mite sick. If ye are goin' down there, ye need yer wits about ye."

When she reached the outside, she drank in breaths of fresh air, reducing the trembling in her limbs. Tynan watched but said nothing as she tried to compose herself.

"I'm sorry," she said.

"Are ye frightened? Is this the panic attack, as ye call it?"

"Not exactly. A panic attack isn't always traceable to a certain cause. Yes. The dungeon…it…it frightens me. When I was visiting the dungeon in my own time, I had a similar reaction."

"They dinnae keep people in there anymore, do they? In your time, I mean."

Alenna shook her head vigorously. "No. People visit to see how prisoners were kept at the castle hundreds of years ago."

"'Tis hard for me to imagine."

Throwing him a feeble smile she said, "We need to get Clandon out." She clasped his forearm lightly. "I can't leave him in there."

"We have to leave him for a time. The guards aren't goin' to let him free without the baron's pardon."

"Then we're wasting time. Let's get back down there." She started toward the entrance back into the dungeon.

Tynan grabbed her arm. "I'll go first."

As they descended, Alenna reminded herself she had to be strong, for Clandon. After what seemed like eons, they reached the depths of the dungeon.

The vault had changed little in six hundred years. Everything within her revolted and jumped, anxious to make her visit to Clandon and then get out.

After she took the last step down, Alenna glanced around. She jolted with fright when something swung close to her, a creak of metal echoing like a small, scraping scream in the shadows. A man hung in the iron maiden swinging from the ceiling. He'd been dead for several days, by the look and smell of him. She stifled a gasp and covered her mouth as she backed away.

Tynan put his arm around her and brought her close. Grateful for his support and his warm body, she allowed him to lead her further into the abyss. Thankfully, for all the large size of the dungeon, few prisoners resided here.

"Ah, so who is this lovely creature, Tynan of MacBrahin?" a voice hissed from the shadows. "Did ye bring her for me? She's a mighty pretty morsel."

Tynan turned with her toward the voice, keeping his arm tight around her shoulders. Two men, chained to the wall, glared at them with glassy eyes. The one who had spoken was filthy, his clothes hanging in rags on his body, his rotten teeth giving his grin a jack o'lantern appearance. Bruises and dried blood covered his face. Alenna recognized the two thugs who had attacked her and Tynan.

Tynan muttered a string of what Alenna suspected were Gaelic curses. "Keep yer mouth shut. I dinnae give a halfpenny about yer bletherin'. And if ye say another word to her, I'll make sure ye never walk out of here alive. Would that I had killed ye the first time I lay eyes on yer filthy cur hide."

"Like as not I willnae live long anyway," the man said. He spat on the floor.

She felt the tension rise in Tynan's shoulders and she put her arm about his waist to caution him against making too much noise.

"Have ye ever seen a man loose a limb?" Tynan asked the man in a deadly soft voice.

The thug shook his head, his eyes narrowing.

"I have," Tynan said. "'Tis no a pretty sight. And I can tell ye that if ye dinnae keep yer foul mouth shut, I will make sure to come down here and remove yer limbs one by one with me sword. And I'll do it in such a way that ye will be alive for the whole time."

His cold words were sharp as a razor and Alenna saw the man's face pale a couple of shades under all the filth. Tynan moved her away.

There was a muffled exclamation as they approached the last cell. "Sir! Mistress!"

Clandon grabbed the bars in front of him and grinned happily. Alenna moved out of Tynan's grip and went to the cell, placing her hands over the boy's.

"Are you all right, Clandon?" she asked.

"Aye. I am well." He didn't look as if he'd been abused or beaten. Yet. "I am happy to see ye both."

"What happened Clandon?" she asked.

"Did ye steal the bread, boy?" Tynan asked.

"Nay, sir. I remembered what ye told me, sir. I dinnae need to steal anythin', since Caithleen's been given' me coins and ye have been givin' me coins, sir."

The boy rattled on about how he'd been snatched and thrown into the dungeon without a by your leave. A guard would only tell him the baron had accused him of stealing bread from the kitchens.

"I swear on me own father's grave, I dinnae steal. Ye have got to believe me." His wide eyes pleaded, pathetic in his small face. "Ye do believe me, mistress?"

"I believe you," Alenna said, pressing his little, cold hands. She looked at the inside of his cell, thankful at least he hadn't been thrown into the oubliette.

The small hole in the ground, situated to the far left of the cell, would have been the death knell for the boy. Approximately seven feet deep, it allowed little room for movement. Those that were thrown in were not fed or given water—they were forgotten. Oubliettes filled with spikes seemed the most merciful. Though the death might be horrible it would be swift. Here the forsaken would die slowly and painfully.

She stepped back hastily as a rat ran from out of Clandon's cell and between her feet. "Ugh."

Clandon actually laughed. "'Tis only a rat."

She managed a smile. "Only a rat, he says."

"And a small one at that," Tynan said, the barest of smiles twitching across his lips.

How could these two have a sense of humor about this? Then Alenna reminded herself that they had always lived with horrors most twenty-first century people could barely imagine.

"How are ye, Clandon?" Tynan asked.

Clandon puffed his scrawny chest out. "I am guid, sir. They cannae scare me." He nodded to the two men chained to the walls. "They tried to scare me, but I told them to leave me alone—bugger off."

Alenna smiled slightly at the boy's choice of words.

"Can ye think of any reason the baron might wish to harm ye?" Tynan asked.

"Nay, sir." His small shoulders sagged as he gripped the bars like a lifeline. "I stay out of his way."

"We'll think of a way to get you out. You have my word," Alenna said.

Tynan gave her a hard glance, as if she might have said something wrong. "Stay quiet, Clandon, and dinnae say anythin' to make the guards angry. Have ye enough to eat?"

"Aye, sir. They have fed me."

Alenna imagined too well what type of rancid gruel they'd given him. "We'll have more food sent down."

"Would ye, mistress?" His eyes widened, an innocent look that warmed her heart. He might be a tough boy but a boy he remained. "I'd surely like some of that bread they say I stole."

Even Tynan smiled this time. "It will be done. We must leave."

Clandon's face sobered, but he immediately bolstered it back to a hearty smile. Tears came to Alenna's eyes at his bravery. Could she say, if she were in this dreadful place, she'd do as well? She doubted it.

Tynan put his hand on her shoulder. "Come. We must go."

She pressed the boy's fingers one more time. "We will get you out of here."

The boy nodded and smiled.

As Tynan led her away, the tears Alenna had tried so hard to hold back trickled down her face. Anger and anxiety for the boy dug at her breast. Tynan didn't appear to notice her tears until they reached the outside.

"Are ye all right?" he asked.

She wiped at the tears. "No."

Looking bemused, he put his arms around her and drew her close. "Dinnae cry."

Without looking at him, feeling a sense of shame at her weakness, she said, "I'm sorry, I can't bear the thought of him being in there."

The pain in her heart overflowed. She buried her head against his shoulder and he gathered her closer. Alenna needed the warm, hard shelter of his arms, needed to feel safe in this savage world. He murmured softly to her in Gaelic and although she didn't understand, the rhythm of the words soothed her. He caressed her back, gently touched her hair, rocking the slightest bit as he might comfort a frightened child.

With a sob, she gave in to the frustrations and dramatic changes that had taken over her life since she'd landed in the past. Her head throbbed again and she realized crying made it worse. Still, it felt so good to let it all out.

When her tears dried she lifted her head to look at him and he grinned. Her heart did a jump. Everything within her recognized the hot, undeniable attraction, the feeling that in his arms nothing and no one could hurt her.

"Are ye quite done soakin' my cloak now, lass?" he asked, looking boyish and all man at the same time.

"Yes."

"Guid. Now let's get ye back to Elizabet's so she might give ye somethin' for yer throat and yer head."

All her life she'd heard of peak experiences. Of moments in a person's life when she knew without doubt her life had shifted inexorably toward a new direction. As they walked away, Alenna knew she had lost an additional piece of her heart to Tynan of MacBrahin.

CHAPTER 16

The first morning rays of light streamed into Elizabet's room as she looked at the bruises on Alenna's forehead and throat. Alenna winced at the pain in her throat and head. Elizabet made tut-tut noise.

"'Tis no as bad as it looks, Tynan, so ye can stop pacin' the floor like a caged animal. Yer makin' us all a-twitter."

Tynan quit striding and sat in a chair. "I am no pacin'."

Alenna gave Elizabet a smile that asked how she endured his stubborn will. Elizabet finished dabbing the pungent cream on Alenna's bruises.

"There. That will take the bruises down." She got up from the small table and poured a goblet of wine.

"Oh no. I don't want any, thank you," Alenna said, wanting all her senses in working order.

Elizabet chuckled and headed for Tynan. "Nay, 'tis no for ye."

Tynan took the goblet without a word and downed half the measure in a gulp.

Johanna came into the room from outside and stopped in her tracks. She barely gave Alenna a glance, but at the sight of Tynan, a large smile spread over her face. The grin boasted a cunning, almost feral intent, backed up by clear feminine interest.

"Tynan," Johanna said as she curtsied to him. "Are ye goin' to the baron's party?"

He smiled slightly, but not much. "Aye." He looked at Elizabet. "I suppose ye are goin'?"

Elizabet hesitated, looking first at Alenna, then at Johanna. "I am nae sure if I like the idea of the assembly. Nae for me and Johanna."

Johanna's veneer of cheeriness slipped. "But—"

"'Tis not decided, Johanna. I dinnae like the idea of women simply being picked by a man and havin' him run off with her for a fortnight. Some would say 'tis a sin against God."

Johanna opened her mouth as if to protest, then subsided as if she thought the better of it. With stiffness in her stance, she retreated to a chair and sifted through a basket of needlework.

Alenna doubted any man would run off with Johanna, based on the sharpness of her tongue and her rudeness, but who knew for certain? Plenty of men could be tempted by her prettiness, to possess her body and care nothing about her mind.

"I must go," Tynan said suddenly. He slammed back the last of his wine like it was water. "I trust ye will see to Alenna until I return."

Elizabet nodded. "Of course."

"Where are you going?" Alenna asked.

"To the baron. 'Tis time I asked him to release Clandon."

"I'll go with you," Alenna said and popped out of her chair.

"Nay," he said firmly. "Stay here. I'll no have him thinkin' this is yer idea. I dinnae like the idea of ye bein' around him, after what happened this night."

"He probably already knows I visited Clandon in the dungeon."

"I can work quicker without—"

"Without me following like a stray puppy?" she asked tartly.

"Aye." Before she could say another word he turned and left.

As she subsided into a chair, Elizabet's tinkling laugh rang out. Alenna gazed at her in surprise. She'd never heard the little woman laugh so heartily.

"What's so funny?"

"Aye, what is so funny?" Johanna asked, obviously equally intrigued by her mother's action.

Elizabet's laughter stopped, but not her grin. "Just this moment I had a vision. And 'tis quite a nice one at that."

"Just this minute you had a vision," Alenna repeated.

"Aye. About Tynan and yerself. It makes me very happy. I see ye together in the future. Yellin', arguin' and…" she paused, her face coloring. She glanced at her daughter.

"Go on," Johanna said, a childish pout forming on her lips. "Tell us."

"Nay, I cannae tell while ye are here, Johanna. 'Tis no for yer ears."

"Humph." Johanna got up and stomped out the door, slamming it behind her.

"I dinnae ken what I am goin' to do about that girl. I wanted her to go because I dinna think she needs to hear more secrets. She is already a terrible gossip as it is."

"She has quite a temper," Alenna said. "But the suspense is killing me. What were you about to say?" Did she really want to know? *Hell, yes.* "Tynan and I were together in what way?"

Elizabet's brilliant smile broke a little. Her ageless face held a glimmer, like a gentle sparkle of snow on a cold morning. Anticipation quickened Alenna's breath. No longer did she consider visions the stuff of fairy tales and impossibilities.

"'Tis very important Tynan learn to trust ye…and to trust himself," Elizabet said.

"Trust me? I thought he'd learned that a long time ago."

"Aye, in a sense. But he is like a babe alone in the night. His fear haunts him. His weakness haunts him. As a warrior, he cannae be seen to have weakness. And as I told ye before, he has built a wall about himself. Now that ye have torn down the wall, he dinnae ken which way to turn."

"I'm not sure I understand."

Elizabet sat forward, talking in a low tone as if the very walls might listen. Alenna also leaned forward to catch the woman's soft voice.

"Before ye came into his life, it was an endless time of trainin' for battles. For workin' hard to get the baron's patronage so that Tynan might forget everthin' he was before he came to MacAulay Castle."

"Why would he want to forget? He told me he left Glenfinnan but he hasn't explained why."

"I cannae tell ye that. He must do that himself. But twill be hard gettin' him to speak of it. Ye have to ken he has been sorely wounded. Worse than anythin' most men have to go through with a woman."

"He was in love with a woman who spurned him? Florie? But he said he wasn't in love with her."

"Nay. Florie is a part of it, but not the whole. Has he told ye about Mary?"

Alenna thought back, but couldn't recall him mentioning the name. "No."

"Ye must ask him about her. If he can tell ye about Glenfinnan and Mary, that will be half the battle."

"But what has this woman to do with me?"

Instead of answering precisely, Elizabet said, "Ye dinnae believe Tynan could love ye. But I see the future. I dinnae see where ye are, but ye are happy and together. And Tynan's child is growin' in yer belly."

Alenna gasped and clasped a hand to her stomach.

"A baby." Heat flowed through Alenna as the implications hit her full force. Pregnant. With Tynan's baby. "No," Alenna said, as if speaking the word would make it so.

Elizabet didn't look fazed by Alenna's adamant denial. "Aye. That is the way of it."

She would have to stay in this time. In this place. "I can't. I'm going back to my time, one way or the other. I can't stay here and make...make babies with him."

Elizabet put up her hands. "I tell ye only what I see."

Perhaps the truth made her head spin, not the bruise on her forehead. Before Alenna could further contemplate the bombshell Elizabet had dropped, the door opened and Tynan strode through, towing Johanna by the arm. The girl jerked her arm out of Tynan's hold and marched directly to the chair she'd sat in earlier. She wiped at the tears on her cheeks.

"Dinnae wander about the castle teasin' every man ye see," Tynan said gruffly to Johanna. Then he turned to Elizabet. "Why do ye let her do this?"

Elizabet's mouth pulled down. "She does what she will most of the time and there is little I can do about it. She has the will of a goat, no doubt."

Despite the girl's impudence, Elizabet always seemed to have an understanding of the girl's attitude. But maybe not. The tranquil world Elizabet built around herself, one filled with potions, lotions and visions, could have a crack or two. As any single mother in any time, Elizabet probably had experienced difficulty raising her daughter. Especially a daughter who seemed intent on catching a man's attention.

Silence settled over the room like a blanket and Alenna sensed the tension rising as Elizabet and Johanna stared at each other.

"I think we should go," Tynan said to Alenna.

"You didn't see the baron yet?"

"Nay. I spoke to Dougald and he told me the baron is no takin' visitors. When Dougald heard of Clandon bein' thrown in the dungeons, he went to the baron himself. The baron refused to release Clandon." He took a deep breath and let it out slowly.

"Dougald saw Caithleen and said she was worried for ye. Perhaps ye should go to her."

Alenna stood and nodded. "You're right."

As they departed and walked along the bailey, her mind turned into a jumble. Just when she thought she had a grip on the situation and a perspective on her purpose in being here, fate threw her a curve. With Tynan beside her, she felt distracted and unable to think about anything but Elizabet's suggestion that she would one day carry Tynan's baby.

Thinking about Elizabet's vision filled her with images that overwhelmed her common sense. Erotic memories of making love with Tynan in the wardrobe swamped her imagination.

"Did you know a woman called Mary?" Alenna asked on a whim, unwilling to wait for a better time to ask. With the way things changed around here, there might not be another time.

He stopped as if he'd been pole-axed. His mouth twisted in contempt.

"Aye," he said hoarsely. "Who told ye about her?"

"Elizabet."

"Bluidy hell!"

"She told me it was important I ask you about Mary."

He started walking again. "She had no reason to tell ye. That's in the past. It doesnae mean anythin' to me."

As his strides lengthened, Alenna quickened her pace to keep up. "If it didn't mean anything to you, you wouldn't be so angry right now."

Tynan heaved a breath indicating weariness as much as annoyance. "Mary was a woman I knew in Glenfinnan."

As they moved into the quadrangle she said, "Elizabet told me that much. Was she the woman you said you'd loved and then lost?"

When he swung on her this time, he grabbed her by the shoulders. Swiftly he steered her into a small enclosure well hidden in a notch next to a tower. The overhanging ceiling and quiet afforded deep, remarkably quiet privacy.

"What are you doing?" she said, balking as he pressed her to the wall and planted his hands on either side of her head. Tynan leaned in close, as if anyone could hear them in this little hole.

Alenna could see the lines at the corners of his eyes and the pure, unrestrained heat within their depths. A hard, conquering, warrior flame warning her to watch out or she'd get burned.

"What I want," he whispered in a tight, soft voice, "is for ye to stop meddlin'. I'm helpin' ye with Clandon because he's a mere boy. I'm helpin' ye with Caithleen because no woman deserves the way the baron is treatin' her. But I dinnae give ye leave to try and understand me."

Her breath accelerated. *Damn him.* An outrageous desire to kiss away the scowl on his face nettled her, dared her to do it. Perhaps she would do it and see if this odd need for him would dissipate like a whirlwind.

"Tynan, it was a simple question. Why are you acting like this?"

"I'm no tellin' ye what happened to Mary," he said, his voice going bass. "She was the only woman for me. I loved her with all my heart and she was murdered. Is that enough for ye?"

She was the only woman for me.

Sympathy and something deeper welled in her at the harshness of his words. So Tynan had loved once. With a spurt of awareness Alenna realized she gave a damn that he'd loved a woman and lost her. A lot more than she should.

Shock radiated through her. She'd allowed him to make love to her and now he'd confessed he could only love one woman. A dead woman.

She shoved back her desire to lash back at him and said instead, "I didn't mean to bring back bad memories. If I could understand about Mary—"

"Then what? Then ye would have me wrapped around yer

little finger, because whenever I dinnae do as ye bid ye would mention her and I would crumble?"

In a fit of frustration she placed both of her hands on his chest and pushed. "No, damn it!"

He barely budged. "What then? Why this burnin' need to ken what happened? Eh?"

As his voice trailed off, she closed her eyes. Somehow, despite her best efforts, the man remained like stone. The sharing she'd experienced with him outside the dungeon had disappeared. The lovemaking had meant nothing to him.

Alenna continued to sense the unmistakable chemistry between them despite his hostility. A burn that threatened to erupt right here, right now, even when discord should have kept them apart.

Although her eyes were closed, she felt his gaze like a feather touch. Could feel him tracing her lips with his gaze, her throat, her breasts...

Butterflies inside her stomach did a pirouette, reminding her the man made her nervous at the same time he generated her desire. Lord help her, she didn't want to open her eyes and see a wall of masculinity in front of her. But since she had little choice, she might as well face the music.

Alenna opened her eyes. The curl of his lips, the tilt of his head dared her. His look defied her to make a move to escape, either from his condemnation or his closeness.

More than anything she wanted to rip the top off the powder keg and discover the real Tynan of MacBrahin. What would he be like if he loved a woman? Would the passion they'd experienced in that wardrobe become even more heated? More incredible?

She licked her lips. "So that's why you say a knight should never love a woman. Because you loved once and lost her and that means you can never do it again."

She placed her hand on his chest again, letting it linger there. He sucked in a quick breath.

"Dinnae touch me like that."

"Why? It shouldn't bother a cold, unfeeling man like you."

Maybe the statement verged on unfair. She knew somehow where this was going to end up. At least she hoped she would be right.

She was.

"Damn ye," he hissed.

Before she could react, he leaned in to her, pressing his warm body against her. As his mouth covered hers she gathered a feeling of triumph to her. This was what she wanted. This is what she needed.

Tynan showing his feelings. Releasing his need and sweeping her into a sweetness she'd never found in another man's arms.

Everything seemed to recede...the sounds of a horse whinnying in the stables, the laughter of children at play, the shout of a peddler selling his wares. All of it paled in significance beyond this drift in time. Everything stilled and hovered with a soft, giving ecstasy.

He fed on her mouth as if he wanted to kiss her into hating him. Instead the kiss fueled her feelings and, with equal fervor and anything but aversion, she responded. If this was his punishment, she wanted more...and more...and more.

Tynan's lips and tongue plundered and took, asking for everything in an erotic dip and retreat dance. His kiss gave tantalizing a new meaning—nothing had ever felt so damned good. A soft moan left her throat as the unmistakable proof he wanted her pressed against her stomach. Alenna arched against him. God, yes. If she admitted it, she wanted his cock inside her again. Heat imploded in her stomach, letting her know her arousal went deep.

Suddenly he broke away from her, jerking back as if shocked

by electricity. His face flushed and his chest heaved. His eyes blazed with the knowledge he'd given her something hot and forbidden. For several moments she couldn't move and when she did it was only to lean against the wall.

"Why did you do that?" she asked, the daze in her mind drifting slowly away.

He didn't answer.

"Please, Tynan. Tell me—"

"Why? Why do ye want to know all about me? I've forgotten Glenfinnan and why I left there. Why can't ye?"

"Because I could understand you—"

"Why do ye need to understand me?"

"Because I care about you, that's why!"

As soon as the words parted her lips, she regretted them. If he knew she cared, he had the power to hurt her. To use her concern against her.

He passed a hand over his jaw, looking bewildered by the way the kiss and her statement had affected him. He took a deep breath and exhaled, as if a burden dropped heavily onto his shoulders.

"It was six years ago. She was but nine-and-ten. We belonged to two different clans and my cousin Angus was courtin' her. Angus was mean and hard and dinnae know how to love a woman. He hit Mary once when she refused his attention."

"Oh, Tynan," Alenna whispered. This explained his fierce protective attitude toward women.

"Mary kept meetin' with me and soon we were in love. I begged her not to become betrothed to Angus, but she wouldnae defy her father, who wished her to marry Angus."

A shudder went through his body and she thought she saw a glimmer of tears in his eyes. "We became lovers, and she came to me one day to say she carried my bairn. I wanted to marry her. She agreed and went to break her betrothal. Sweet Mary believed that Angus wouldnae want her any longer if he knew she'd been unfaithful and carried my seed. She'd be free to marry me."

Tynan stopped. Pain etched his eyes with a muddy, deep agony. Dark pain for Mary and for himself. When he spoke again, his voice halted and hardened, as if he could force down the agony if he tried.

"He killed her."

Three words, said slow and solid.

"Tynan." She reached for his shoulder and pressed, wanting to give him what comfort she could.

"I was in a rage ye cannae imagine."

Alenna could imagine, but she said nothing.

"She was found at the home he was makin' for her. His sword…'twas found at the site with her blood on it."

"What happened then?"

"He ran the night he murdered her. I thought to hunt him down like the animal he was and kill him."

"You didn't?"

"Her maither and father begged me nae to go. They had seen Angus' rage and thought he might kill me. I dinnae care. I thought of nothin' but takin' his life, as he had taken hers. I tracked him into the deepest, most dark area of the Highlands, but he escaped. I searched for months, but never found him. He disappeared like a ghostwraith."

"You never heard about him again?"

"I heard some months later he had been killed in a fight over another woman. Would that I could have been the one to kill him." His voice thinned and for a single moment she imagined he might release the rage. Drive his fist against the stone wall behind her, smash the solid hate and repressed fury into oblivion. He leaned against the wall, once again bracketing her with his arms. "Now ye ken about Mary."

Tears stung her eyes, but she forced them back. He didn't need her to cry again. He didn't need to see her empathetic reaction to his loss. But it hurt her to see him in this mental pain. A suffering that had festered for years.

"I should have gone with Mary to speak to Angus," he said.

"Tynan," she said softly. "You couldn't have known Angus would kill her."

"I should have gone with her. She would be alive today."

"No."

He stepped back from her. "Let us seek Caithleen. She needs ye."

As they left privacy behind, Alenna felt as if she'd altered and aged. Wiser, though perhaps no stronger, she'd discovered her past pain meant nothing in comparison to what this man had endured. He'd come through solid and determined. A survivor. She could hope she would fare so well and be so strong in the days to come.

LIKE THE BARON'S HEART, the donjon was colder than a Highland snowstorm. A tomb awaiting the arrival of the newly dead.

Although used to the brutal elements of the Highlands during winter, Tynan felt the chill like a death sentence. If he'd taken to fancy, the eerie feeling might swamp him like a bad dream, drowning him in the evil he sensed simmered below the surface of his lordship's noble title. He wished he had the facts to expose the baron for what he was. Instead he'd waited and waited to gather the evidence of the man's true nature. He'd yet to succeed.

Tynan waited in the antechamber off the bedchamber that served as the baron's personal quarters. He was worried about Clandon. Obviously the baron planned something concerning Alenna and Caithleen, and Clandon's fate might be a part of that plan.

Caithleen would lose her status as the baron's concubine.

Tynan became more certain with every moment that Alenna would be the baron's new mistress within days.

As he waited for the baron to appear, he recalled the shattering kiss he had shared with Alenna earlier in the day. She'd provoked him with her pushing, her boldness. Yet this very boldness set him off—more and more he lost control when he was with her, unable to reject her. She drove him mad.

When he'd pressed her against the wall, he'd wanted to lift her skirts right then and press deep inside her silken warmth. Take her until she cried out and he felt the hot clasp of her pleasure once more. Being inside her had bewitched him and he regretted releasingplanting his seed inside her.

Nay.

He did not.

God help him, but he would give almost anything, do almost anything to take her again and plant his seed so far up inside her she would blossom with his child, and every man would know that she was his.

But despite this ramming need, he reigned in his lust with a reminder that Alenna didn't belong with him, and if he took her she once more would surely die…just as Mary and Florie had died.

Perhaps he'd already doomed her. And just that thought alone kept him from taking her again. Even so, he realized he fought for more than Clandon and Caithleen. He fought for Alenna's favor.

There. He'd admitted it. When it came down to it, he should want Alenna to hate him. Yet everything within him tightened with pain at the thought she might think ill of him. Aye. Her response to his kisses and caresses, her willingness to take his seed into her sweet body said she did not hate him, and for that he was grateful.

Tynan smiled. He was more than confused—he was bluidy mad. How many times had she said that she thought him a barbarian? Yet when she'd taken his cock into her hot body and fucked him into insanity, he thought he'd never stop coming, shooting endlessly into her—

He heard footsteps coming toward the chamber and tightened his hand on the dagger at his waist.

"Tynan."

Tynan turned and bowed as the baron came into the room. "My lord."

The baron had dressed as if ready for the assembly. "May I offer you refreshment?"

Tynan strode forward until he stood within a few short feet of the baron. "Nay. I have little time."

A barely imperceptible nod tilted the baron's head. "Then pray tell me what brings you here."

"Clandon. He is in the dungeon."

"He was caught stealing bread from the kitchens and shall be punished."

"I would ask for the boy's freedom."

One of the baron's eyebrows twitched, but the rest of him remained still as marble. "On what grounds?"

"He is a truthful boy and wouldnae steal."

"But he was caught with bread from my kitchen in his hands."

Tynan pressed his suit. "Did yer lordship see him do it?"

The baron stiffened, his face going indignant. "You would not find me near the kitchens."

"Then who accuses him?"

Tynan saw it...a slight slip in the austerity of the baron's face. A resentment at the questioning.

"Kitchen servants," the baron said.

"And what witnesses are these? I would speak with them."

"I will give you no names. I will not have witnesses alarmed."

Taking another tack, Tynan said, "I plead then for mercy. As a boy, he has no the understandin' of a man. Though I give him money, 'tis no much. Sometimes he finds himself hungry. Ye can see from his bony body he gets little to eat."

The baron cracked a chill smile full of satisfaction, deceit and no regrets. "You are most generous."

"If yer lordship shows pity, all in the castle will see that ye are a merciful master. If yer lordship would allow me to take the boy as my ward—"

"Enough!" The baron's expression stiffened even more than Tynan thought possible.

Tynan knew everything came down to a battle of will or of birthright. Perhaps both. Tynan wondered if he might find himself in the dungeon with Clandon.

The baron strode about the room for a few moments, then went to a window to peer out, as if he could see the whole world through the little slit. Everything in his bearing said that the world belonged to him.

"I think not," the baron said, his voice flat.

He turned and flashed a harsh smile. "Many who would have pleaded for the boy would be in that dungeon with him right now, for challenging my authority. But you have always served me well. Give me no reason to doubt that loyalty."

Tynan knew when his battle was lost. Haste or further argument would make matters worse. Time to retreat and come back with another attack, at another time.

Tynan bowed. "Aye, my lord."

With that solemn agreement, Tynan left the room.

CHAPTER 17

Alenna slipped the kirtle and surcoat of blue over her head and smoothed it down with her fingers. As she arranged the band and veil on her head, she wished for a mirror. She enjoyed the clean scent of lavender soap, thankful Caithleen had an extra piece of the soap to give her. Nothing had felt better than rinsing her hair over and over, after a scrubbing with the soap.

She thought she might freeze to death in the cold room before her hair dried, but she couldn't stand to let her hair go more than two days without a wash.

As she fastened the veil under her chin, she realized lack of conveniences became more a way of life the longer she resided in this time. So much had changed since she'd dropped through time into this bizarre place, it seemed far more than a month had passed. Less and less did she think of Demi and her other friends in the future. Even her connections to Caithleen and Elizabet became tighter, more meaningful than those relationships she'd had in the twenty-first century.

In truth, she hadn't thought much about returning to her time at all lately.

Why?

She knew why, but admitting it didn't come easy. *No. No.* She couldn't say it. She wouldn't say it.

Tynan.

Alenna took a deep, shuddering breath and tried not to think about him.

Reluctantly she put on the heavy necklace the baron had given her. As the large garnet nestled between her breasts, the heavy, cold press of the necklace felt like a harness. A stamp of ownership. Skin prickling in distaste, she walked to one of the windows and watched the light drizzle raining down. Winter seemed well upon them. Tonight she'd need the cloak Tynan had given her.

Tynan. Damn him. She couldn't stop thinking about him.

Contemplating the man set her blood on fire, in more than one way. She felt a driving need within her to see him. Touch him. And yes, if she really admitted to herself...kiss him and take him into her body again. God, how she wanted him.

Alenna turned away from the window with an impatient sound.

She wondered what Tynan was doing, where he was, what he was thinking. Her extreme desire for him grew every time she saw him. How did she stop these feelings that flowed through her whenever he came near? How?

Like a piece of wood caught in the vortex of a tornado, he drew her to him, but Tynan drifted from extreme to extreme. Sometimes he seemed a tender and giving man...other times a cool, hard, unforgiving warrior. Yet her trust had heightened tenfold after his care of her at the dungeon. The tender way he'd held her in his arms, his story about Mary...it had broken barriers and allowed her see into his soul. Somewhere, in that hard shell of a man, love remained.

Determined, she forced her mind away from thoughts of Tynan and back onto what would happen tonight at the assembly. Tynan's refusal to help her set up Dougald and Caithleen hadn't deterred her from the goal. If he wouldn't help, she'd make sure Caithleen made it clear to Dougald during the party that she wanted him. Although hesitant to be so bold, the girl had acceded to Alenna's assurances of success.

Certain Caithleen might escape the baron's clutches for a fortnight, Alenna began to fear for herself. What if the baron picked her tonight? The idea sickened her. What the hell was she going to do?

Caithleen entered the room, her feeble smile a poor attempt at masking her true feelings. Tension had etched lines into her face, disguising her youth, dark circles marring her pretty eyes.

Frantic for news of Clandon when Alenna first returned to the donjon, Caithleen admitted the baron had thrown Clandon into the dungeon when she'd talked back to him one too many times to suit him. He'd hit her when she'd pleaded for her brother's safety. She acknowledged that her pleas drove the baron into a rage and he beat her across the back with a switch. Soreness made it difficult for her to move.

Alenna's stomach churned with rage and she worked hard to calm down. Even now the anger ate at her like a wild beast.

"Aye, but that's a lovely dress," Caithleen said. "Tynan will take one look at ye and want ye as his partner."

Alenna scoffed. "I'm not important tonight. The goal is to get you away from the baron."

Plucking nervously at her long hair, which hung loose down her back, Caithleen cast a glance at the door. "Do ye think this will work? If he hurts Dougald, I dinnae think I could live with it."

Reaching for her young friend's shoulders, Alenna spoke firmly. "Dougald is tough."

"Tough?"

Alenna smiled. "Strong. A warrior of superior strength."

Caithleen looked into the air, a dreamy expression erasing

her apprehension and replacing it with a porcelain smile. "That he is." Caithleen touched the necklace around Alenna's throat, then jerked her hand back as if she'd received a bite. "'Tis an evil thing."

"You know I don't want to wear this necklace."

"Aye. 'Tis as ye say. He commanded ye to wear it. Ye had no choice."

Alenna sighed. "I had a choice, but if I didn't wear it, God knows what he'd do." She gave Caithleen the brightest smile she could. "No. I think I'll do well to stay away from men tonight. Or any night from now on."

Caithleen's smile said she didn't quite believe her.

* * *

TYNAN'S GAZE swept around the great hall. As minstrels played a song, loud laughter and chatter rose high to the cathedral ceiling. Couples danced about the room, their steps intricate and precise. Sounds of revelry reached an annoying din.

All the merry making did little to expel the gnawing jealousy building within him. Since the assembly had started two hours ago, Alenna had barely spared him a glance, dancing first with one man and then another. Now she danced with the baron.

Tynan sat at one of the trestle tables and brooded, as the men around him laughed and eyed the women they planned to take for a fortnight. Swinging his gaze in Alenna's direction, he watched as she danced awkwardly, obviously unsure of the steps. Still…tonight she looked…

Enchanting.

Did she have any idea how she made his cock ache? He was jealous of the material that clung to her long arms, her breasts and waist. He watched the material fishtail, sweeping the floor as she danced. She looked bluidy happy, grinning like a wee jester.

With jealousy came a streak of despair.

Their last encounter showed she desired him, but he wanted more. He felt he knew her well, yet knew her not at all. More than a burgeoning need for her body, he had a need to learn things about her she had yet to reveal.

After his audience with the baron proved useless, he wallowed in a helplessness he hadn't felt since Florie's death. A spike of pure mental agony wrenched his soul. He could not let the same fate befall Caithleen and Alenna as had befallen Mary and Florie. He hadn't protected them from the evil that rotted men's hearts.

His fingers clenched his wooden goblet and he was half tempted to rip Alenna from the baron's arms. To take her away from the danger hovering over her like an ax at the executioner's block. Damn her. Ever since she'd appeared like a ghost in his life, his ability to see a clear goal, to know what do next, was frayed.

Tynan glared at the goblet in his hand, realizing he needed his wits about him more than he needed wine. Formulating his goals, he straightened his back. If he continued to fail in his duty, in his convictions, his life would not be worth living.

Somehow he had to keep Clandon safe as well, and this meant getting the boy away from the area entirely.

How could it be arranged?

And if Alenna wasn't careful, the baron would take his base heart and wretched needs—

Damn the baron to eternal hell. And damn himself for this infernal desire for Alenna. The baron's heart might be made of stone, but Tynan's heart turned to bluidy mush whenever she came within his presence. He closed his eyes and remembered her words.

If you never have love at least once in your life, you have nothing. Even if you lose it.

He'd found himself returning to those words over and over

again. When she'd come to his door, bruised and needing his help, he discovered he could not refuse her anything. Their sexual encounters should have satisfied him, but they only made him long for her with a deep, heavy ache in body and soul.

Tonight the baron was vigilant. Tynan saw the way he looked at Alenna. The idea of Alenna being forced...of being trapped under that man's body as he rutted over her, made Tynan's stomach churn. Tynan turned away his morose thoughts and noted Baron Carruthers sat at the head table, close to Caithleen. The man had a wife, but he'd left her at his castle, and his lascivious glance landed first on Caithleen, then Alenna.

"Humph," Tynan said to no one in particular.

Dougald slapped him on the back. "What ails ye? Are ye still pinin' for the lass?"

Tynan grunted. "I dinnae ken what lass ye speak of."

Dougald laughed loud enough that the other knights at that end of the table looked his direction. "Why Alenna, of course."

"If ye ken what's guid for ye, ye'll keep yer mouth shut," Tynan growled.

"Och. The man's fair in his cups over her."

The men at their side of the table laughed.

"Ye are no exactly sober," Tynan said, wondering how much ale Dougald had consumed.

"Aye." He lowered his voice so only Tynan could hear. "But this is my last sip. I want to be able to do my duty tonight."

Tynan had no illusions about what the other man meant. Too much drink meant he wouldn't be able to service whatever wench he chose for the game.

"Now ye are another matter," Dougald said as he slapped his friend on the back again. "If ye keep drinkin', ye'll no be able to—"

"I told ye to shut yer trap."

Dougald laughed. His glance flickered to Caithleen and his

eyes grew warm, then he whispered, "I'm takin' Caithleen for the game."

"What?"

"I'm choosin' her tonight. I think she likes me."

"I have it on guid authority she likes ye very well."

Leaning forward, Dougald once again stared at Caithleen. This time they made eye contact.

"Eh? What authority is this?" Dougald said without taking his gaze off Caithleen.

"A secret source."

"Now ye sound like a damned bluidy spy."

Tynan kicked him under the table.

"Ow! What—"

"Keep yer mouth shut. Do ye want someone to think we're plottin' against his lordship?"

Dougald winced. "Yer in a right nasty mood. Are ye no goin' to do the game?"

Tynan didn't answer. Shoving aside the rest of his wine, his gaze went once more to Alenna. He gritted his teeth. What choice did he have? He couldn't let the baron, or any other man, trap Alenna in his clutches.

He turned to Dougald. "I need to speak with ye outside before the games start."

* * *

"I'M SO glad the baron let ye talk with us," Elizabet said. She smiled at Alenna and moved to give her room in the circle of women that included Caithleen, Johanna and another woman Alenna hadn't seen before.

Surprised that Elizabet had come to the event, she asked, "I thought you weren't coming?"

Elizabet gazed about the room as if she expected someone to jump up and bite her. "Aye, but Johanna convinced me she would ignore any man who wished to dance tonight. She is here merely to watch others." Taking a deep breath she continued. "Ye escaped the baron's clutches, I see."

"I told him I was tired of dancing." Alenna spoke the truth. Her feet were tired and she wanted out of the baron's grasp.

The unidentified woman grinned at her. She looked to be about forty, with a kind expression and mischief in her eyes. Almost as tall as Alenna, her long hair fell down her back in a length of grey. Braided with brilliant cords of green and blue to match her luxurious blue attire, her hair was obviously her crowning glory.

"This is Marie," Elizabet said. "Her guidman is Steward to Baron Carruther's estate. He wasnae able to make the journey to MacAulay Castle."

Alenna curtsied. "How do you do?"

The woman curtsied as well. "I have heard from Elizabet that ye are but new arrived here. Tynan of MacBrahin's cousin."

"Aye," Alenna said.

Marie leaned forward slightly and whispered, "Is it true what they say of him? I hope he picks me tonight."

Alenna darted a glance in Elizabet's direction, but Elizabet did nothing but smile.

"What is it they say about him?" Alenna asked.

"Pish. How is it that ye havenae heard?" The older woman lowered her voice even more. "He can satisfy a woman until she's screamin' for him to stop."

Alenna felt a blush spread across her cheeks like a heat wave. Admittedly, the woman's question didn't embarrass her as much as the image forming in her mind of Tynan making love.

"He can ride a woman all night before he satisfies himself," Marie said as if she already knew the answer to her first question.

Before Alenna could formulate a coherent answer, the baron

clapped his hands together and thus silenced the room. With the quiet came dread. No doubt he meant to start the games.

The baron lifted his goblet to the crowd. "Honorable ladies and gentlemen. I am glad you are able to attend tonight and that you will be able to stay with us here at the castle for a fortnight. It gives me great pleasure to join with you in this special game. You all know how it commences. A man will choose his lady for the next dance. And during that dance, he will declare his intentions toward the lady. If she accepts his terms for the fortnight, he will shout to the room that she has accepted. The first man to receive agreement of his terms is the winner. And the man receives more than just the beautiful lady."

The baron lifted a small, black box from the table. "Inside this box is a precious item, that no one but myself has seen. 'Tis the man's payment, to do with as he chooses." The baron slapped his hands together again. "Start the games!"

The baron turned his gaze directly onto Alenna and she shivered. What was she going to do?

As the minstrels played a new song, her throat tightened and the bruises on her neck throbbed with the memory of the baron's cruelty.

She knew what she must do.

She would approach Tynan and ask him to choose her for the fortnight. Of course she would make it clear he couldn't take her in the carnal sense. Would he accept her terms?

Elizabet grabbed Alenna's arm and said unnecessarily, "The games have begun."

Alenna looked around the room, her pulse leaping. She shouldn't feel this way. Her heart pounded knowing any minute the baron would pick her. Images of what deeds the baron might have in mind made her skin crawl with revulsion.

Dougald advanced toward the group of women. His boyish, flirtatious smile landed squarely upon Caithleen.

"He's comin' for me," Caithleen said, her voice a soft whisper.

"He's a braw one," Marie said, her hands on her hips, her stare assessing Dougald like a piece of livestock.

Dougald stopped in front of Caithleen, bowed and held out his hand. "If ye were to dance with me, I would be most honored."

As Caithleen nodded and put her hand into his, Alenna looked about the room for the baron. Seated at his dais table, he observed the group without a hint of malice.

Relieved, she watched as Dougald led Caithleen to the dance floor.

Mission accomplished.

She saw the baron stand and start toward her. Fear battered her chest, cutting off her breath. Elizabet clasped her arm again.

"The baron comes this way," she said, her voice an urgent whisper.

"Aye," Marie answered. "And he's not a bad one either."

Little did the dimwitted woman know.

Alenna held her breath. Soon he'd reach for her hand and he'd lead her to the dance floor. She had to get to Tynan now.

When Tynan's big form appeared in front of her, his hand outstretched to her, she started in surprise.

"Tynan." Her voice sounded breathless to her own ears.

He bowed, his gaze sweeping over her in an unmistakable ravening assessment. Flustered, she forgot to curtsy. When Tynan moved slightly, she saw the baron come to a dead halt in the middle of the room, his face flushed, his jaw tight.

"Dance with me, Alenna," Tynan said softly.

Music faded into the background. The sound of ribald laughter and hale talk vanished. She could only see the man in front of her and the possibilities in his words. When had he last looked at her that way? Something had altered within him. How she knew she couldn't be certain, but every centimeter within her detected the transformation. Maybe it was in the way his dark gaze never left her, or the way he touched her.

Alenna knew he would defy anyone to come between them.

Tonight he wore a black shirt covered by a plaid he had secured at his shoulder with a brooch. He wore something that would eventually evolve into the modern day kilt and she surreptitiously admired his strong legs. Everything about him spoke of primitive needs, and he didn't look as if he planned to take prisoners.

Dazed, she didn't take time to look at Elizabet or at Marie.

Alenna put her hand in his and he led her to the dance floor without another word. Whispers of speculation echoed around them, but she couldn't have cared less.

As they danced his gaze caught hers and held, while they moved through the steps Caithleen had taught her earlier in the day. Each precise and gentle movement of their bodies as they came closer and paced away resembled a mating dance. Within her imagination erotic scenes flowed and brought a flare of heat to every inch of her body. The music seemed to talk to her and draw her closer to him. The lute and cymbalum hummed in an oddly carnal tune, when she never would have expected such simple sounds to be so thrilling. As the music drew them together yet again, they stayed close for several moments longer than they should.

"This ornament," he said, staring at the necklace. "The baron gave it to ye?"

"Yes," she said. "He wanted me to wear it tonight."

Tynan nodded. Alenna couldn't tell if he disapproved of her wearing it, and she wished she didn't care whether he approved or not.

"'Tis a mark of ownership, this necklace," he said.

Ownership.

The word stung. Suddenly the heavy jewelry felt like a dog's collar. She wished she could take it off. Here. Now.

"He can't buy me."

"Nay. He willnae buy yer soul but he will try."

That the baron would be certain of her total acquiescence frightened her.

"I won't let him," she said.

This seemed to pacify Tynan somehow and his eyes grew warm.

"Ye were surprised," he said in her ear, then gently pushed her away so she could twirl.

When she came back to him and clasped his warm hands Alenna asked, "By what?"

"That I chose ye. Ye dinnae expect it."

"No," she said softly.

His fingers laced through hers and he drew her hand to his lips, pressing a kiss to her knuckles. The warmth of it tingled up her arm.

"And ye dinnae want it."

He said it like a fact, but it sounded like a question on her ears. "No," she said unwilling to tell him the truth.

"Would ye have the baron? Would ye have his dirty hands and body upon ye, before ye would have me again?"

The question shook her. "No."

Alenna knew her monosyllabic answers enticed him to go deeper with his questions, but she couldn't say more. He would have to excavate the truth from her inch by inch, like a psychoanalyst extracting answers from a patient. Agonizing footfall by footfall. She knew what paralyzed her. The fear that if Tynan made love to her, she wouldn't be able to resist him, and another piece of her heart would fall.

As the music increased in tempo, his gaze grew hotter and hotter, smoldering with erotic possibilities. "Then ye do want me?"

"I was going to ask you to dance, and then you came to me before the baron could offer—"

"Do ye want me?"

She couldn't say it. She couldn't.

"Go with me now. I'll no take ye unless ye tell me ye want me. Whatever ye choose, ye will be safe with me."

He offered her shelter in the Black Tower. He offered her his body. He didn't offer her his heart.

Perhaps, if he had given his heart…

"Will ye come with me?" he asked again.

She must have him. "Yes."

He stopped immediately and held her hand aloft in his, so all could see their connection. "She has accepted my terms!"

Loud and deep, his voice boomed so no one could fail to hear him. All around them people started to clap and smile.

Not the baron.

He stood behind the table at the dais, his eyes dark with something Alenna thought might be anger, or even jealousy. But, no. The man had no heart. The only feeling he could have would be animosity, because he'd been thwarted in his goal to possess her.

"Silence!" The baron roared. Every noise came to an abrupt halt. For a terrifying second she thought the baron would say their choice was not acceptable. The baron cleared his throat and picked up his goblet. "To Tynan of MacBrahin and the lovely Alenna."

All around them people held up their goblets in a toast and took a drink.

The baron set down his goblet and retrieved the small black box. He came around the table, down the steps of the dais and straight toward them. As he approached, Alenna stood still, fear pumping through her veins harder than water bursting a damn.

Everything seemed to slow to a crawl. No doubt when she drew a deep breath, everyone in the hall would hear her. Her heart started a fearful tattoo and her palms grew sweaty. Tynan gripped her hand tightly until it almost hurt, as if he feared she'd escape. Indeed, something could happen. Something appalling and horrible and she'd be torn from him forever.

Struggling to control this ridiculous fear, she thought of how well she'd survived until now in this alien world. But maybe nothing was scarier than the truth. She'd admitted to Tynan of MacBrahin she would accept his offer, and instead of taking advantage he'd said he offered her shelter.

Not love.

Not a few minutes of wild distraction.

Protection without any strings or obligations.

Whether Alenna wanted it to or not, another modicum of her heart that had dangled free, waiting for Tynan to claim it, fell to him anyway.

She had to do this for Tynan. She couldn't lose control and go screaming from the room like a ninny. As her breaths pushed in and out she concentrated on slowing them down, on bringing her muscles back into command. Loosening and relaxing, she gentled her death grip on Tynan's hand and dared to look at him. Full of serious reassurance, his gaze said everything would be all right.

The baron stood in front of them, his eyes glassy and arrogant on the edge of drunkenness. Perhaps he would have challenged Tynan if he'd been sober, but even this seemed doubtful. He'd look like a fool in front of these people, and she guessed he wouldn't enjoy the embarrassment.

The baron nodded to them and bowed. He handed Tynan the box. "Take this with my compliments, Tynan. You have won a lady of great virtue."

"Thank you, my lord."

A challenge formed in the older man's expression, as if the game was not concluded and yet another prize waited to be won.

"Open it and show all what you have won."

Tynan opened the box and revealed a garnet ring that matched the necklace Alenna wore around her neck.

Alenna gasped.

Her ring. The garnet ring.

The baron had her ring from the dig. How and where had he acquired it?

Tynan took the ring and solemnly lifted her left hand. Alenna's heartbeat quickened as he slipped the heavy jewelry onto her ring finger, then looked at her. His gaze was hot, intent and full of a million promises she feared and wanted all at the same time.

The baron cleared his throat. "Would that I had been more swift of foot, Tynan."

Tynan kept his hold on her hand and nodded. "Had I seen ye were so intent, my lord, I would have yielded."

Alenna knew his assertion meant nothing. Tynan made small talk to appease the nobleman's ego.

"Go in peace," the baron said and backed away from them. Then he turned from them and clapped his hands. "Start the music."

Tynan didn't wait, didn't try to engage her in another dance. He led Alenna through the crowd, accepting with grace the slaps on the back from his friends and the women's knowing gazes.

Dougald and Caithleen blocked their path. As Caithleen approached, a sweet, delighted smile on her face, Alenna felt tears form. Caithleen hugged Alenna and whispered in her ear.

"Thank ye. Thank ye for helpin' me. I didn't think Dougald would come for me."

Alenna drew back. "Be happy."

After Tynan shook hands with Dougald, he clasped Alenna's hand and pulled her through the remainder of the crowd. She hung back a little, dazed by everything that had happened and by a strange anticipation.

Tynan had won her.

The idea of a man winning her should have rankled. Instead, sweet longing and piercingly hot desire tangled inside her.

At the doorway a cold, driving wind screamed like a hundred banshees and blew rain into their faces, lashing at their clothes.

Once outside the donjon, she disengaged her hand from his. "Wait."

"Nay. There is no time to wait." He grabbed her hand again and walked with her toward the tower.

"But—"

Before she could say another word, he turned her about and yanked her against his chest. And then his lips came down hard on hers.

CHAPTER 18

Startled by the suddenness of Tynan's embrace, Alenna didn't move for several seconds. As he kissed her with almost frantic intensity, she subsided against him in pleasure.

Despite the rain soaking her, warmth flooded her entire body. He didn't cajole her, he devoured, using his tongue to arouse her. It was hot, wild and burning.

Suddenly he drew back, putting her away from him. He grasped her arm and tugged her onward. She trotted alongside of him, her breath coming in gasps.

When they reached the tower, Tynan wrenched the door open. Once inside he secured the door and turned back to her. As he stood in front of the door, his looming presence assured no escape. His gaze burned like a brand, holding her captive, reminding Alenna of the first time she'd tried to escape this room. Then he'd taken her in his arms and kissed her with a passion she'd never before experienced. Every time he'd kissed her, her pleasure had increased, her need had blossomed. Back and forth she'd argued with herself, denying this desire that raged within her and didn't show any sign of dissipating.

She dangled over a cliff, unsure whether to jump or to step back. To jump meant an uncertain fate. To step back meant this ache in her soul for fulfillment, for connecting with this man, would remain unanswered.

As he swung away and lit the candles on the table, Alenna stood as stiff as a board, befuddled by aching desire and trepidation. Tynan would never harm her, that she knew for certain, but the moment crawled out until tension drew her muscles tight. He turned back to her.

"Now ye can yammer all ye like," he said quietly, as if nothing of consequence had happened at the great hall.

"For your information, I wasn't planning to yammer." She crossed her arms and turned away. "Thank you for...for saving me by accident from the baron."

"Eh?"

"I know you didn't really want to do this. You did it out of a sense of obligation and because you hate to see women abused by other men. You've done a very honorable thing."

Arms at his sides, his fists clenched, he moved closer until he towered over her. "Ye dinnae ken."

"What don't I understand? You saved me from the baron. I was just surprised. I thought you said you weren't participating in the games."

He swallowed hard. "I couldnae stand the thought of ye bein' taken' by that—"

He stopped, and at his revealing words, her heart turned over with dawning wonder. Silence hung like a cloak over their heads, until she could barely stand the quiet.

Finally Tynan asked, "Are ye all right, sweet?"

The softness of his words and the gentleness of his expression made her throat tighten and tears come to her eyes. She couldn't look at him or speak.

"Jesu," he whispered and reached for her. Drawing her into

his arms, he gathered her close until she felt the heat of his hard chest, his loins, his rock-solid thighs. He pushed his hand under her veil and smoothed her hair with his fingers, rubbed her back with soothing strokes. "I cannae stop my need for ye any longer. I had to get to ye before the baron."

"You saw him coming for me? But you said—"

"I did see him. But I was already on my way. If he had tried to leave with ye, I would have taken ye from him."

Surrendering to the joy she felt at his words, Alenna put her arms around his waist and sank into the comfort he offered. A silence wrapped around them, filled with unspoken confessions.

When she found her voice, she said, "Did you ask Dougald to choose Caithleen?"

"I dinnea have to. When I told Dougald how she was bein' hurt, he had no doubt about takin' her with him tonight."

"Thank you," she said, a lump growing in her throat.

Tynan drew back from her the smallest bit. She removed her arms from about his waist, placing her hands on his chest. Underneath her fingers his heart beat steady and strong. The feel of him beneath her fingers, the male scent of him, the steady regard of his gaze was all she needed for now. The roof could fall down around her and she wouldn't care.

With infinite care he leaned down and touched her cheek with his lips, cupped her face gently with one palm. His lips lingered and pressed. Comforting and warm, his palm slid along her skin, reaching around to remove the band holding her veil in place. The silky material glided along her sensitive skin as he removed the veil, tickling and arousing almost as much as his fingers. He cupped the back of her neck and his other arm went around her waist.

"Do ye know how much I want ye?" he asked.

Doubts crowded her mind. "I wasn't sure…"

"Not sure?" Tynan asked as he pressed a kiss to the tip of her nose, then to her forehead. "Ye have bewitched me with a spell so deep I cannae escape. Shall I call ye a witch?"

A smile parted her lips. "Is that a compliment?"

His mouth traced her cheek and the dazzling pleasure of his simple touch rocked through her.

"Ye are sweet and wild, and I ache for ye," he said huskily.

As his mouth touched her ear Alenna gasped. Nothing now made any difference, nor meant anything except having his hands on her. His lips on hers. His cock deep inside her.

"Ye have tempted me beyond my guid sense, Alenna."

"As if you had any sense to begin with."

He grunted, reaching down to lightly smack her butt.

Alenna gasped. "You…you…"

"Big hairy oaf?"

A giggle slipped from her.

The glimmer in his eyes turned serious. "If I take ye tonight, I'll want to take ye every day of the fortnight."

His bold words ignited the firestorm banked inside her. With a perverse sense of pleasure, she asked, "Why do you want me?"

Instead of answering with words, he touched his lips to hers. A feather brush, that sizzled with heat and flitted away in a second.

"Why?" she asked.

"Ye are a wee silly clootie, if ever I saw one. I've wanted ye from the first time I saw ye."

"Well, you were aroused. I mean in bed…and the first time you kissed me I could feel—"

"Like ye feel me now?"

He cupped her buttocks in both hands and pressed his solid erection into her belly.

"Yes," she whispered.

"Like ye felt me when I slid deep into yer body and gave ye pleasure?"

She flushed with heat.

He tilted her chin up with his index finger. "I'll protect ye from the baron. From anythin'. When I saw ye there in the great hall tonight, I thought I'd die if I couldn't be inside your sweet body, but if ye want this night to end right here, right now..."

No. She wanted him and would no longer deny it to herself or to him. She reached up and twined her arms about his neck.

"I want you," she whispered. "I can't stand this any longer. Please."

Happiness slammed through Tynan as he took her mouth, molding her warm lips. The heat of his need drummed in the heavy beat of his heart, the hammering of his pulse and the unmerciful throb in his cock and balls.

There was no going back. No stopping the stampede as it rushed toward them, all thoughts of restraint melted. Memories of Mary and Florie disappeared under the sheer weight of his desire. He would die if he couldn't have her.

With a deep groan he plundered her mouth, tracing her lips relentlessly with his tongue until she parted them and allowed him to push deep within.

Alenna pressed herself tight against him, groaning as he kissed her again and again. As his tongue caressed hers, moving in and out of her mouth in an erotic tempo, her nipples hardened and the arousal between her legs rose to a tormenting pitch. With an animal need she grasped at him, returning the steady thrust of his tongue with her own.

Never mind what the consequences would be. Never mind that someday she would be forced to leave him. Right now she wanted to live to the full extent her heart and body would allow. Everything in her pulled tight, begging for release.

Seconds flowed into minutes for Tynan as he plundered her mouth, caressed her back, reached to cup her breasts. With his thumbs he traced circles over her cloth clad nipples and delighted in hearing the gasps and whimpers of excitement erupting from her throat. He wanted to rip the dress off her and taste those budding nipples with his tongue, but excitement slammed through his body and made his fingers tremble.

Tynan had to have her now.

Now. Now. Now.

Tearing his lips from hers, he pressed his forehead to hers and gasped for breath.

"Have ye never done somethin' wild in yer life? Somethin' ye had to do or die?"

"No," Alenna whispered, feeling his hands delineate her ribs, trailing a pattern of heat, sparking an earthquake tremor within her body.

With deliberate steps Tynan backed her up until she felt the stone wall behind her. He lifted her against the wall, shoving her skirts up and situating himself between her thighs. She wrapped her legs around him and with his powerful body he held her in place. The hot, startling feel of his naked cock against her hot, wet folds made her lips part and her eyes widen. Staring into her eyes, he dared her to look away, and she saw the fever of his need reflected. Gently he nudged her folds with his erection, barely parting her. A tiny sound ripped from her throat almost unwillingly.

He answered with a sound of deep, male appreciation. A soft, sexy smile covered his mouth. "I willnae hurt ye."

A flush moved from deep in her loins and traveled to her throat, brushing upward to her face. In the past her lovemaking with men had been so tame. She'd never imagined a need this hot…this uncontrollable.

"Ye have never felt a man's need like this?"

"Never," she whispered, a small gasp uttered with pleasure as he pushed a little further into her.

His boldness, the straightforward taste of his passion drew her deeper into a frantic need for completion. She wanted this quick joining as much as he did. With tiny thrusts he tested her, dipping a little way inside, retreating, dipping. All the while he stared deep into her eyes.

Another whimper came from her throat. The heat of his steady probing set a throbbing deep into her loins. She ached high up inside, her body drawing him inward to her wet, sensitive folds.

"It has never felt like this," she said, gasping in pleasure.

He made a primitive sound, deep in his throat and his lips captured hers, hot and sudden. As his tongue sought hers he thrust firmly and his cock thrust all the way to her cervix, forcing another sound of startled excitement from her throat. Alenna's fingers grabbed at his shoulders, then she slipped her arms around his neck. He filled her, he completed every inch until her entire world pinpointed down to this moment. This unbelievable urgency. Eager for his taste, she kissed him frantically, meeting his tongue with a fervor all her own. She squirmed on his cock, loving the thickness stretching her to the limit.

She expected him to thrust against her with haste after their eagerness to join. Instead he gyrated slowly, each stroke a gentle, though thorough penetration that generated pleasure so exquisite she felt dizzy with the sensual tumult. Time disappeared and divided as Tynan moved slowly within her, turning her world into a sensual delight.

She raked her hands through his hair, assuaging her need to feel the texture of the dark strands. And yet it wasn't enough. As she strained against him, savoring each movement of his body, she explored his shoulders, feeling the muscles strain as he held her against the wall.

She tore her lips from his, gasping with her need for release. Her excitement had never charged forward so quickly, nor had her need been as potent.

"Oh God," Alenna whimpered, shuddering, burying her face in his shoulder. "Please. Please."

She couldn't move her hips, but the heat of his steel-hard cock caressed, and her sensitive walls trembled around his cock.

"Aye," he said, his tone hoarse and strained with passion. "Aye."

He thrust harder, spearing into her core with jabs that drew out the animal in them both. Hearing his deep moans of satisfaction, she shook with pleasure.

"Aye," he said again, his breathing fast and heavy.

She strained against him, moving to give them both the result they needed. Behind her closed eyelids, a red fire sparked and her world coalesced. Her pussy convulsed around his hot length and a scream rent her throat. She worked her hips as the climax slammed through her, shaking as the liquid heat melted her with bliss.

He shoved and shoved, deep, hard.

And although she'd never known it was possible for her, the pleasure peaked yet again and again, again…a series of explosions that eased and spiked with each thrust. Alenna cried out as the climaxes threatened to blind her forever, until one last tremor of enjoyment remained. He tore his mouth from hers as he drove hard and buried his face in her neck. A shout left his throat as he shook, trembled. She shivered in delight as his hot seed bathed her inner walls.

Tynan thought his breath would never return. The ecstasy he'd felt buried deep inside her incredible hot channel had to be a dream. Nothing could ever feel as exciting as this. He realized his heavy weight held her against the wall and not only did he remain buried within her, but her legs stayed about his waist.

Her body trembled, and when her inner muscles clenched around him yet again, he grunted.

"Jesu, sweet, yer killin' me."

He watched Alenna intently as she smiled, soft and slow. She clutched at his shoulders and moved her hips. The slight friction sent a hiss through his lips.

"Ye'll be the death of me if ye keep on doin' that."

Mischief lit her eyes. "Little ole' me?"

"Wench."

"Don't call me that—"

He silenced her with a kiss. He didn't want to let her go. He kissed her lips softly. Not once, but twice. Three times. As Alenna twined her arms about his neck and tightened her hold, he felt his body harden inside her.

"I want to feel you around my cock again," he said roughly.

"Oh God," Alenna said, like a fervent prayer. "Yes."

But Tynan didn't ask what she was praying for.

Softly she kissed his cheek, caressed his lips with her fingertips. The heat he saw in her eyes warmed his heart as well as his body.

Keeping her clasped tightly to him, he headed for the pallet. Gently he laid her down, regrettably leaving her body at the same time. She reached for him.

"Nay," he said. "I would have ye naked this time."

In an infinitely small corner of her mind a warning flashed. It threatened to hold her back from the wild desire gathering within her once again. Shoving it ruthlessly away, she watched as he removed his plaid.

"Hurry," she said.

His smile appeared somewhere between amused and shocked. "Nay. I willnae."

He was teasing her. The infernal man was teasing her.

Slowly he allowed the plaid to fall to the floor. With a quick, startling move, he drew the shirt over his head and it fell to the floor. His boots followed. She stared at every impressive inch of him.

"Oh my." The words were out of her mouth before she could stop them. He was the most magnificent male animal she'd ever seen.

Yes, she'd seen those broad shoulders, muscled chest and

powerful arms before. She'd seen those stalwart legs sprinkled with dark hair. She'd felt the heat of that impressive cock deep within.

She hadn't seen them together in one totally amazing package. She was hot for another taste, for another fuck to send her into oblivion.

"Is that meant to be praise, then?" he asked.

She smiled. "Yes."

Tynan's answering grin was cocky and arrogant. As he came toward her she slid back on the bed to make room for him. "Nay. Come to me."

Alenna did as he asked, and as he brought her close he helped her remove her garments one by one until she stood naked in his arms. He stared at her breasts until they burned, and a hard throbbing started between her legs as he gazed at her belly, then to the soft down at the top of her legs.

"So bluidy beautiful," he said, awe in every deep, husky tone.

She thought she'd found happiness when he'd driven her over the edge of passion minutes before, but his regard, the feral intensity in his eyes surpassed any physical passion. With reverence he brought her against him, kissing her softly, gently. Using his lips and tongue with expert skill, he brought a fire deep into her softest center.

He found her secrets. Secrets Alenna had kept hidden from other men. Testing, his fingers took her wetness and circled her hot opening. He teased her with flicks of his fingers across her clit, fondling and playing. His tongue tasted one nipple with steady, mind-melting touches, driving her insane with his gentle touch. He moved to her other breast. Tynan treated her to a double dose of lunacy when he suckled her nipples and thrust two fingers deep into her.

She opened her eyes and watched as a wicked grin spread over his face. Gently he lowered her to the bed. He separated her legs with his hands. As he knelt between her legs he touched her gently from ankle to thigh, and all the while he watched her, observed her reactions. With every sensation that battered at her, she feared for her heart.

She couldn't hold out for long.

She was in danger of falling hard for him.

Alenna ceased to think as his tongue smoothed over her clit. A gasp came from her throat, as much from surprise as excitement. A man had never feasted on her as if she were fine wine and a precious delicacy. As he traced his tongue around her folds, swirling and licking, she arched her hips, wanting so much more. She grasped his head, plunging her fingers into the thick waves. She groaned, thrashed, the ecstasy hovering just out of reach. He parted her folds and settled his mouth over her clit in a kiss, sucking on the sensitive point until she whimpered with the exquisite feeling. Seconds later he drew her wetness downward with his fingers, touching between her buttocks.

Alenna gasped and stared down at his head nestled between her legs. Over and over he spread her moisture down, bathing her until he could slip one finger deep into her backside.

"Tynan." She gasped as his forbidden touch drew her excitement into a frenzy. "Yes. Yes."

Tynan couldn't believe how delicious Alenna was, pleased that she accepted his touch where not every woman would allow such liberties.

Without reserve he devoured and consumed her until he felt her trembling increase. He moved his finger inside her, preparing her for another type of lovemaking he hoped she'd abide. He wanted to slip into all of her, spew his seed deep in her mouth, in her cunny and, in her tight nether hole until he possessed her in every way.

He couldn't stop. Like a stallion bent on charging into the fray of battle, he pursued her pleasure more than his own. On and on he pushed her toward the edge, wildness mixed with a tenderness he'd never felt for another woman. A sense of urgency drove him to bring her to the border, then hold back until she begged him, pleading for release.

He thrust his finger, licked her clit, wanting her so fiercely a growl slipped from his throat.

"Say ye want it. I need to be inside ye. Everywhere inside ye."

She moaned. "Please. Please, Tynan."

He caressed her tight channel as he licked and sucked her clit. Rapidly, he brought her over the brim.

Her back arched as she came, cries erupting through her throat. Immediately he crawled up her body and lowered his hips between her thighs. He posed his cock at her tight anus and started to work it into her hole. She gasped.

"Hurt?" he asked, concerned.

"No. Please. More."

He slipped his arms under her knees and tilted her hips back so that her buttocks rose high and aided penetration. Gratified, he worked his hips back and forth, easing one increment, one inch at a time into the well-prepared opening. He took it slow, even though sweat beaded on his forehead and his heart pounded so hard he thought it might burst from his chest.

Alenna took him within her with a sense of destiny. As if she had always known, from the very first time she'd seen him, that they would be together like this. She'd never wanted anal sex with another man, but with Tynan she wanted it so much she almost screamed for him to take her hard.

With a long, steady push he slowly took her, and as his big cock found its path and surged up her back hole, she cried out in pleasure. *Oh God. That felt...incredible.*

He trembled as he held her, as he delved with agonizing slowness until he could go no farther. She abandoned all coherent thought as he rode her. With every movement, his control thrilled her in a part of her she'd never known existed. She needed him to show her the most animal, the most out of control side of him.

He kept his thrusts slow and deep, pressing inside her with a rhythm that surged in her heart and along her veins. She arched against him, taking his mouth in a deep kiss. She dictated the kiss, pushing her tongue into his mouth. Exploring, she moaned in satisfaction when he made a deep sound of pleasure and slightly increased the tempo of his thrusts. The sensation of his cock caressing her in this new place drew her into a wild, staggering bliss. He controlled her entirely, his thrusts firm but gentle and she sobbed with excitement, her panting, moaning breaths a testament to how much she liked it.

He found one nipple, teasing it with flicks of his tongue, and she arched against him again, whispering his name softly. As he watched her he thought it was the most erotic thing he'd ever seen. Her face flushed, her lips parted as her breath came swift. Although the pleasure threatened to erupt from him, he kept his thoughts steady on making her cry out in ecstasy. He suckled her nipples, nibbled and licked ceaselessly.

Every gasp, every writhing twist of her hips made Tynan shudder with pleasure and he slowed. She pushed up against him.

"Tynan," she gasped.

He knew her agony but he wouldn't relent. He wanted Alenna to know his touch, his lovemaking, as she'd known nothing else. No other man would ever be able to erase the feel of his cock plundering her depths. He eased in and out, the steady thrust and drag of her tightness across his aching flesh quickening his breath.

As his breath came heavy and fast, she knew he wanted her to challenge him. To show him her thoughts could never be for anyone but him. God, how could they be for anyone else?

"Alenna." He groaned her name, guttural and harsh as he quickened his pace.

Alenna was going to die. No way she could survive the pleasure. A cry burst from her, coming between a gasp and a scream. A river of heat sprang from deep within her and swelled to encompass her entire body. And like a drowning woman she let it take her. With a powerful thrust he stiffened and quaked. A loud, harsh cry burst from his throat as he thrust again, and once more. Then he sank upon her and was still.

CHAPTER 19

Tynan couldn't sleep. The sounds of laughing and merrymaking outside had calmed, alerting him that the night grew late.

Alenna lay in his arms, her soft breath stirring the hair on his chest as she nestled close to him in sleep. He brushed a tendril of soft hair back from her face. The sight of the bruise on her forehead stirred fierce, protective feelings and he brushed her cheek with his fingertips, savoring the softness of her skin.

A sigh parted her lips and she snuggled against him like a trusting child. Certainly she was not a child but a grown woman who had shown him powerful passion. With the giving of herself she had set every inch of his body on fire and had at the same time shown him his weakness.

He couldn't resist her.

Gently he kissed her forehead. She sighed again and smiled in her sleep. He touched her skin with increasing desire, savoring the softness of her femininity as if this were the last time. Sweeping his fingers along her body, he stroked a rosy nipple. She moaned…a sweet, yearning sound that fueled his desire high.

When Alenna didn't open her eyes, Tynan leaned down and brushed his tongue around and around the hardened tips of her breasts. She moved in his arms, sighing with pleasure, but still she didn't open her eyes. He ministered to both nipples, licking and tasting, sucking and nibbling gently with his teeth until her breath came fast. He enjoyed the texture of her hard nipple on his tongue, drowning in the scent and feel and taste of her. She had full breasts, but they weren't large, and they fit easily in his palm as he cupped and stroked.

Finally she opened her eyes. The softness in their depths caused his heart to pound. What he saw there frightened him. Scared him so much he knew he had to hide behind the passion. Had to immerse himself in her body and her arms, so he wouldn't think about feelings and wouldn't wonder what would happen when their passion ended.

Eager to brand himself upon her, he urged her over on her stomach. He palmed her back, careful not to massage too hard. His fingers dipped between her folds and found them pleasingly wet. She trembled as he explored her pussy, his fingers slow and gentle but relentless. He dipped three fingers into her pussy, widening her, preparing Alenna for a fast coupling. He wanted her writhing, screaming, demanding. He wanted to show her no one else mattered. With his other hand he fisted his cock and stroked. Jesu, he must have her soon or go mad.

Instead he held back, not wanting to cause her discomfort in any way. He slid his fingers back and forth, caressing her inner walls, spreading her cream all along her pussy lips and reaching deep inside her. As arousal grew, her musky scent flowed all around him. His heartbeat throbbed in his chest as excitement pushed him to act.

When her cries started to escalate, he pulled his fingers from her heat. He drew her hips up and with a relentless shove, plowed straight into her.

She cried out. "Tynan! Oh God!"

He froze, caught up in a mix of emotions. "Did I hurt you?"

"It feels so good. Please. Please more."

Gratified, he set to work, but this was work he would gladly drown in, gladly give her anytime, anywhere. He pumped, stroked with steady, relentless plunges into her body's silky grip. He stroked her supple back, watched her heart-shaped ass wriggle as he palmed her flesh.

By all that was holy, he'd never seen anything more bonnie.

His breath rasped in his throat as he closed his eyes, gripped her hips and increased the pace. Her euphoric cries and pleas for more cut through the air. Before long her tight channel pulsed around him and she cried out, sharp, whimpering cries of soul-staggering ecstasy. He erupted inside her, unable to hold back. Dizzy with pleasure, he jammed into her and spilled inside Alenna with stream after stream of hot seed.

As they came down from the pleasure, he pulled out of her grip and eased her down beside him. Alenna sank into his arms with a sigh, her smile replete and thoroughly content. She fell asleep again, nestled close.

A desire to cherish her, to give her anything and everything she wanted flowed like a warm wine in his blood. That she hadn't spoken, hadn't insisted on talking about what happened between them, made him glad.

Because he was terrified.

He'd vowed so long ago never to make love to a woman again.

Celibacy did not worry a man when he put his body through the paces, training for battle, working his muscles each day until he fell on his pallet too tired to think of anything as basic as animal needs. This woman from the future had changed everything. Her intelligence and determination whittled away at the fortress he'd built.

The ache in his soul increased as he gazed at her. His commitment to stay away from the raw attraction he felt inside crumbled, despite her foreign ways and stubbornness. What could he say about her bravery?

How many other women did he know that could have faced the baron and fear of dungeons, all for the sake of a young boy? How many women did he know that would risk their life to save Caithleen? Risk her life to save him twice. Why had fate sent her through time to him?

The noose around Tynan's heart squeezed so hard it hurt.

He could not. Simply would *not* love her.

Shifting Alenna out of his arms slowly, he rose from the bed and hastily dressed. Maybe if her sweet skin didn't press against him his head would clear and he'd think more like the man he'd been yesterday. Sweet lord, help him. Going back to yesterday wouldn't help. Returning to the time before she appeared from the mist would not help. For now he knew the overwhelming pleasure of sharing her passion.

He covered her with a plaid and left the bed. He stared blankly around the room, as if he'd entered a foreign land. Alenna had dazed him. Stunned him with the force of emotion she'd generated and he felt a strange hollowness.

What if she left? What if she went back to her time?

A lump closed his throat and he had to take a gasping breath to relieve the sensation.

Finally his gaze dropped to the table. The necklace.

He didn't recall removing the glittering gems from her neck last night. But then he'd been too consumed with fire to care. Even now she still wore the ring he'd placed on her finger.

Turning away from more wealth than he'd seen in his life, he went to the hearth. After stoking up a fire, he lowered himself into a chair. Putting his arms on the table and his head on his arms, he thought about what he should do.

Outside the wind screamed like a woman who had lost her only love.

* * *

Alenna woke as the first light of day broke through the shuttered window and the icy air penetrated the generous plaid covering her nakedness.

She reached for Tynan but encountered only cold fur.

Fear traveled like an arrow into her and she sat bolt upright. The last embers of a fire burned in the hearth. Tynan sat at the table, his head down on his arms. Why had he dressed when he could stay in her arms?

"Tynan?"

He slept on. She took in everything about him. The blue-black sheen of his hair as it lay against his stubble-roughened cheek, his thick lashes, the curve of his lips that could smile, frown, or give her such powerful ecstasy.

She reached out to touch him. He came awake with a start as he sat up. His gaze scoured the room, as if he expected intruders.

"What is it?" he asked sharply, standing up so quickly the chair fell backward with a clatter.

Alenna smiled. "Nothing. You're here freezing your butt off, instead of staying warm in bed with me."

He didn't smile. She searched for a way to decipher what she saw in his eyes. A wariness and distrust. No…something far deeper. Then she recalled when he'd told her he'd once loved a woman and had regretted it. She'd witnessed the same look at that time. He bent to retrieve the chair, righting it back onto the legs.

Alenna reached for him, instinctively seeking his warmth and his arms. "What's wrong, Tynan?"

Instead of embracing her as she expected, he took her arms and put her away from him. Hurt went straight through her in a raw punch.

Like a restless animal, he paced the floor, then came to an abrupt halt in front of her. "I cannae do this."

"Do what?"

"Last night. I should have just taken ye from the feast … not…"

His lack of ability to form words, his hesitation, was unusual. The determined man with the clipped speech she'd come to recognize as vintage Tynan had disappeared.

"I took what only yer guidman should."

Was that all that was bothering him? Her honor? Of course. He was a man of the fourteenth century.

Alenna came closer to him and she saw him take a deep breath as they almost touched. "As I told you, I wasn't a virgin. And no one in this time expects me to be. I was supposed to be married once, remember?"

"I had no right. I'm not your guidman."

Reaching up to touch his face, she caressed his hard jaw, rough with dark stubble. "I'm from the twenty-first century. People sometimes take lovers and they don't have to be married. Obviously, it's not that much different now." She shrugged. "I've seen that from the way people took to that party. And here you had me thinking that I should worry about my reputation, and the baron was bold enough to tell me that I shouldn't live with you because it was unseemly." She grinned. "All of you are big liars."

Tynan took her hand from his face. He stepped away and tossed wood into the hearth to make a new fire. The rejection in his actions hurt like a bee sting, and with that came anger. Had everything she'd seen in his eyes been an illusion? She'd seen warmth, tenderness and raw need. Maybe, God help her, even a little love.

"I'm sorry I took advantage—"

"Stop apologizing," Alenna said, feeling her tether snap. "Once and for all, you didn't take advantage of me. I could have refused your offer at the party. Instead I put my hand in yours and left and came here with you." She took a sustaining breath and willed him to listen. She moved closer as she spoke, until she stood near him. "You didn't force me to do anything I didn't want. It was the most special experience of my entire life."

Still he poked at the fire, refusing to look at her, his face granite hard. He acted as if nothing that had happened the last few weeks had transpired. She was back to square one. Back to the day she'd first arrived.

"Tynan, what we had last night…what we have now. I don't want to lose that…it's special…"

A flicker of last night's passion flared in his eyes. She fed on that look and hoped it would grow.

The flame died like a snuffed candle. "I cannae make love to ye again."

Alenna licked her dry lips. All the air seemed to suck right out of the room. "I don't understand. What happened to make you…why are you so cold?"

"I let drink and passion cloud my mind. No more."

As if ice had seeped into her chest, her heart felt heavy and frozen. "Tynan, you loved me like I've never been loved before. You took me away from more than the party." Tears backed up in her throat and burned like an open sore. "You took me out of that vile man's reach."

"And that was how ye repaid me?" he asked as he stopped messing with the fire. "By lettin' me take ye?"

His words, sharp and succinct, blistered her so much that she almost slapped him. Instead she spoke without thinking, without a care as to how he might react.

"How dare you! I did not give you my body as payment. How could you think that? How could you?"

When he gazed at her this time, she saw regret in his eyes. It wasn't enough.

She took a shuddering breath. "I made love with you."

"It isnae love," he said bluntly, coldly. "It cannae be."

She'd never known until that instant what it felt like to have her soul torn out and stomped underfoot. Certainly her breakup with her fiancé had hurt like hell. But nothing prepared her for the hollow ache occupying the spot where her heart once resided.

"No," she said softly, the fight draining from her like blood from a wound. "It was sex. A bed partner for a fortnight, just like you said."

When he said nothing, her heart dropped the final notch.

"Forget it," she said, stomping back to the bed. With haste she threw on her dress. When he came up behind her, she whirled on him. "Where is my cloak?"

She filled time, asking a question that didn't matter in the scheme of things. She had to escape. To ponder what had happened, before she broke down in tears for the second time in two days.

"What are ye doin'?" he asked as she swept by him into the outer room.

"I don't know." She put on her cloak and marched toward the door.

"Wait," he said. She had no time to get the door open before he blocked her way.

"Why should I wait, Tynan? Give me one good reason why I'm here. Because if I stay with the baron he'll treat me like a whore? Beat the life out of me whenever he feels like it?"

"Aye. I told ye that stayin' here ye would be safe."

Alenna made a snorting laugh. "Safe? Hardly. You're here."

"I willnae touch ye again. Not even to kiss ye."

Obviously he didn't plan to move from the door anytime soon and she didn't relish the thought of fighting him to leave.

"Is that what you really want?" she asked.

His mouth opened, then closed. Finally he said, "'Tis how it must be."

"God, you are so full of it."

"Full of what?" His brow creased in mystification.

"I think I see now what your problem is, Tynan of MacBrahin."

When she used his entire name he stiffened, as if his mother had announced an oncoming punishment. Perhaps he remained susceptible to her in a small way. With the slightest trace of hope Alenna pressed her suit.

"Mary's death wasn't just a tragedy to you. It scarred your heart in such a way that the only way you can justify the pain is to blame yourself," she said.

His gaze turned hard as rock. "I am to blame."

"You didn't murder her. Angus did."

"When I took her—" His voice faltered and he cleared his throat. "When she became full with my bairn, I killed her. She would still be alive if I hadnea taken what wasnae mine to take."

"She might have still married Angus. You don't know what would have happened." His silence spurred her on. "You are still in love with her and you can't let go of that love."

"Nay, I dinnae love her…I cannae love—"

"Yes, you can. Admit it. Her death hurt you deeply."

"Aye," he said, the reluctant syllable slipping across his tongue. "Any woman I…any woman I take is cursed to die. I willnae see that happen to you."

It came to her then. She saw it in the grim set of his mouth and the anguish in his eyes. Mary's misfortune certainly didn't complete the entire story of what tortured his soul. Florie had been pregnant and had been taken from him.

Alenna sank onto the pallet. "What else, Tynan? What else keeps you from me?"

He dropped to his knees in front of her and when he looked at her, his gaze had lost its chill. Tynan begging for her sympathy? That this big, strong man needed her understanding came as a sobering thought. Did she honestly have that much control over him?

His hands rested on his trews-covered thighs, and for a wayward momentfraction Alenna remembered touching those rock hard limbs...tracing her fingers over him. A renewed pulse of desire drummed in her, but she shoved it down. Not now. Maybe not ever again.

"I cannae have another woman die because of me. 'Tis my curse. My mother, when I was ten—" He broke off and swallowed hard. "My father beat her to death in front of me own eyes. And I stood there. I was so scared I dinnae move. I let the bastard beat her, Alenna."

"Oh, Tynan," she whispered, laying her hand on his cheek gently. "I'm so sorry."

"When she was...dead...he told me that it wad be a lesson to me. If I disobeyed him, he'd do the same to me."

"You were a child. You couldn't have done anything to save your mother."

"Aye, I could have. I stood there like an ox and listened to her screams."

She cupped his rugged face between her palms and caressed his cheeks with her thumbs. "You were in shock. Your mother's death was your father's fault. And Mary died because of Angus. Florie died under the hands of a murderer. Other people did these horrible deeds. Why are you blaming yourself?"

He didn't answer, and with a sinking sense of inevitability, Alenna saw stubbornness engulf his expression. He believed in this curse, in these horrible tragedies, more than he did her. If he could set her aside so easily, then maybe he'd read the writing on the wall more clearly than she had.

Their passion couldn't continue.

"I cannae do this to you. I've got this demon inside of me."

"There is no demon."

Tynan reached up and pulled her hands from his face, but he held her hands within his. "You mean too much to me to let anything happen to you."

She stood slowly, forcing tears away with effort. "Goodbye, Tynan."

He stood with her as she headed for the door. He stepped in front of her, as he had other times when she'd attempted to get away from him.

"Yer not goin'. I've vowed to take care of ye. 'Tis the least I can do."

"No, Tynan. You're right. You've got to let me go. I can't stay in this room with you for the next fortnight without wanting to make love to you. Without needing your touch. There, I've admitted it. I want you and I know you want me. But you can't or won't let me in. Not where I want to be. Just let me go." Alenna sucked a breath in and knew it sounded like a sob.

A flicker of something like pain passed over his face, momentarily shifting his steely countenance.

"What are you going to do? Keep me prisoner here? Tie me to the bed or the chair?" she asked, turning her words hard. "Would you be like the baron or the other men who abuse their lovers or their wives? Their daughters?"

She saw the fight leave him…the horrifying idea he might in some way be like his own father, like Angus. Like the murderer who had ended Florie's life. She had used his own fears against him and the shame burned her as deep as a knife wound.

"I'll stay with Elizabet, if she'll let me, until I find a way to escape this Godforsaken century. Out of your life," she said, choking the words out.

Slowly he moved out of her way. As she went out the door, anguish gripped her, powerful and devastating. Tears flowed into Alenna's eyes and she almost sobbed. Slamming down the impulse to scream, she left and never looked back.

* * *

Tynan's black mood deepened when he saw Dougald standing at his door later that day.

"What the bluidy hell are ye doin' here?" Tynan asked, scowling.

"I've a guid reason for comin' by. Can we speak? 'Tis most urgent."

Tynan nodded reluctantly and let Dougald inside.

As they settled down at the table Tynan said, "This better be worth it."

Dougald glanced around the room. "Where is Mistress Carstairs?"

"'Tis none of yer concern."

At Tynan's rough statement, Dougald grunted. "Ye are in a most foul mood this morn. Considerin' the way ye ran out of the donjon last night I would have—"

"I dinnae wish to speak of it."

Dougald shook his head. "What has got to ye? Before Mistress Carstairs arrived ye used to have some humor. Now ye do little but snarl. Is there no help for it?"

Tynan let the truth of the words soak into him. Aye, he'd been a bastard sometimes since Alenna had arrived. "Ye ken how I am. Would ye seek to change me now?"

Dougald sighed in exasperation. "Nay."

"Then what have ye come here for, other than to counsel me on women?"

"The baron sent a message out, sayin' he wants us to go to Ruthven's stronghold and negotiate a peace."

"Eh?"

Dougald shifted in his chair as if eager to take some action. "He wishes to talk with us today."

"There are many ears and eyes here I no longer trust," Tynan said. "But ye ken how I feel about the baron."

"Nay. Ye have no told me everythin' about what ye suspect."

Tynan knew he'd been so caught in Alenna's web he hadn't spent time with his friend and hadn't explained the suspicion growing in his gut. He wouldn't let Alenna distract him from important matters any longer.

"Caithleen has suffered at his hands. She told me what he's done. And I saw the marks the Baron made on her back," Dougald said.

Dougald was a fine man, and even though Tynan had heard from Alenna what Caithleen had suffered, he knew Dougald believed in few people but the very innocent. In fact, their friendship would not have been solid but for the battles they had fought and won together against Ruthven's forces.

"Then ye will ken what I say next to be true." Tynan reached for a flagon of wine and poured them each a goblet. Reaching for his own portion of wine, he slammed back the bitter liquid and grimaced.

"I believe the baron has murdered many women," Tynan said.

"Murder," Dougald said, a stunned look dulling his usually bright eyes.

"Though I cannae prove it, he has murdered most of his mistresses. Florie, to be sure. And he might do the same to Caithleen and Alenna. I've stayed here and kept my fidelity to the bastard so I might seek the truth. I wanted proof of his murdering soul."

Dougald's stunned expression changed to anger as he slammed his fist down on the wooden table. "Why would he stoop so low?"

"Ye forget. I have seen men much like him, many years ago."

Recognition dawned over Dougald's face like a new sunrise. "Yer father? Angus?"

"Aye. My father. And Angus." Tynan's pain twisted in his gut like a knife. "'Tis a curse I see their black souls better than others. Mayhap my own dark soul sees a kindred evil within them."

He recognized a beast and a devil when he saw one.

And Baron MacAulay was the beast.

"Nay," Dougald said. "Ye are no like that man. Dinnae ever think that. A more noble soul I have yet to meet, Tynan."

His friend's kind words couldn't comfort him. He struggled for a way to ask Dougald something he might not agree to support. "When yer fortnight with Caithleen is over, do ye want to keep her with ye?"

Dougald's face reddened. "Aye." He gave Tynan a sheepish grin. "Aye. I love her."

Tynan managed a small smile. "Love? Are ye cuif? The baron may want her back."

"I have been thinkin' on it. Caithleen and I will go away together."

"What of Clandon?"

"We will get him out somehow."

Resigned that Dougald had lost his heart to Caithleen, Tynan said, "Then 'tis settled."

"How are we to stop the baron?"

"When we go to the Ruthvens to negotiate, we must show Baron Ruthven we are on his side. We will help him bring down MacAulay Castle."

"He might as soon kill us as look at us."

"Aye. He might."

With a sigh, Dougald reached for the wine, slammed it back and poured himself another portion. He held up his goblet.

"To the love of a guid woman. Now that I have had it, I can die a happy man," Dougald said.

Despite the heaviness in Tynan's chest, he laughed. "Aye. For the love of a guid woman."

After they consumed the draught, they poured another.

"To the most beautiful women we know. Caithleen and Alenna!" Dougald said.

"Aye!"

As the wine simmered his blood, Tynan still sobered. The plan weighed on his soul. If all went well, the baron would no longer be able to hurt women or defenseless boys ever again.

If his plan failed, if Ruthven decided to cut Tynan down where he stood, he would never see Alenna again. She would be at Baron MacAulay's mercy.

CHAPTER 20

The dungeons remained as dismal and dank as the last time Alenna descended into their revolting depths. Despite her resolve, the stench nauseated her.

Having Elizabet by her side gave her strength. The woman's serenity, her sense of peace, made entering the hell pit more palatable.

As she descended the steps, Alenna shoved aside the fear threatening to close around the edges of her being like a smothering, ghostly shroud.

"Are ye well?" Elizabet asked, her voice unruffled.

"Yes."

"I'm glad ye thought to bring the bread," Elizabet said.

Alenna succeeded in bribing her way into the dungeons by giving the guards two loaves of bread Elizabet made earlier that morning. She had a loaf of bread left to give Clandon, as well as rabbit meat. While the thought of rabbit made Alenna's stomach lurch, she imagined Clandon would appreciate it. She'd thoroughly cooked it, though she doubted Clandon would have cared much, considering the slop they fed him now.

Once in the dungeon, she noted the two thieves chained against the wall. Both of them hung from their shackles like wet rags. Sores covered parts of their bodies and one of them had been whipped. The man who had accosted them during her last trip to the dungeon appeared alive, but his eyes were closed.

"Ghastly," Elizabet murmured as they scooted by the pitiful pair.

"A swift death would have been easier for them than this," Alenna said, turning her gaze away. "Why couldn't the baron just have killed them?"

Elizabet's eyes burned with a special fire of distaste, something Alenna couldn't remember seeing in her eyes before.

"Because the man is without a soul. He'll do whatever to whomever he likes. And make no mistake, his nastiest work is yet to come."

"Have you heard if Caithleen and Dougald have left the castle?" Alenna asked softly, as if the walls did have ears.

"Nay. She willnae leave the castle knowing Clandon is in this pit."

"Damn it," Alenna hissed. "But I thought Dougald planned to take her out of here?"

"Well, if she's as stubborn as ye are, lass, it no may be possible for Dougald to change her mind."

Alenna wanted to scream. Her only consolation came in knowing Caithleen had Dougald's protection.

When they reached Clandon's cell, they could see that his skinny body was propped against one of the slimy walls and his eyes were closed. Alenna's heart practically stopped. Quickly she clasped the bars.

"Clandon!"

The boy's eyes popped open.

She smiled and sighed with relief as he jumped up and ran to the bars.

"Are ye doin' well, young lad?" Elizabet asked, smiling.

"I'm doin' well," he said, eyeing the bundle under Alenna's arm.

"I've brought you something to eat," Alenna said, quickly passing him the bundle. "Bread and meat."

"Zounds!" He took the food with enthusiasm and tore at the bundle like a child digging into presents on Christmas morning. He stuffed the bread into his mouth.

"How long has it been since you ate?" Alenna asked.

"Only last night. Some sort of pig's swill."

She thought he looked thinner, and her worry grew rather than subsided.

"Tynan tried to get me out," Clandon said between bites of bread and meat.

"What?" Alenna said, taken by surprise. Another part of her knew she shouldn't be surprised.

"Aye, he did. But the baron said no."

"How do ye ken this?" Elizabet asked.

"Dougald told me. He came to see me last night and brought Caithleen with him. He tells me they are goin' away soon and they will take me with them."

This news heartened Alenna's soul. At least Caithleen had been able to see Clandon. But if Tynan hadn't managed to extract Clandon from the dungeon, what made Dougald believe he'd be able to win the boy's freedom?

"He has a plan?" Alenna asked.

The boy nodded. "Aye, though he dinnae tell me what it was. He feared if I would be beaten by the guards and he no wanted me to be able to tell."

So far the boy had managed well. She could only hope his imprisonment wouldn't be much longer.

"Elizabet and I are going to talk to the baron after we leave here. We may be able to get him to see reason."

Behind them came a thin laugh, high and edged with an eerie quality. A quiver shimmied over Alenna's skin.

Alenna and Elizabet turned to the men chained to the wall. The man who had provoked Tynan leered at them, his grin as nasty and sickening as she remembered. She turned away, ready to ignore him. Clandon stopped eating and stared at the man, his expression filled with loathing.

"Could ye spare me some bread, missy?" the man asked.

"Not on your life," Alenna said.

"Not even for word to help the boy and yer man?"

Leaning back against the bars of Clandon's cell, she glared at him. "What type of word?"

The man tilted his head to the side and she could see a festering cut on his neck. Amazing the man hadn't died already.

"Ye dinnae think that little tussle me friend and I had with MacBrahin was to rob him, do ye?"

"What?" Alenna asked, uncertain she'd heard him correctly.

"We was hired to kill him, but I guess we dinnae ken his strength. We came upon ye for sport, but we was lyin' in wait for MacBrahin." He jerked his head in the direction of his deceased friend, his detestable grin exposing his black teeth. "Jack here, rest his soul, he were the one that got cut bad. But me friend Will, he got kilt by MacBrahin."

Alenna gave a scathing laugh. "And you want me to give you food for that information?"

"We was hired by the baron. Would have gutted MacBrahin, too, if it had no been for yer pryin' arse."

Dread seeped into her heart like an icicle. Never mind that she'd tried for hours to harden her feelings. She couldn't. At least not where Tynan's safety was concerned.

"Why would the baron pay ye to kill his best knight?" Elizabet asked so softly that Alenna barely heard her.

The slimy man chuckled, the high-pitched sound grating on Alenna's ears.

"He wanted him dead and paid us well for it too. But here I am, more's the pity."

She couldn't feel charity or anything other than loathing for the man. She wouldn't give the man bread for information that may not be true.

Elizabet turned back to Clandon, finished listening to the miscreant. "We'll see to it one way or the other ye get out, Clandon."

Clandon's disposition had turned, his dark eyes blighted by a haunted expression. "Ye have to help him, Mistress."

"Tynan?" Alenna asked, though certain who he meant.

"Aye. I was thinkin' I am safer here than he is out there." He gestured toward the small window high on the wall behind him. "He is a great warrior, but..."

"'Tis all right, Clandon. We will get ye out of here soon and we will tell Tynan what this beast behind us said," Elizabet said.

The man sniggered again. This time his tone had turned harsh and hoarse. "Well, ye might be too late, at that."

Alenna turned swiftly and glared at the man. "What are you jabbering about?"

"I ain't sayin' more until I get some of that boy's bread."

Alenna hesitated, but Elizabet turned to Clandon and held out her hand. "Give me a bit of the bread."

Clandon passed a portion of the bread to Elizabet. Alenna reached for Elizabet's arm. "Don't."

"I am no beyond a little charity," Elizabet said. "Even for a man as horrid as this one."

Alenna gauged the stubbornness in her friend's eyes for several moments before she relinquished her grip on Elizabet's arm. Elizabet crossed the room and stuffed the bread into the vile man's mouth quickly. He growled as he chewed and Elizabet backed away swiftly.

His black eyes sparkled with unholy zeal as he devoured the small portion of bread. Crumbs fell from his mouth. Perhaps it was his last meal, Alenna thought with revulsion. She saw the nastiness, the despicable lack of remorse for anything and everything he'd done in his life. She imagined his foul deeds would easily fill a book.

When he'd consumed the bread, he licked his lips. "There's a chance the great Tynan of MacBrahin won't live to see the day pass if he leaves this castle."

"What are you talking about?" Alenna asked, annoyed and fearful.

"The baron said he'd see to it that if I failed, he'd send MacBrahin on a false errand of truce to Ruthven's castle. Ruthven will kill MacBrahin for sure. Or mayhap he will have him killed along the way." The odious man's rheumy eyes crinkled at the corners as he grinned. "And there's more like me that can be bought to do the deed. Mark my word."

Elizabet made a sound of disgust. "May God have mercy on yer soul."

Like a man on his last edge, his laugh echoed with alarming insanity. Turning away, Alenna and Elizabet moved back to Clandon's cell.

"Do ye think he speaks the truth?" Clandon asked.

Elizabet nodded, her face grave and thoughtful. "Aye. We must seek out Tynan and warn him."

Alenna's eyes filled with tears. "We've got to find him immediately and make sure he doesn't leave the castle."

As they walked by, the man spat at them, but they moved away too briskly for him to hit them. His curses followed them out of the stone prison.

Once into the fresh air, Alenna took a revitalizing breath, but her heart filled with anxiety for Tynan. "Would the baron have a reason to kill Tynan?"

Elizabet nodded, worry lines etching her forehead. "Lord help us, I think he would. Ye have no idea how truly evil a man he can be."

Apprehension added heaviness to Alenna's heart. Elizabet's

declaration made her suspicious. "What else do you know, Elizabet?"

"I wish now I'd said somethin' much earlier. I might have kept some of this from happenin'."

"What do you mean? Tynan is the baron's best warrior. And Dougald is not far behind. Why would he cut down his own defenses?"

Elizabet shrugged. "Some evil cannae be explained."

Fear for Tynan bludgeoned Alenna's senses, quickening her heartbeat as they headed toward the Black Tower. "We'll find him before we go to the donjon and see the baron."

"Alenna! Elizabet!" Caithleen rushed up to them, gasping. "Ye must come at once. Tynan and Dougald are goin' out of the castle walls to negotiate a truce with the Ruthvens. Tynan almost came to seek ye out but I said I would find ye."

Alenna exchanged glances with Elizabet.

"So the man told at least part of the truth," Alenna said.

"Where are the men now?" Elizabet asked Caithleen.

"Hurry. They are waitin' at the outer bailey for us."

When they reached the outer bailey, Alenna saw the two knights upon their huge horses. Garbed in their chain mail, Tynan and Dougald hadn't donned their helms.

Caithleen and Elizabet hurried toward them but Alenna hung back, her steps slow. Weight settled on her shoulders like an anvil. If Tynan left the castle, he might not return. Tell Tynan to go and she may never see him again, dead or alive. Her steps quickened. He must go. His life, when it came down to it, was in more danger here in the castle.

Dougald dismounted from his horse as Caithleen ran to him. As Dougald gathered Caithleen into his arms and kissed her with abandon, Alenna felt the anvil around her neck grow heavier. She stopped in her tracks. Obviously absorbed in each other after a single night of passion, Caithleen and Dougald appeared made for each other. She envied their impetuosity.

She sensed someone staring at her. Elizabet stood next to Tynan's horse and looked back at Alenna. Tynan sat upon his horse, back ramrod straight, the chain mail and accessories sitting on him like fine clothes on a gentleman.

The power of his attention reminded her of what had happened last night and this morning. If she lived to be a hundred, she'd always remember the touch of his hands on her skin as he'd slipped his fingers into her pussy, plucked her nipples. His lips as he'd kissed her, sucked her clit. His cock as he'd made love to her more fiercely and more tenderly than any man before. More than that, she would never forget the way he looked at that moment. Greedy fire burned in his gaze, as if he could devour her with one look.

Slowly she walked toward him. When she reached him, Elizabet stepped away and spoke with Caithleen and Dougald.

If Alenna expected Tynan to jump down from his horse and take her in his arms, the way Dougald had embraced Caithleen, she was mistaken. Instead he gripped the reins with his gauntlet-clad hands and gazed at her with smoldering eyes.

He cleared his throat. "We will be gone a day or two. 'Tis several miles to Ruthven's castle and we dinnae ken what will happen when we arrive."

Composure she'd worked hard to keep threatened to crumble. She abandoned her pride and tears once again filled her eyes.

Her turmoil was so great it seemed to cut off her air supply. "That horrible man in the dungeon said the baron wants you dead."

Tynan's eyes narrowed into dark slits. Slowly he dismounted, coming down close to her. Alenna wanted to step back, didn't want to smell the masculine scent that had wrapped around her in passion not so long ago. As he clasped her shoulders, his heavy gauntlets felt cold and impersonal. Yet when he leaned down to whisper in her ear, she felt a shiver of pure feminine reaction dance through her body.

"Speak softly of this matter," he said, the warmth of his breath tickling her ear. "There are other things the baron may have done. He may have murdered his mistresses, including Florie."

Alenna gasped and he brought her a little closer. "Ask me not how I ken. There is no time now. But ye must not let anyone ken that ye ken the things the baron has done."

"No, I won't," she whispered. "But if you leave...I...I fear for the safety of the castle."

Pain seemed to tug at one corner of his mouth. He nuzzled his face into her hair and brought her flush against his chest. "I dinnae want to leave ye here alone, Alenna. I fear for ye."

His words, spoken in a soft hush, challenged her defenses. That this strong warrior actually cared enough about her to show fear stunned her. Immediately she had to reassure him. If he worried for her too much, his own safety might be jeopardized.

"I'll be fine."

Brushing his lips against her cheek he said, "Dinnae do anythin' to put yerself in the baron's path."

Could he read her mind? She couldn't tell him she planned to ask the baron for Clandon's release.

Instead she asked, "Will you take care?"

As he put his arms full around her waist, she dared herself to look into his eyes again. She tried to read what she saw there. Ice and fire. Pain and glory. He'd seen it all and there was no one she believed more capable of coming back alive.

"With Dougald by my side, all shall fair well," he said.

"Without you here, the castle will be defenseless," she said again, knowing that her words meant nothing.

"Nay. We have left all the foot soldiers and knights here."

But I would feel safer if you were here. Like I do right now, in your arms.

Tears pricked at the corners of Alenna's eyes and she pushed them back with an effort. She couldn't let him see her cry.

"What if it's true and the baron means to hurt you? What are you going to do?"

"Then, when I am sure that my friends here are safe from the baron, I will leave here forever."

Another pain punctured her soul. "Where would you go?"

"Anywhere I would no be haunted by…"

When he didn't complete his sentence she waited patiently. Still, a minute went by in silence.

"Haunted by memories?" she asked.

"Aye." He closed his eyes for a moment.

As he opened his eyes she thought she perceived a smoldering intensity, like hot need. He leaned closer…closer…

No.

She couldn't let his lips touch hers. If she did she'd never be able to let him go. Alenna pushed against his chest, aware of Elizabet's speculating stare. Tynan released her and abruptly remounted his horse.

Dougald still held Caithleen in his arms, his hands caressing her hair, his gaze deeply locked with hers. A trickle of happiness for the couple managed to lighten Alenna's disposition.

"Dougald, ye had all night and half the day for that," Tynan growled. "Let us be off."

Dougald gave Tynan a grin, kissed Caithleen passionately, then disengaged himself from her clinging arms. Tears fell steadily down the young woman's face and the sight of the girl's sadness caused the lump in Alenna's throat to swell.

"We will stay together, all three of us," Elizabet said. "At my lodgings. Then the men shall have no more worries about our safety."

"I will worry yet, but 'tis a guid idea, I'm thinkin'," Dougald said as he mounted his destrier.

As Tynan and Dougald started toward the gatehouse, the portcullis was drawn up and they rode through to the barbican. As he left, Tynan turned slightly to gaze at Alenna, his expression as bleak as a storm-filled sky. She gathered her last perception of him deep into her memory and stored it in a safe place. When she lost sight of him, her heart beat fast, drumming in her ears, and for a second she wondered if she might faint.

Elizabet waved to the departing knights but Alenna couldn't move. Stunned by the force of her feelings, she barely breathed. What if Tynan was killed? What if—

"Alenna," Caithleen said at her elbow. "All will be fine."

The three women looked at each other with equal parts despondency and confusion.

Alenna now understood the agony passing through a modern soldier's wife or girlfriend when her man went off to an uncertain fate. Disquiet ate at Alenna's gut like worms. She knew if anyone could survive the savage land outside these gates, Tynan could, but that didn't make his departure easier.

Caithleen wiped her eyes with the back of her hand and straightened her spine. Though her eyes glittered with tears, she firmed her expression. "I will get my things out of Dougald's chambers. We can than then move into Elizabet's."

"I will go with you," Elizabet said.

"Nay. I will meet you at your rooms."

Alenna and Elizabet watched Caithleen as she dashed away into the crowd milling about the outer bailey.

"She needs time alone," Elizabet said. "Let us see the baron. Are ye sure this is what ye want to do? Ye know Tynan has tried pleadin' with the beast?"

For several seconds Alenna didn't reply. She tried to inject the bright, unusually warm day into her emotions. She took a deep draught of the breeze pouring over the walls of the castle.

Even the sanctity of nature had little effect on her at this moment.

Alenna gave considerable thought to what she planned. Meeting with the baron was a dangerous proposition, but she had to do something to free Clandon without Tynan's assistance. "Tynan can't help me anymore."

"I saw when ye left last night that ye were dyin' to be in each other's arms."

Any thought of being with Tynan, any memory of the wild lovemaking they'd experienced last night and this morning made her flush. Struggling to forget what an incredible experience it had been, she turned and walked off. Elizabet immediately came along beside her.

Alenna dodged a boy and a hound as they raced by her. The boy laughed as the dog pranced about his heels. "Clandon needs us now."

"Aye, but are ye sure 'tis the best way to go about it?"

"We've discussed it and didn't come up with any other choice. You wouldn't want me to wait until Clandon's been in there for God knows how long would you?"

Sighing heavily, Elizabet said, "Nay. I wouldnae. Nor would I think that I'd been so wrong about ye."

Alenna stopped walking. "Wrong about me?"

"I saw Tynan and ye in the vision, plain as the mornin' sun. Ye were together and ye had a child in yer belly. And Tynan looked at ye with love in his eyes. Just as he loves ye now."

Alenna made a scoffing noise. "He doesn't love me."

"He does."

In frustration Alenna began walking again. "We talked about this earlier."

"But 'tis no like a vision of mine to be this mighty and yet be so wrong. I'm sure of his love for ye."

Alenna's laugh mocked. "His love? Impossible. The man can't love me because he won't love me. I should have known. I should have realized that what he felt…what he felt was only physical. But no, I had to weave a dream around him."

"'Tis more than a dream."

Ignoring her statement, Alenna plunged ahead. "He won't love me because he's still caught in his fear. Afraid that he's some monster and that loving a woman…making love to her is her seal of death."

"Can ye blame him for thinkin' so? Most common in any man to wonder if an evil eye had been placed upon him."

Alenna stared at her friend. "Tynan isn't any man. He's amazingly…modern for someone of this time. Sort of."

Elizabet's lips curled in a smile. "Tynan is no different from any man who has suffered in his life." Elizabet took Alenna by the shoulders. "All of us have our clooties. 'Tis the little bairn in him that cannae make the bad dream go away. Night after night it haunts him. I'd hoped ye were the one woman that could break him free, lass."

"He's on his own. I tried. I talked to him. I shared my…"

"Your love with him? Did ye tell him ye loved him before he left?"

When Alenna didn't answer, Elizabet said, "He may be a fine, braw man, but he's just a man. And they dinnae always say what they feel. Aye, he's much afraid of what will happen. But that only shows that he loves ye. To him, the way to protect ye is to keep ye from him."

Alenna's anger and tears mingled. She knew if she didn't take a deep breath into her lungs, the tears would flow and the resentment soon after. She'd never felt so weak in her life as she did at that moment.

"But he's beating himself up over things in his past he couldn't prevent. His mother, Mary and Florie died at the hands of other men. Tynan isn't like that. He's…he's gentle and he's…" She shook her head vigorously. "I can't love him. I can't." She remembered the garnet ring sitting in the box at the Black

Tower. "I've the means to leave this time. But I won't love him and then leave."

Elizabet made an exasperated noise and released her hold on Alenna's shoulders. "What is this cannae? He cannea and ye cannae... pift! But I've seen ye both do many a brave thing. Ye are bolder than any lass I've seen, goin' to the baron right now... goin' to the dungeon to see Clandon. Life is short and ye must take what love ye can when it comes yer way, or forever regret it."

Something in the small woman's eyes and tone reflected that she'd done such a thing. Taken life by the bootstraps, hauled herself up more than once and plunged straight ahead. Had she also loved and lost?

"What's worrying you, Elizabet?" Alenna asked.

"I fear I'm losin' my way with me daughter." The words came out clipped and sharp. "Johanna, as ye have seen, was no at home this morn'."

"Yes," Alenna said cautiously.

"She left last night without me hearin' her."

"Oh no." As Tynan had tried to pound into her skull, plenty of danger lurked in this environment. A young girl like Johanna would be defenseless among the night predators. "If she's in the castle, we should be able to find her."

"'Tis what I hope."

"Then after I've seen the baron, we'll search for her."

As much as Alenna wanted to leave this century, too many things remained unfinished. She couldn't depart without knowing Johanna was safe and Clandon free. Once their security was assured, she could forget this experience like a bad dream and return to where she belonged. Though leaving Tynan behind would burn like a fire from hell, she forced the painful thought away and moved onward.

When they reached the donjon, they found the guards pliable to allowing them to enter when Elizabet gave them a steady gaze. Undoubtedly the men believed the concept of the evil eye.

Alenna and Elizabet ascended to the third floor chambers and entered the large sitting room. As always, the room felt like a meat locker. Elizabet waited while Alenna went to baron's bedchamber door and knocked.

A girlish giggle came from within the room. Seconds later another sound came to Alenna's ears as clear as day. Johanna's voice.

CHAPTER 21

Shocked, Alenna turned her gaze to Elizabet.

"Johanna is in there," Alenna whispered. "I heard her voice."

Elizabet's lips firmed, disgust and outrage covering her normally gentle features. "The vile bastard."

Before Alenna could stop her, Elizabet knocked loudly. "Johanna!"

"Elizabet, don't!" Fear spiraled in Alenna's breast.

"I willnae let that bastard take my child. I willnae let him do to her what he did to me."

"Elizabet—"

The door swung open abruptly and Elizabet took a step back.

The baron stood in the doorway, shirtless. Beyond him, Johanna lay on his bed, covered with a plaid. Her smile resembled a cat that had been caught licking the cream.

Alenna felt her stomach do a slow, nauseated flop.

With perfect composure the baron lifted one eyebrow and then glowered. "How dare you come blasting into my chambers? Can you not see I am busy?"

"How could ye do this to her? How could ye!" Elizabet said with pure venom.

"I'll do as I damned well please."

Elizabet's face turned purple with a rage Alenna had never seen before.

"That is my daughter, ye bastard—" Elizabet tried to push her way past him but he blocked her. "How could you do this to your own—"

He gave Elizabet a hard shove. Sprawling backward, she lost her balance. Alenna gasped and reached for her, but she fell hard against a table and struck her head against the floor. Alenna heard a sickening crack.

"Oh my God!" Alenna gasped, kneeling next to the prone woman.

"Mathair!" Johanna jumped from the bed.

"Leave the slut be!" The baron snatched at Johanna's arm and held her back.

Alenna searched for a pulse in Elizabet's neck. That's when she saw the small trickle of blood come from Elizabet's nose. "Oh God."

She looked up at the baron, who stood in the doorway and made no move to help or showed any remorse.

"Well, well," he said. "Who would have thought she would be jealous of her own daughter."

He laughed and the cold, hard sound slid over Alenna's skin like a reptile's tongue. Alenna shivered as realization made a sickening path through her mind. Alenna located Elizabet's pulse and then leaned over to listen for a heartbeat. Relief came from her throat when she heard Elizabet take in a breath.

Alenna looked up and saw Johanna take a length of bed covering, wrap it around herself like a toga and attempt to walk past the baron again. This time he let her go.

A sob came from Johanna's throat as she dropped down next to her mother.

"She's alive but she may be badly hurt," Alenna said. She looked at the baron, hoping to appeal to any sense of charity left in the man. "We need to help her."

A thin grin parted his lips. "She's not worth it—"

"Damn it, just help me get her to the bed. Then send for help."

Fear spiked in her when she realized what she'd done. She half expected the man to kill her on the spot. Instead, her sharp words had the effect she'd hoped. Despite the baron's vile personality, preying on the weak made him overconfident. Alenna tired of playing games with this low-life.

He reached down and picked up Elizabet, his expression stone harsh. Alenna held her breath until he placed her on the bed. Johanna shuffled to the bed and climbed up to sit on the edge. Tears rained down the girl's face, and for the first time Alenna saw vulnerability in the shallow, petulant girl.

Alenna turned to the baron. "She was only protecting Johanna—"

He snorted. "She is too late." He moved closer to the bed. With lightning speed he reached out and grabbed Johanna by the chin. "She is a whore...just like my sweet daughter here—"

"What?" Alenna asked, uncertain she'd heard the incriminating, vile statement correctly.

Johanna wrenched back and almost fell on top of her prone mother. Her eyes widened, terrified and disbelieving.

He laughed and the crazy sound reminded Alenna of the prisoner in the dungeon. "Johanna is my child. And she is mine to do with as I will."

Sickness rose into Alenna's throat and she covered her mouth and took a deep breath.

He turned away from Johanna and advanced on Alenna. Alenna stepped back until she came up against a table. "Didn't Elizabet tell you? Or did she keep that wee secret all to herself?"

A thousand questions came to mind. How could Elizabet

have stood being in the same castle with this man? Despite the number of questions assaulting her mind, Alenna feared for Johanna's life, Elizabet's life and her own. Evil seemed to be etched in every wrinkle on the baron's face.

Johanna sat on the bed, holding her mother's hand and shivering. The vacant look in her eyes said she would be useless as an ally.

Apparently, the baron took Alenna's momentary acquiescence for compliance and smiled. "I see you understand the way of things. Elizabet is not the saint you thought. We had a... liaison all those years ago, when this castle was still under my father's power. Then she disappeared and I didn't see her again until six years ago, when she came back and demanded money for her upkeep and her bastard child."

"You gave her money?" Alenna asked.

He shrugged and then looked at Johanna like an indulgent father. A very sick, obscene father. "Enough to keep her in the rags she wears. I could have sent her away but when I saw this tempting bit of flesh, I thought it might be nice to have her when she was grown." He reached for Alenna, yanking her close to him so she pressed against his smelly body. "Now you are a tempting morsel. When I came into your room that night—"

"You!" Alenna gasped. "You came into my room—"

"Aye. 'Tis unfortunate you woke so soon. We might have had a wee bit of fun."

"How dare ye!" Johanna's piercing shriek battered Alenna's ears.

Alenna turned in time to see Johanna hurl a heavy pewter goblet directly at the baron's head. He dodged the thrown object with ease, then reached across the bed and pulled Johanna by the arm over her mother's legs and onto the floor. Johanna cried out in pain as the sheet fell from her body.

"Stop it!" Alenna grabbed at the baron's arm. "You're hurting her!"

He shoved her back and she hit her hip against the table with a bruising force. The pain radiated down her leg and she groaned.

"Bitch," he hissed, reaching down to yank Johanna up by her arm. Moving quickly he grabbed Alenna and started toward the outer chamber.

As he dragged Johanna and Alenna along behind him, he cursed. "Whores!"

Alenna stumbled and landed on her knees. Pain slammed into her. The baron jerked her up again. "Stand up, bitch!"

Kicking open the door, he yelled down the staircase, "Guards! Guards!"

He loosened his grip slightly and Alenna saw her chance. Kicking back at him with the heel of her shoe, she made a solid connect to his knee. She heard his cry of rage and pain as she jerked away from him and started down the stairs at the fastest pace she dared. If she could get outside before the guards realized—

As she rounded a turn she ran right into a burly guard.

"Seize her!" The baron bellowed down the tower stairway.

The guard took no chances and landed a blow to Alenna's midsection with his forearm. The pain doubled her over as the impact forced the air from her lungs and she almost fell. The guard, though, had other ideas. He dragged her back up the stairs. Her diaphragm seemed paralyzed and she wheezed.

The guard pitched her into the room and she landed at the baron's feet on her hands and knees, head hanging down as she tried to suck in air.

Any moment she expected another blow. Instead, she felt Johanna's gentle hands on her back.

"Alenna," Johanna whimpered.

Alenna lifted her head and saw nothing but the baron's legs.

"You can't escape from me, Mistress Carstairs. And you've been a very, very wicked girl. Guard, take them to the dungeon."

* * *

DARK CLOUDS, pregnant with snow, hung like shrouds over the sky. A cold wind thrashed the tall grass as Tynan and Dougald made their way over the last mile to Ruthven's castle.

Tynan's body and mind tossed with troubling thoughts he couldn't deny. As they urged their warhorses to pick up the pace, Tynan thought of Alenna, alone and vulnerable.

If his plan succeeded, he would make certain Ruthven's men understood no women or children could be harmed in the attack. Above all, Tynan wanted to get to Alenna first and assure her safety.

God help him, how he wished now he'd taken a deep, passionate kiss from her before he'd left the castle. If something happened to him, it would be his deepest regret that he hadn't sampled her sweet lips again. She did care for him, at least a little. He'd seen the worry in her teary eyes.

Shoving thoughts of her away with an effort, he concentrated on the task ahead. Perspiration ran down the back of his neck and he flexed his fingers inside his gauntlets. They had but a mile to go before they reached Duncarval, the Ruthven's stronghold. As yet they'd seen no sign of Ruthven's soldiers. With their flag of truce flying, they hoped no soldiers from Duncarval would attack.

"Do ye think Baron MacAulay trusts us?" Dougald asked suddenly.

"He does no believe we'll betray him."

"Are ye sorry to do this?"

Giving his friend a hard look, Tynan said, "Nay."

"Do ye believe what that scum told Alenna? That the baron sent the man to kill ye?"

"Aye."

"Why would he do it?"

"Mayhap he saw that Alenna and I...that I lusted for her."

Dougald's laugh boomed out over the countryside. "Lust?"

"Lust. 'Twas all—"

Dougald laughed again. "I've seen the way ye look at her. Why do ye deny that ye love her?"

Tynan refused to answer, knowing he couldn't…wouldn't love Alenna. Not saying it…not giving these feelings a name meant they didn't exist.

Silence covered the men until a short time later.

"I am worried about Caithleen, and about what William of Ruthven will say when we tell him what we have in mind," Dougald said.

Tynan threw a confident smile in Dougald's direction. "Never ye mind. We can hope Ruthven is a man of reason and his fault is he hates Baron MacAulay. To us, it might be our savin' grace."

As they reached the crest of the hill, Tynan took a breath and prepared himself for the sight of Duncarval.

Standing like a colossal sentinel over the entire countryside, Duncarval was slightly smaller than Baron MacAulay's stronghold. Though Ruthven had fewer holdings than MacAulay, he remained powerful in his own right. His family had once consisted of a wife and three sons and a daughter. His eldest son died in a skirmish with the English several months ago. Above all, Tynan wanted to hear what Ruthven said about rumors that he besieged MacAulay Castle as revenge for his daughter's alleged kidnapping and death at the hands of MacAulay.

"Let us move along. No sense in waitin' here," Tynan said.

They moved down the hill and soon came to the Duncarval's outer defense, a very large, deep-looking moat. Tynan saw movement in the towers and knew someone watched. Dougald made sure he hoisted the flag of truce high. Moments later the drawbridge came down and several knights on horseback crossed the bridge and proceeded toward them.

"Dinnae make sudden moves," Tynan said, certain their lives

hung in the balance. Outnumbered, Tynan knew he'd be able to kill his share and Dougald the same. Still, he didn't want a fight, any more than he'd wanted to leave Alenna at the castle.

The six knights halted in front of them and took off their helms. A sign of trust, no less. One knight at the front of the pack moved his horse forward, until his animal stopped close to Dragon. Tall in the saddle, with long, blond hair, the man looked rough and coarse.

The man spoke in Gaelic rather than Scots or English. Dougald, who didn't understand much Gaelic, let Tynan speak. Moments later, the blond knight turned his horse away and beckoned to Tynan and Dougald to follow.

"What did he say?" Dougald asked. "It dinnae all sound friendly."

"The baron will see us," Tynan said, leaving out the harsh words the man had peppered them with. Threats that assured him if he made a wrong move and attempted to slaughter William of Ruthven, the both of them would be put to death before the morn.

As they crossed the drawbridge, Tynan sent up a prayer, hoping he hadn't made the biggest mistake of his life.

***

As ALENNA LEANED against the wall behind her, the dungeon stayed as silent as a graveyard at midnight.

She shivered as cold seeped into her bones like the insistent call of death. As a cramp struck her right leg, she moaned and closed her eyes.

Her side ached where the guard had hit her, but nothing else appeared broken or otherwise damaged. She stayed upright for as long as she could. Soon her back ached and a thin, annoying throb started in her temple. After four hours in the semi-darkness of the dungeon, she sank against the wall and slid into sitting position on the floor.

God only knew what lived on the floor with her.

She thought of the garnet ring and wished she wore it now. Then she could have transported herself out of this nightmare that had no end. A sharp pang of hunger drew her attention away from the ring. Placing her hand on her stomach, she wondered how she could even think of food at a time like this.

"Are we goin' to die here?" Johanna asked, her thin voice scarcely filtering through the murkiness of the dungeon cell.

Alenna glanced at Johanna, who sank onto the rancid floor next to her. Johanna's hair hung in a stringy, dirty tangle along her pale cheeks, her once-sharp eyes vacant and shocked.

Thank God the baron had allowed Johanna to put on her clothes before throwing them both in this hellhole. Spared the humiliation of being paraded through the castle nude, Johanna's clothing also offered protection against the unheated dungeon.

"No," Alenna said, as much to soothe herself as anything. "We'll find a way out, or the baron will come to his senses."

Alenna doubted the baron would release them but she hoped the fib would make Johanna feel better. Although not a psychology expert, she'd witnessed enough of the baron's antics to know nothing more than sheer, ruthless blood thirst motivated the man.

Serial killer. Definitely a sociopath.

Her skin crawled when she thought of Johanna being taken by the baron. *Incestuous bastard.* Alenna took a deep breath and let it out slowly, realizing she could easily work herself into a frenzy.

Elizabet.

How could she have given so little thought to Elizabet's plight? Elizabet might be dying or already be dead. Self-recriminations piled high as she thought how she might have avoided their predicament. Going to the baron had been stupid. Utterly stupid.

Tears came to her eyes. Alenna hoped against hope she would awaken and find this entire trip through time a cruel, demented nightmare.

"Mistress!" Clandon called from the next cell.

Alenna couldn't see Clandon because of the stone wall between them. But, she could see his hands as he poked them between the metal bars of his cell. She glanced over at the empty shackles and the vacant iron maiden as it swung from its hook like a birdcage.

"Mistress," Clandon said again, breaking her out of her nightmare thoughts.

"Yes, Clandon."

"Are ye well?"

"We are well," she said, knowing it wouldn't help to admit otherwise.

"What if the baron finds Caithleen?" he asked.

Although beaten down by circumstances, Caithleen didn't realize how capable she'd become. Was there a chance she might help them escape? How would she know where to find them?

"I'm sure she's making plans to hide. If she realized we aren't coming to meet her at Elizabet's—"

"Mistress, we have to help my sister," Clandon said, a pleading edge climbing into his voice. "The baron will kill her. He will!"

"First we must find a way out of here," Alenna said, knowing they had to start at the beginning. "We can't do anything from here."

Clandon sighed. "The walls are thick, the bars hard. How can we get out?"

For too long Alenna had allowed weakness to dominate her actions. Back in her time she'd allowed her fiancé to dictate her actions and as a result had lost her job. She couldn't do that now. For death stood around the corner, its ugly face ready to claim them.

"We'll think of something," Alenna said.

She leaned her head against the wall and tried to think, tried to keep the fear from overwhelming her. Sympathy and her own need for comfort drove her to approach Johanna. Johanna huddled against the corner, staring out of the cell. With both hands she gripped the metal bars like they were her anchor in a raging sea.

Alenna knelt next to Johanna, but the girl didn't move.

"We'll be all right." Alenna made a statement of faith. "If we don't find our own way out, Tynan will come for us."

Even if he didn't love her, she knew he'd fight for her and do anything to help her.

A spark of life interrupted the glassy consistency of Johanna's stare. "What of my mathair?"

What could she say? The girl might break down if she told her Elizabet might die. Then again, Johanna had endured a hard life and had survived. Johanna might be tougher than she looked.

"Ye dinnae think she is alive," Johanna said, retaining a tight hold on the bars.

Alenna gripped Johanna's shoulder. "Your mother is strong. If anyone can survive, she can. Just as you can."

Johanna's gaze drifted to hers. "I did an evil thing." Johanna's voice reminded Alenna of a small child. As if she'd retreated into a safer past. "An evil thing."

"What do you mean?"

"The baron. I...I let him...I let him..." Johanna's arms began to shake, then it transferred to the rest of her body. "He's my father but I dinnae know it. I swear I dinnae know it."

"It is no fault of yours," Alenna said.

"I should not have gone to him."

"Why did you?"

Johanna shrugged her thin shoulders and shifted until she no longer gripped the bars. "I was angry at mathair for not lettin' me go where I pleased. She treats me like a child."

"She worries."

"She treats me like a child."

At the girl's petulant tone, Alenna wondered if all the fight had left Johanna. "That doesn't explain why you went to the baron."

"I thought he could...I fancied him takin' me as his mistress. Just as he had Caithleen. I dinnae ken he hurt Caithleen until mathair told me. But I dinnae believe her. I thought she was doin' it to keep me away from him."

Family dynamics, Alenna thought fleetingly. Even in this day and age, teens and parents clashed. "Your mother was trying to protect you."

Johanna nodded and her eyes filled with tears.

Alenna knew she had to distract Johanna. "We need to think about what can we do for ourselves. With the three of us working together, we may think of a way."

The barest of smiles moved Johanna's lips. "Nay. We are doomed for our evil."

"We are no evil!" Clandon banged something against the bars. "'Tis the baron. I spit on him."

"Clandon, hush," Alenna said. "The guards may hear you."

"Beggin' yer pardon, Mistress."

"It's all right. I don't want to attract their attention. We don't know what they might do." She turned her concentration to Johanna. "We haven't done anything evil."

Johanna's eyes widened and her tears fell once more. "I have. God is punishin' me."

Alenna realized Johanna often did foolish things. But after Alenna's wild night with Tynan, she felt imprudent herself. One part of her regretted their lovemaking while the other part knew she had experienced something rare and soul deep with Tynan.

"I don't think God expects us to be perfect," Alenna said.

Johanna's tears slowed. Alenna thought she could see a new respect in the girl's expression.

"I'm sorry for all I said to ye before. For my spiteful ways. I… I have always had a feelin' for Tynan. Thought mayhap someday he'd care for me. I see that…that he loves you."

Alenna's heart swelled as she fought back tears. "I'm not sure it is love."

Johanna nodded vigorously. "Oh, aye. 'Tis love if I ever saw it."

Smiling, Alenna said, "Love or not, it isn't getting us out of here right now. Let's think how to escape."

Alenna knew it was the only way the three of them would remain sane.

CHAPTER 22

"You are either the most addle-pated sirrah I have had the pleasure of meeting, or you are the bravest of knights," William Sewall, Baron Ruthven said to Tynan quietly.

Shifting in his throne in the great hall, the tall man looked down on Tynan and Dougald with an imperial glare. Thin, with sharp features and a long face, the baron appeared to be a man from whom time and tragedy had taken its toll. Equal parts cunning, resolve and sadness lurking under the surface of Ruthven's lined face.

Tynan knew attempting to get help from a man he'd called enemy a short time ago verged on madness. Now that he had laid out his plans to Ruthven, when he most needed strength, he felt like the lowest rag-picker. As a knight from an enemy camp, he knew his position was weak. Behind him, three guards stood ready to fight him if he made any move they saw as threatening. He'd taken a gamble that could cost his life, Dougald's life and the lives of those he held most dear.

Alenna.

He must do this for her. To hell with himself. Her safety mattered to him above all things.

Baron Ruthven waited for an answer.

Dougald stepped forward when Tynan didn't speak. "Forgive us, my lord. Our journey has been hard and laden with foul weather."

Tynan almost smiled at his friend's feeble excuse. Both of them had endured far more difficult campaigns than the short jaunt to Duncarval.

Baron Ruthven gestured to a servant standing at attendance in one corner. "We shall have wine and bread." The baron gestured toward a side door. "Let us speak in privacy."

As they retreated to a side chamber, the baron hung back to give his guards instructions to stay outside the door and permit no one but the servant to enter.

Once settled in the small antechamber off the great hall, Tynan felt more at ease. A roaring fire in the hearth immediately worked to warm his bones. While not concerned about food, he knew he needed food to keep up his strength.

"What say ye again to our plan, my lord?" Tynan asked. "Do we assume too much?"

Baron Ruthven smiled, his grin two parts menace, another part understanding. "You assume much. Though perhaps not enough to sign your death warrant."

The servant came in with the wine and bread. After he departed, they ate in silence for long minutes. Tynan knew under all that calm resided a steel-hard vigilance. He'd seen these traits in many great men. The ones that survived this long, with this much power, didn't break under strain of any kind.

"You say you believe him to be mad and this is why he should be removed from his castle as lord. These are charges for which he could have you executed," Ruthven said.

"Aye," Dougald said. "We have come to grave times. My

woman is in danger, as is Tynan's woman. No innocent shall be safe from this man's vile and ungodly ways."

"Does he speak of the devil as his king?" Ruthven asked, leaning forward. "Say you he is in league with Beelzebub?"

Tynan shook his head. "Not that we ken, my lord. As we told ye, we believe he killed a woman who was his mistress. Perhaps he has killed more woman." When he saw the baron's features darken, he pressed his point home. "He has had ten mistresses. We heard yer daughter was taken from Duncarval several years ago and that ye believe it was the baron who stole her."

The baron's eyes turned cold, penetrating and deadly. "She was taken on a journey back from her aunt's. She had almost reached the castle when her caravan was attacked. All the knights who accompanied her were slaughtered." He leaned forward in his chair and glared at Tynan. "You say you've been a knight to MacAulay only four years?"

"Aye," Tynan said.

"How did you ken she'd been taken at all and that it may have been the baron's doing?"

Tynan pushed back his wine, aware the gesture could be seen as defiant. "I spoke with many inside the castle I'd trust with my life. Some have been at the castle many years. They said a beautiful woman not more than six-and-ten was brought to MacAulay Castle, nigh on ten years ago. When she came in, she was bloodied and beaten."

"God's blood!" Ruthven slammed his hand on the table. The door to the antechamber swung open and a guard stepped in. Ruthven waved the guard out. "Go on with your tale, MacBrahin."

"They say her name was Bella and that she was kind to all, though her heart was always far away."

Ruthven cleared his throat and took a draught of wine before responding. "Mirabella was betrothed to one of the knights killed during her capture. It was a love match. Many said I was madinsane to allow such a low born—" Apparently realizing he was forgetting himself, Ruthven stopped. "It was not a match I would have approved of, had my daughter not made me see...made me see that some things must be done for love beyond all else."

Tynan could hardly believe what he heard. Tynan would not have expected a man as hard and as ruthless as Baron Ruthven to have such feelings about love. "Then ye ken why Dougald and I have come to ye. We do this for love."

He spoke before he could hold back and this time he recognized the truth of his own words.

I love Alenna.

"My woman is in danger, my lord," Tynan said. "I would do anythin' to keep her safe. Dougald and I are but two knights and cannae overthrow MacAulay on our own."

Tynan watched as the older man's expression faded from suspicion to a haunted air. As the reality of what Tynan said pressed in on him, he appeared to shrink into his chair.

"Aye," Ruthven said, his eyes hard as chips of stone. "Aye. I will help you."

* * *

A DAY and a night drifted away slowly for Alenna and soon the noise from the outside world beyond the dungeon seemed part of a reality she might never witness again.

Late into the evening, after Johanna fell asleep on the floor and Clandon lay quiet, Alenna stayed alert. She couldn't possibly sleep, not knowing what fate had in store for them. Though she tried to be strong, she imagined living out her days in this vermin-infested cell, with disease and suffering her companions. How long could she expect to remain sane? Would starvation kill her before then?

Closing her eyes to the darkness, she wrapped her arms

around her knees and wished for sleep. At least if she could rest she would know temporary oblivion and peace. In the cloak of darkness she allowed her tears to flow, hoping they would have a cleansing effect and release stress.

She cried for Tynan, knowing he must be in terrible danger. What if Ruthven had slaughtered Tynan already?

All hope was lost if Tynan was dead.

God, I love him. No matter what, I love him.

There. She'd finally admitted it. Somehow she had fallen hopelessly in love with a brazen, brawny, barbaric Scot from a different time with a distinct set of rules. Call her a fool, but it had happened. Alenna wanted more than nights of passion with him, she wanted his love. She knew she had his affection, but she also recognized he'd left his heart with a woman called Mary.

A sob slipped from her lips and she covered her mouth with her hands to stifle the sound. Above all things, she knew she had to believe in Tynan and his ability to survive. Intelligent and strong, he would make it through this venture alive. She had to trust that somehow he'd help her, Clandon and Johanna.

What of sweet Elizabet? Alenna's heart clenched painfully and she sniffled as another sob managed to escape her throat. Had Elizabet survived? What of Caithleen?

Alenna had never made a habit of praying, but she clasped her hands together now and put all her thoughts into wishing all her friends safe. Exhausted, she dropped into a fitful sleep, where misty dreams danced in her head like vengeful demons.

As a new day dawned, she woke to strange sounds not a part of the norm in this dreary, death-laden place.

"Run for yer lives!"

The shouting from outside the dungeon windows startled her and she jumped to her feet. She wished the tiny window were low enough so that she could see out.

"Mistress, do ye hear that?" Clandon asked from his cell.

"Yes."

Johanna stirred as more shouting broke the morning air.

"What is happenin'?" Johanna asked as she sat up and brushed her hair back from her face. Dark circles ringed her eyes.

Increasing sounds of commotion outside continued for an hour, until it became clear the castle had come under attack.

"Without Tynan here, the castle will fall," Johanna said, wringing her hands like a timorous old lady.

Alenna couldn't deny the foot soldiers relied on Tynan for guidance and direction. "This is a large fortress with many soldiers. Even without Tynan the castle isn't entirely helpless."

Clandon laughed. "Mayhap 'twould be better if it fell."

"Clandon," Johanna said. "How can ye wish it? If the castle falls, we all die."

Hysterical sobs issued from Johanna's lips.

Alenna grabbed her arms and shook her gently. "Johanna, please. I realize you're afraid but we have to be ready to defend ourselves."

"With what?" Johanna wailed the question.

Alenna looked around their barren cell. Wooden bowls and goblets remained on the floor, accumulated from the two meals they'd been served since their imprisonment.

"I don't know," she said, frustrated. "But we must try. We are not helpless. We'll work together."

Johanna swallowed her sobs, but tears spilled over her cheeks. "Mayhap…mayhap I could sell myself to one of the guards."

"What?" Alenna asked, incredulous.

The girl took a deep breath. "Aye. I wasnae a maiden when I went to the baron. I…I once—"

"I won't allow you to do that. Your mother wouldn't want you to sacrifice yourself."

At the mention of her mother, Johanna sobbed again. "Why did she keep it from me?"

"Keep what from you?"

"That the baron is my father."

"I don't know, Johanna. But she must have had a reason. Probably because she knew what the baron was like. And he wouldn't claim you as his own daughter. You wouldn't really want him for a father, now you know what he's like, would you?"

Johanna's tear-streaked face reddened. "Nay."

Alenna patted her back, attempting to give what comfort she could. "Your mother may be safe."

"She will hate me, even if she is."

"Why would she hate you?"

"All this is my doin'. I was fashed, ye see. I would have my way. If I had no gone, my mathair—"

"She is alive. I feel it."

Her assurances appeared to calm the girl somewhat.

"Please, mistress," Johanna said between sniffles. "I could call for a guard—"

"No," Alenna said. "You can't put yourself at risk."

"The guards might let us take our leave."

"For your favors? I don't think so. I think they fear the baron far more. They'd worry what would be done with them if they let us go."

Clandon laughed. "No if they be busy."

"What do you mean?" Alenna asked.

"If there is war, they cannae be payin' much leave to us," Clandon said.

A loud noise, like cracking wood and the rumbling of rocks falling, heralded something momentous happening not far from their area.

"Lord save us." Johanna put her hands to her mouth.

Fear did a new dance in Alenna's stomach. If the castle

crashed down around them, they were essentially helpless. Another deep terror tore her heart. If Ruthven attacked the castle that meant Tynan had failed to bring a truce to fruition.

It meant Tynan might be dead.

Closing her eyes, she saw Tynan cut down by an arrow, or perhaps hanged. Suddenly the walls loomed close, the air too thick and hot.

She pictured Tynan full of vigor and life. The man she'd known hours ago, the man who had loved her like she'd never been loved.

Please, please let him be safe.

Alenna took deep breaths to restore her equilibrium. Concentrating on the problem at hand would keep her from dwelling on Tynan's welfare.

Was Ruthven attempting another attack? Unless he had a significant force of men, how could he hope to take this mighty castle? Alenna tried to estimate how large the household of men might be, including knights, soldiers and servants.

Perhaps two hundred individuals? No, that sounded too low. If she counted all the numerous knights in the baron's employ, the number skyrocketed.

As the pandemonium continued outside, Alenna smelled smoke.

"Oh my God," she whispered.

"The castle is on fire!" Clandon shouted. "There be smoke comin' in our windows!"

She looked up. Just as he'd said, a small stream of smoke filled the upper part of the chamber.

* * *

TYNAN TURNED toward the castle and watched as a spear came hurtling from between a crenelle high on the battlements. The spear impaled an unsuspecting fool who had wandered too close to the castle walls. With a hollow cry, the man tumbled into the moat with a splash.

Shouting curses, Ruthven ordered his soldiers to hold their positions. Battlements were heavily armed with archers and other soldiers, ready to rain projectiles down on anyone who came near.

Although some progress continued in the assault, Tynan didn't like what he saw. Smoke poured from the center of the castle. He estimated the wooden beam roof of the great hall had caught fire.

His stomach twisted. Since he'd realized he loved Alenna, he had a difficult time thinking about the battle at hand. As he'd returned to MacAulay Castle, guilt beleaguered his every step. Part of him believed he should have taken Alenna with him. At least now she'd be safe at Ruthven's castle. But he knew if things hadn't turned out for the best at Ruthven's, her life wouldn't have added up to a half-penny.

Alenna was in danger because of him.

Every time he cared for a woman, something bad happened to her.

No! No. As God is my witness, this time things must be different.

Alenna had changed his entire world.

If anything had happened to her, he'd gladly offer himself to a stray arrow or fiery barrage of missiles. The mere thought of losing her hit his gut like a hot poker.

I cannae live without her.

Alenna had come to this time to save his life. But not only had she saved him from death.

She'd saved him with her love.

Alenna wouldn't give herself body and soul to just any man. Yet she had given Tynan the deepest pleasure a man could know, both in body and spirit. Either way, she was in grave danger right now and thoughts of her pushed him forward. He had to get inside and find her.

"Jesu, please let her be safe," he whispered.

Dougald joined Tynan, and they stood near the huge trebuchet as soldiers prepared it to fire another missile at the castle walls. Moments later Ruthven approached on his horse.

"We have been at them for a day and have made progress. But not enough. I shall send some of my men back to fetch the other trebuchet," Ruthven said.

Dougald turned his attention from the soldiers loading the mechanism with stone shot. "Nay, my lord. Soon we can attack the walls by foot and on horseback. The roof of the great hall is alight."

"It would take hours to get another trebuchet here," Tynan said.

Ruthven looked at the catapult machine just as a soldier severed with an ax the rope holding the appendage. The stone hurled high into the air as the weight on the other end of the arm came crashing down.

As the massive stone hit the top of the tower that housed the dungeon, it cracked loudly with the sound of stone crashing inward. Soldiers yelled in unison their satisfaction. The rumble of falling masonry echoed like thunder behind their cheers.

Ruthven smiled. "And do you think MacAulay will surrender, because his castle is burning down around his ears?"

Tynan shook his head. "Nay. I shall have to go in and get him."

Ruthven turned his glare on Tynan. "Not if I get him first."

"Aye, my lord."

Ruthven grunted. "How long shall these walls hold out? We have made penetration through two towers and masonry is falling even now from the front curtain wall."

"A few more blasts should do it," Dougald said. "I'll tell the men to ready the batterin' ram."

As Dougald headed down the slope, Tynan gazed out over the damage already inflicted on the sturdy fortress. The numerous arrow slits in the curtain walls meant the structure of the walls themselves weakened under continuous attack. More bombardment would accomplish destruction.

"How thick are these walls, MacBrahin?" Ruthven asked.

"About twelve lengths, my lord," Tynan said. "Thicker than most castles can boast. Your soldiers and knights will overwhelm them when they let down their guard."

Ruthven turned a curious expression on Tynan. "You seem very certain. Yet you trained and worked with these men for four years. Have you so little confidence in them?"

"Nay. But the garrison will be weak. Tired. Men will fear for their families. We can stay here as long as it takes. They dinnae have enough supplies to keep them from starvin'. I asked the baron to keep the supplies up, but he dinnae pay mind to it."

"Then 'tis his idiocy that will kill him." Ruthven smiled narrowly. "You are an interesting man, Tynan of MacBrahin. If you survive this siege, I would offer you a position as knight in my household."

Tynan felt his gut sour. He didn't think he would ever return to being a warrior after this. After betraying the baron, after putting so many people who had trusted him in mortal danger, the guilt rode him hard. Perhaps he could return to Glenfinnan. Perhaps…

No.

None of it mattered if he could not be with Alenna.

"I dinnae know what I will do. I willnae make any vow 'til I ken what will be."

A cry went up as another projectile hit its mark, making a significant hole in the gatehouse. The battering ram would have an easy time making a void large enough for the charge.

Tynan took little notice of the flurry of activity. All his concentration went in to how he would rescue Alenna. When he reached her, he vowed she would know two things—that he loved her and that he never wanted her to leave him.

* * *

COUGHING as smoke filtered into their cells, Alenna, Clandon and Johanna stayed low to the ground.

A loud boom overhead shook the building and Johanna screamed. A part of the wall of Clandon's cell collapsed.

"Clandon!" Alenna ran to the hole between their cells and peered through.

"I am fit, mistress. If they keep goin' I will soon be out of here." Grinning at her through the hole, his voice relayed the cheerful refrain of a boy heady with the desire for battle.

Night had descended on the castle many hours ago and the constant assault battered Alenna's ears and nerves. Even with the coming early hours of the morning, the attack hadn't lessened. A red glow, no doubt from the flicker of flames consuming various parts of the castle, cast a strange light inside the dungeon. Hell had come to MacAulay Castle.

Alenna shivered with a chill deep in her bones. Her despair increased by the hour, as all their discussing and planning came to nothing. They could form no ideas on how to escape the formidable prison.

"If we leave here," Johanna said, "I willnae disobey me mathair again."

At least Johanna had regained hope that Elizabet might be alive. "I'm sure she'll be glad to see you."

Several moments later, footsteps echoed down the stairway leading to the dungeon. Johanna seized Alenna's arm. A soldier emerged from the darkness carrying a torch, and behind him stood the baron. Alenna straightened, lifting her chin in a gesture of defiance.

"Most delighted to see you, my dear Johanna. And you, Alenna, of course," the baron said, an inane smile plastered on his face. He turned to the guard. "Unlock the door."

"What have ye done with my mathair?" Johanna asked.

"Never you mind."

The baron reached in and snatched Alenna by the arm, dragging her from the cell. Then he slammed the door. Johanna grabbed the bars.

"Where do ye take her?" Clandon called out. "Leave her be!"

Not deigning to answer, the baron dragged her upstairs. Fear surged through Alenna's veins like fire.

"Ruthven has come for you, hasn't he?" Alenna asked.

The baron stopped immediately, glaring down at her. Smeared with soot from head to toe, he laughed and tightened his grip on her arm. "And your traitor lover shows him the way."

Was Tynan truly all right? Perhaps Tynan had convinced Ruthven to be on his side. But her joy dissipated like a whiff of smoke at the baron's next words.

"If he wants you, he will have to come and get you. And I will be waiting for him."

"You've lost," she said. "Surrender. Maybe Ruthven will show you mercy."

She yanked her arm from the baron's excruciating grip.

The guard cuffed her on the back of the head and she fell to her knees on the stone steps. Pain in her knees far outweighed the throbbing in her head, but dizziness kept her from rising.

The baron rounded on the guard. "You simpleton! 'Tis I who will punish her!"

The baron pulled her up again and she swayed. Relentlessly he drew her up the steps two at a time. Alenna's heart pounded in her chest, fright making her mouth dry and her legs weak. She knew she would die unless she thought of some way to save herself.

Tears filled her eyes for all the people she had failed.

She'd failed herself, her friends, and most of all Tynan.

Once outside the stuffy dungeon, acrid smoke filled her lungs and she coughed and covered her mouth and nose with her hand. All around her, shouting and screaming echoed about the castle like the tormented souls of hell. Hearing cries from the battlements above, she saw men pouring over the top of the walls nearest the gatehouse and barbican.

A flaming arrow came over the wall nearest them and landed directly in front of the baron. He stepped back, bumping into her. He turned swiftly and grabbed her arm to pull her along.

Alenna glanced at the guard. Shorter than she, but heavily muscled, he looked capable of inflicting significant damage. Though she probably couldn't overpower two men, what choice did she have but to fight?

Now or never.

She yanked her arm out of the baron's grip, stopped and turned, wedging a knee in to the groin of the unsuspecting guard. As the guard doubled over in pain, she took off at the fastest run she could manage among the free-for-all.

"Get her, you fool!" the baron's rasping cry filled the air.

As she ran, Alenna realized she might be in as much danger from the chaos around her as she had been in the baron's clutches. If she could hole up somewhere—

She remembered the alcove Tynan had pulled her into that day and headed for it. At least it would be out of the direct fire and she could plan what to do next. All around her, men engaged in hand-to-hand combat. She dashed around clusters of fallen bodies.

An arrow sailed by her head and slammed into a soldier wrestling with another man. He crumpled and fell dead at her feet. The other man turned on her and pulled out a dagger. Alenna backed away and stumbled straight into a solid body.

Two powerful arms came about her. "Bitch!"

The baron had her.

She struggled, kicking her heels back, but his arms crushed hers to her side. "Let me go!"

Before she could scream, a blow to the back of her head turned her world into piercing pain and blackness.

CHAPTER 23

Meat locker-cold shook Alenna's frame, her body quaking as she woke.

So cold.

Sharp pain lanced her head and she gasped, reaching up to press her hand to her forehead.

Dazed, she couldn't recall anything. Shivering, she opened her eyes and realized the baron had her under the arms and pulled her along the ground like a sack of potatoes. All around them, the battle continued, mixed with horrendous noise and a horrid stench she'd never smelled before.

Did fear have a scent?

Tremors racked her frame. Dizziness swamped her, and something warm trickled down the back of her neck. For a second, the idea she might die seized her breath.

No!

She didn't want to die. She wanted more than anything to tell Tynan she loved him and would stay with him in this century. No matter what, she couldn't leave him—now or ever.

Alenna opened her eyes and noted the baron moved in the direction of the donjon. Gathering her scattered thoughts and ignoring the throbbing pain in her head, she made a decision to get away now or be killed. It was as simple as that.

"Bitch," the baron said. "Wretched whore. You are like all the rest. All the rest."

With the last strength she possessed, Alenna shifted, throwing him off balance as she struggled against his painful grip.

He dropped her and she rolled away from him, coming up against another body. She hopped up, dodging the baron as he rushed for her. He slipped in mud and tripped. Stepping back, she almost fell over another body.

As she looked down, Alenna saw the man lying at her feet clutched a knife in his dead hands. She snatched it as the baron leaped to his feet. An animal roar left the baron's throat as he charged her. Everything seemed to slow down. She had time to see the feral grin of triumph on his face, obviously sure of his victory. Madness stamped its brand on his hate-distorted face, a clear testimony to his insanity.

"I'll kill you!" He dashed toward her.

Lashing out with the knife, her own screech of fright and anger tearing from her throat, Alenna caught him across his right cheek.

Howling, he lurched back, blood streaming down his face. Expletives split his lips as he held a hand to his damaged skin and staggered toward her.

Run.

Run.

The baron laughed, the insane sound chilling Alenna's veins like an ice water bath, his bloodied face a grimace of mingled pain and depravity.

Suddenly, out of the corner of her eye, she saw a man she'd recognize anywhere. Powerful joy surged inside her and strengthened her will.

"Tynan!" Alenna cried out, half in warning and half in welcome.

Tears threatened her eyes but she blinked rapidly. Now was not the time to weep, but to survive.

She had seconds to take in the sight of his handsome face. Blood ran from a cut on his forehead and his eyes burned with battle lust. Then the baron leapt upon her, jerking her in front of him and holding the knife to her throat. Her heart pounded heavy in her chest and she gasped hard for breath.

I'm dead.

She expected to feel the knife split her throat.

She would never kiss Tynan again.

God, please keep him safe.

"Alenna!" Tynan came to a halt several yards away, his breath coming hard, his feet spread apart, his sword secured in one hand and a knife in the other.

"You wouldn't dare," the baron said, a stream of blood coming from his mouth and splashing on her shoulder. "The wench is mine. I will have the pleasure of seeing the pain in your eyes as I kill her, Tynan of MacBrahin."

Hatred for the baron blazed in Tynan's eyes. She caught his glance and held it for a split second, willing all her heart into one gaze. Did he know how much she loved him? Could she convey all she felt, other than stark fear, into her eyes?

"Nay," Tynan said, still breathing hard. "Ye have done enough killin' and rapin' in yer time. Ye will be executed for the murder of William of Ruthven's daughter, Mirabella. Release her." Tynan gritted each word through his teeth. "Or I swear I shall gut ye like a fish."

The baron laughed. An evil, putrid sound that made her flesh crawl with disgust. "Nay. It shall be I that guts you."

The baron nuzzled her neck then brought his dagger closer to her throat. "Come closer and she dies."

Alenna saw everything as if it were in slow motion, as

another soldier came from behind Tynan and started for him. "Tynan. Behind you!"

Tynan swung about with his sword as the man charged. Tynan welded the sword with such power he sliced the man's head clean from his body.

She felt the baron's grip slacken and instinct drove her. She shoved back, stomping on the baron's foot. He howled and loosened his hold. As she wrenched from him, Alenna felt pain slice through her arm and she cried out. Stumbling out of his way, she tripped and fell on her back.

Tynan raced toward the baron, a cry issuing from his throat as he attacked. The baron growled as he pulled his sword from the scabbard and parried Tynan's first thrust with the sword. Tynan drove the baron back with one strike and then another.

Alenna sat up and clutched at her wounded arm. Lightheaded, she used all her will to remain conscious, watching as the two men fought.

Tynan quickly took the advantage as he drove back the baron.

Like a strange ballet the two men sidestepped, parried, rebuffed. Tynan's superior size and strength quickly gained the upper hand. Moments later, Tynan dealt the baron a fierce blow to the shoulder, driving the man to his knees.

With blinding speed Tynan swung his sword, a battle growl issuing from his throat as he gripped the sword in both hands.

He lopped the baron's head from his shoulders.

The baron's headless body dropped to the ground like a sack of flour.

Alenna watched in shock and relief as Tynan stood over the dead man. Tynan's breath rasped hard in his chest. He turned toward her and his fierce battle expression faded, the hardness leaving his eyes, replaced by weariness and unmistakable relief.

Alenna sobbed as he strode toward her. Sinking onto his

knees beside her, he pulled her against him and kissed her forehead, her face, her lips. His breath came harsh and labored.

"Thank God. Thank God," he whispered, his voice deep and strained.

She let the sobs escape, bursting through her throat in great heaves that made her cough and choke.

"Sweet," he murmured, looking down at her. "Ye are safe now. No one will ever hurt ye again. Ye are safe." He saw her injured arm and cursed. "Oh, God, sweet, ye are wounded."

Alenna tried to answer but instead gasped in pain, the croak coming from her throat like a plea.

He ripped part of her dress away and used it to bind her wound. Gently he picked her up in his arms and strode with her toward the Black Tower. In a daze, she realized the fighting had ceased. Smoldering ashes, the sounds of the wounded and dying, the cheers of the victorious heralded the end.

"It's over," she whispered as he held her tightly in his arms.

She looked into those brown eyes she thought she'd never see again. For a moment he stopped and stared down at her. A tentative smile barely touched his hard lips.

"Aye. 'Tis over." Tynan kissed her with a hot, sweet taste of passion remembered and yet to come.

"I...I thought I might never see you again," she murmured.

"God's bluid, sweet," he rasped, his voice husky with fatigue. "Ye will be the death of me yet."

"Not today." She smiled through a rain of tears as she clutched him close. "Not today." When he managed a weak smile she asked, "Have you seen the others? Are they safe?"

"Aye. Dougald has taken Caithleen and Clandon outside the castle walls. When I first fought my way into the castle, I went to the donjon. Elizabet was there with Caithleen. Caithleen said ye had been taken to the dungeon. Dougald and I freed Clandon and Johanna and then I came for ye."

As they went toward the Black Tower, she realized they

walked in the same spot where she'd been hurled through time. She realized she didn't care if she returned to the future. She had all she needed right here, right this moment.

Once inside the tower, Tynan placed her gently on the big bed and sat beside her. Among the smudges of dirt and blood on his face, she saw the glitter of tears in his eyes. The sight melted her heart with tenderness. She reached up to touch his dear face.

Crushing her to him, he whispered into her hair. "Sweet, I love ye. I love ye more than life itself. When I saw the baron holdin' a knife to yer throat...I thought—"

She pulled back slightly and touched her lips to his gently. "Shhh...I'm here with you now."

"Alenna," he whispered, "I would do anythin' for ye, I love ye so much. Dinnae ever leave me."

Happiness swelled within Alenna, reaching a height which hours ago she never could have dreamed. She kissed him over and over and whispered the words she knew he longed to hear.

"And I love you, Tynan of MacBrahin. I'll never leave you."

* * *

As ALENNA WALKED in the fresh, crisp morning air, she realized her heart was free from worry.

All around her signs of the castle's devastation loomed, but Ruthven had ordered repairs and for a month steady progress had been made. Once again the walls of MacAulay Castle, under the protection of Baron Ruthven, bloomed into a place of commerce. Alenna had never seen the people look happier and more industrious as they went about their daily business. They'd discovered the new lord of the castle could be a generous and kind man. Soon Baron MacAulay's cruel shadow would be erased from the castle.

But there were some things that couldn't be erased.

She pressed her hand to her stomach and smiled tenderly. Elizabet's prophecy had come true in more ways than one.

Alenna had been overjoyed by the last month's events. Through all the death and destruction, many good things happened. Among them was Elizabet's quick recovery from her head wound. Johanna had weathered her horrible experiences, seemed to be the stronger for them, and had entered into a better relationship with her mother. And just that morning Caithleen and Dougald had married in the chapel.

Alenna quickened her steps back to the Black Tower, eager to be with Tynan. Last night, as he'd held her in his arms, he'd said he had something to ask her. Anticipation ran straight through her blood. Could he be ready to propose? If not, she planned to propose to him. It might not be the done thing in the fourteenth century, but she didn't care.

Although content to stay in the fourteenth century, she hadn't lost her independent ideas. In fact, she'd managed to teach Caithleen a thing or two. Caithleen had proposed to Dougald.

Smiling, Alenna instinctively felt for the ring on her finger. As she turned the ring around so the garnet faced out for the world to see, the answer struck her like a bolt of lightning from the cloudless sky.

The ring.

She'd been almost in this same spot, close to the Black Tower when she'd discovered the ring and been hurled through time. Now, as she looked at the gem on her finger a soft mist enveloped her, appearing as if by magic.

No. Oh no.

While she'd known the ring was the catalyst for her return to the twenty-first century, she'd never been certain how. Now she knew, and the reality of the mist clouding the world around her with its cold breath set a pattern of fear and sadness into her heart. She knew the mist would take her back to the twenty-first century and she would never see Tynan again.

And he would never know she carried his child.

So this explained the legend of Tynan losing his love. She had entered his life in a swirling mist and would leave just the same.

She heard the sound of horse's hooves clopping and looked through the gathering thick fog. Tynan sat upon Dragon. She saw Tynan's mouth open as if to speak and he reached out to her.

She held her hand out to him, desperate for one last touch. "Tynan!"

He urged Dragon into a gallop and headed straight for her. For several seconds disorientation made her sway and her surroundings swirled before her eyes.

She was falling.

Seconds later, she opened her eyes and found herself sitting on the ground. As she looked up she saw Tynan standing next to her. Joy blossomed in her heart like a new rose.

"Thank God," she whispered. "You...you're here with me."

His soft smile of happiness lifted her senses until she almost shouted with the ecstasy. Looking around her, she realized instantly something had drastically changed. "It worked, Tynan. We're together."

He gazed around, confusion clear in his deep eyes. He helped her stand and then brought her close to his side, arms around her.

"Sweet Alenna, is this what I ken it is?"

Curtain walls completely repaired, the castle didn't look quite right. And there were plenty of other changes that couldn't have occurred in the last few seconds. Including the test pits, right next to where they stood.

"I think so, Tynan."

Alenna knew something monumental had happened when two people walked out of the Black Tower wearing parkas, jeans and athletic shoes.

"My God!" Tynan said as he held her closer. "'Tis no as it was before. What has happened?"

She turned in his arms and looked at his ragged fourteenth century clothing. "Well, you could pass for someone in creative anachronism, I suppose."

"Eh?"

She smiled and looked up at him. "You're in my world now, Tynan of MacBrahin. There is a lot you're going to need to learn."

His eyes widened almost comically. "But how? Why?"

Slowly she urged him around the corner, out of sight of the tower. She showed the ring to him.

"The ring, Tynan. Somehow this ring was what transported me through time."

He held her hand and stared at the jewelry as if he'd never seen it before. "This is the bobble ye thought I stole when I first met ye? This ring?"

"Yes. But now I know the ring was always the baron's...in the past."

"But how did it come to ye in the future? How did ye have it before?"

"Remember I told you I was looking for artifacts and found this ring in the test pit next to the Black Tower? I'd just slipped the ring on when I was hurled back through time."

He nodded solemnly. Slowly, he removed the ring from her finger.

"What are you doing?" she asked.

"Do ye want to stay with me always?"

"Of course—"

"In this time, Alenna? Or in my time?"

She saw his eyes, warm with love for her, and her heart did double time.

"Wherever you are is where I want to be," she whispered.

"Then I'll stay here with ye," he said and deftly dropped the ring down a drainage hole near the wall.

She gasped. "Tynan!"

He turned her toward him, putting his arms around her again. "I am sorry, sweet, but I dinnae wish to take any chances that time might rip ye from me. When I...when I saw that mist gatherin' around ye, I knew I had to get to ye. I could no stand the thought of losin' ye. I love ye."

Alenna sighed, gratified by the heat in his gaze and the warmth of his smile. He kissed her softly, his lips molding to hers for a sweet second. As she broke the kiss, she remembered his beloved horse.

"Where is Dragon? I mean, he didn't come forward in time with you."

A line formed between his brows as he frowned. "I jumped off him as I reached the mist. I'll miss him sorely. He was a guid warrior." When a plane flew overhead, he almost jumped out of his skin. "The flyin' machines Elizabet told me about?"

"Yes. But there's more." She cleared her throat. "I suppose I should ask you before you have a chance to change your mind."

"Ask me what?" he asked gently.

"Will you marry me?"

"Eh?"

She nudged him gently in the ribs. "Will you marry me?"

Tynan grinned. Then he kissed her again. A hot, bone-melting kiss that set her on fire. Alenna heard someone laugh.

"Nice costumes," a teenage boy said as he strolled by. They broke from their kiss.

"Costumes?" Tynan asked.

"What is the date?" Alenna asked the boy.

"September 25," the boy said.

"What year?" she asked.

The boy screwed up his face. "Two thousand and twenty-four."

Tynan's mouth fell open.

"Close your mouth, dear," Alenna said as the teenage boy strode away. "I'm back on the same day I left. I can't believe it!"

Just then Alenna saw Demi striding toward them. She waved. Happiness at seeing her friend surged within Alenna.

"We have a lot of explaining to do," Alenna said.

"What kind of clishmaclaver will ye tell them? Would ye rather I speak?"

"I'd better do the talking. I'm wearing a dress from the fourteenth century and I've got a gorgeous hunk of a man at my side."

"Hunk?"

She sighed. "Never mind." Alenna reached up to thread her fingers through his thick hair. "You didn't answer my question, Tynan."

His expression softened, his smile one of deep love. "Aye…I mean, yes. Yes, I'll marry ye…you and love you all my livin' days. How did ye…you ken I was goin' to ask ye today?"

"I didn't. I didn't want to wait any longer."

"Ah, dinnae give me that." Shifting on his feet, Tynan gave her a wary look. "Now that we're in yer…your world, I suppose ye will be givin' all the orders from now on?"

Alenna winked and laughed. "Yes. Sometimes."

His face sobered slightly. "I will miss our friends in the past."

Sadness toned her initial feelings of happiness down to a dull roar. "I wish they could have come with us."

"Nay. They wouldnae be happy in this world."

Allowing all the love she had for him to show in her eyes, she reached up and cupped his face. "I have something else to tell you before Demi gets over here."

"Aye?"

"Remember Elizabet's prophecy...where she saw me carrying your child?"

For a moment his expression remained blank, then flashed to joy. "Jesu!" He pressed his hand to her stomach gently. "My bairn? Yer havin' my bairn?"

"Yes. It's been more than a month. I think it was the night we first made love—"

His lips smothered her words, and in front of all the tourists, Tynan of MacBrahin kissed her so well everyone could see they belonged to each other.

"Alenna," Demi said from right next to them, so they practically jumped out of each other's arms.

Alenna smiled at her friend. "Demi, meet Tynan of...I mean Tynan MacBrahin. He works at the castle and—"

"I am her hunk," Tynan said matter-of-factly.

Alenna felt her face flame as Demi laughed.

"Well, I'll say you're a fast worker," Demi said, grinning and winking at Tynan.

When Demi took his hand and shook it, Alenna almost laughed at the droll expression on his face.

Demi turned to Alenna. "Where on earth have you been? I've been looking all over for you. I was about ready to call security. Where did you get that costume?"

"I've been a little distracted. I wasn't feeling too well and Tynan...uh...took care of me.

Demi looked at Tynan and gave him a huge grin. "I'll bet. He looks a little frazzled himself."

Linking her arms through Tynan's and Demi's, Alenna started walking and they were forced to follow.

"Demi, have we got a tale for you. You're not going to believe it. Oh, by the way, I owe you five pounds," Alenna said.

Demi's eyebrows twitched. "You saw a ghost?"

Alenna nodded. "Much more than that, Demi. Much more."

Alenna smiled and looked at Tynan over Demi's head.

With a sexy smile promising love forever, he winked at Alenna.

"Much more," he said.

IF YOU ENJOYED BRIDGE THROUGH THE MIST...

If you enjoyed Bridge Through The Mist and read it as an ebook, click here to go right to the sign up page for my newsletter or stop by my webpage at www.deniseagnew.com. By the way, if you visit my webpage, take a look around. I write more than just horror.

Thank you so much.

ABOUT THE AUTHOR

Denise A. Agnew is the award-winning author of over 70 novels and several optioned and produced screenplays and TV pilots. Her film Secrets Beneath The Floorboards (written with Marie D. Jones) premiered on Lifetime Movie Network October 2023.

Denise's record proves that with paranormal, time travel, romantic comedy, science fiction, thriller, historical, romantic suspense and horror writing under her belt, she enjoys writing about a diverse range of subjects.

Denise is also a Writer/Producer (Where's Lucy? Productions), a paranormal investigator (SOS Paranormal Investigations), Reiki Master, Certified Creativity Coach and Evidential Medium. As a Creativity Coach, Denise assists anyone in the creative arts, including writing, to maintain lifelong creativity. Denise lives in Arizona with her husband. You can find additional information about her other books at deniseagnew.com.

facebook.com/denise.a.agnew
instagram.com/creativemedium888

GLOSSARY OF SCOTS TERMS & SLANG

Athair ... father

Bairn ... child

Brathair ... brother

Braw ... handsome

Clishmaclaver ... chatter

Clootie ... devil

Cuif ... foolish

Destrier ... war horse

Fash ... trouble

Guidman ... husband

Kelpie ... water horse

Ken ... understand

Gloamin ... evening

Mathair ... mother

Spae ... foretell

Spaewife ... fortune teller

Sumph ... stupid, soft

Taet ... little

Taet Doup ... little ass

Taupie ... stupid young woman

Trews ... pants

Trebuchets ... a type of siege engine for hurling weights and missiles.

Whingin' ... Complaining, worrying

Wud ... wild

Made in the USA
Middletown, DE
09 September 2024